Nanda Devi

Nanda Devi

ERIC SHIPTON

Vertebrate Publishing, Sheffield
www.v-publishing.co.uk

Nanda Devi

Eric Shipton

 Vertebrate Publishing
Omega Court, 352 Cemetery Road, Sheffield S11 8FT, United Kingdom.
www.v-publishing.co.uk

First published by Hodder and Stoughton Limited, 1936. This edition first
published in 2019 by Vertebrate Publishing.

This book is a work of non-fiction based on the life, experiences and
recollections of Eric Shipton. In some limited cases the names of people,
places, dates and sequences or the detail of events have been changed solely
to protect the privacy of others. The author has stated to the publishers that,
except in such minor respects not affecting the substantial accuracy of the
work, the contents of the book are true.

ISBN 978-1-912560-10-3 (Paperback)
ISBN 978-1-910240-16-8 (Ebook)

Produced by Vertebrate Publishing.

Contents

Shipton's Legacy for Mountaineers by Stephen Venables

Eric Shipton was one of the great mountain explorers of the twentieth century. As a young climber he was brave and skilful, with a prodigious flair for pioneering new routes on remote peaks, far from any hope of rescue. During the course of his life that bold vision broadened to encompass immense landscapes and he was drawn increasingly to the wide canvas of exploration, with the result that we sometimes forget what a brilliant natural climber he was. However, whether we view him as an explorer, or climber, or both, his greatest achievement was to unlock the secrets of so many mountain ranges. The mountains he discovered – and the manner in which he discovered them – remain an inspiration to all who have attempted to follow in his steps.

I first came across his name in 1972. I had just started climbing, I was filled with dreams of far off mountains and was devouring everything I could on the subject. One book in particular seemed to enshrine all my half-formed aspirations. It was Shipton's autobiography, *That Untravelled World*. Here was a man who had dared to follow his dreams and whose sense of enchantment sparkled from every page of unadorned prose.

Soon I got to know all the other books and followed Shipton's travels in more detail, discovering the intricacies of the Nanda Devi adventure, the repeated attempts on Everest and the breathtaking scope of the great Karakoram explorations told in my favourite of all, *Blank on the Map*. I couldn't afford to buy first editions and had to rely on borrowed library copies. So I was delighted when a new *omnibus Eric Shipton: The Six Mountain-Travel Books* assembled all his early narratives into a single affordable volume, complete with well-captioned photos, additional articles, clear maps, pertinent appendices and an eloquent Introduction by Jim Perrin. It remains a treasured and constantly rejuvenating source of inspiration.

Since first reading Shipton's books, I have got to know some of the people who actually climbed with him – Scott Russell in the Karakoram, George Lowe and Charles Wylie in Nepal, John Earle in Patagonia. They all found him a delightful companion, a great conversationalist, an enthusiast but also a gently provocative rocker of the establishment. And it's that same engaging personality that speaks through the books; they are immensely readable.

As Jim Perrin points out, the writings would be remarkable if only for their sheer geographical scope. From his astonishingly bold, assured, pioneering debut on Mount Kenya, to Everest, to Garhwal and the Karakoram, to Turkestan, to Patagonia, Shipton's explorations covered immense areas of wilderness. But it was the manner of those explorations that made them such a continuing inspiration to modern mountaineers. Few of us cover as much ground; none of us has equalled the record of the 1935 Everest reconnaissance expedition that made first ascents of twenty-two peaks over 20,000 feet; most of us would baulk at the frugality espoused by Shipton and his famously austere companion, Bill Tilman; but the ideal – of achieving more with less, travelling uncluttered, attuned to the landscape – remains an aspiration.

As Harold Evans famously pointed out, a picture can be worth a thousand words. It was Eric Shipton's 1937 photos of the Latok peaks, the Ogre and Uli Biaho that inspired the next generation. In a sense he threw down the gauntlet for John Roskelley, Doug Scott, Jim Donini and all those others who brought modern techniques to the soaring granite towers in what is now northern Pakistan. More recently the spire that bears Shipton's name has been a recurring magnet for modern American climbers like Greg Child, Mark Synott and Steph Davis. Shipton had the grand vision to reveal vast tracts of previously unexplored mountain country; his modern followers are enjoying the fruits – whether it is the fine detail of a vertical rock tower or the broader sweep of the great Karakoram ski tours carried out by people like Ned Gillete, David Hamilton and the Odier brothers. For myself, with Phil Bartlett and Duncan Tunstall, it was thrilling, in 1987, to try and emulate Shipton, making a serendipitous first ascent above the Biafo Glacier, before continuing over Snow Lake to the same Khurdopin Pass he had reached with Scott Russell 48 years earlier, at the outbreak of the Second World War.

That war saw Russell incarcerated in the infamous Changi jail in Singapore, while Shipton languished more comfortably in one of the few proper jobs he ever had – as British Consul in Kashgar. There he wrote his first volume of autobiography, *Upon That Mountain*. He ends the book on an elegiac note, describing his last evening on Snow Lake before returning to a 'civilisation' embarked on a cataclysmic war. 'The great granite spires of the Biafo stood black against a deep blue sky. At least this mountain world, to which I owed so much of life and happiness, would stand above the ruin of human hopes, the heritage of a saner generation of men.'

Elegant prose from a man who, as Peter Steele's excellent 1998 biography revealed, was dyslexic and relied heavily on editorial help from some of his many girlfriends. If only some of today's celebrity adventurer authors could be given similar help. But it's not just down to writing style. All too often the authors are simply ticking lists, notching up goals. With Shipton the journey was everything, the tantalising view into an unknown cirque more important than the prestigious summit. Despite his obvious natural flair as a climber, he became increasingly drawn to the bigger picture, the far horizon. And by all accounts he could be hazy about logistical details. Hence the Everest putsch of 1952, when he lost the leadership of what was likely to be, finally, the successful expedition. The irony was that Shipton had taken part in more Everest expeditions than anyone else alive. As an outraged Charles Wylie pointed out, 'he was *the* man, he was Mr Everest.' Of course, the replacement leader, John Hunt, was in his very different way just as charming and charismatic as Shipton, and he ran a brilliant show. But, as Hunt was the first to acknowledge, it was Shipton who had assembled his crack team, including the two New Zealanders, George Lowe and Ed Hillary, who both played such key roles in 1953. And it was Shipton who had, in 1935, first employed the aspiring young Tibetan, Tenzing Norgay.

Even the most selfless, unworldly saint would be aggrieved at losing his chance of global fame. Shipton had obviously thrilled to the opportunity, in 1951 and 1952, to be first into untouched country along the Nepal–Tibet border, all the way from Makalu to Menlungtse, but for a jobbing mountain lecturer and writer, success on Everest itself would have brought useful kudos. The sense of missed opportunity cannot have been helped by the subsequent break-up of his marriage. For a while he began to resemble a character from a Benjamin Britten opera – an outcast, an oddball, a penniless misfit.

There the story might have ended, had it not been for the redemptive solace of mountain wilderness and the realisation of new challenges. Like his former climbing partner Tilman, Shipton began a whole new career of exploration in the far south, rejuvenated by the stark empty spaces of Patagonia and Tierra del Fuego. And here again the world he explored has become a magnet for modern climbers. His gruelling first crossings of the great southern icecaps remain a template for today's sledge-haulers, including his younger son, John Shipton, who is increasingly following in his father's steps. Likewise on Tierra del Fuego, where one of today's most imaginative and ascetic mountaineers, Andy Parkin – and his frequent companion Simon Yates – is drawn repeatedly to the mountain ranges Shipton first unravelled. And on the great spires of Cerro Torre and FitzRoy, virtuosos like Rolando Garibotti, Ermanno Salvaterra, Kelly Cordes and Colin Haley still exemplify the Shipton ideal of travelling light, paring down, achieving more with less.

As for that most vulgarised of all mountains – Everest; there too, during a golden age of new possibilities in the seventies and eighties, Shipton's ideals were finally realised. The Australian route up the Great Couloir and the Anglo-American-Canadian route up the East Face, which I was lucky enough to join, were both pulled off by a handful of climbers, without oxygen equipment, and without the help of high altitude porters. As for Reinhold Messner's audacious solo ascent of the North Face – or the remarkable forty-one-hour dash up and down the Japanese-Hornbein Couloir by Erhard Loretan and Jean Troillet – they probably exceeded Shipton's wildest imaginings.

There is one other quality – seemingly modern but actually timeless – that many modern climbers share with Eric Shipton, and that is the decision to follow the path of their own choosing. There was a wonderful moment in the early thirties when Shipton realised that expeditioning really could become his life, that he could continue to play this endlessly fascinating game, in his case never losing that vital sense of curiosity. That is what makes these books so compelling to every generation that follows. As he wrote in his coda to *Upon That Mountain:*

> There are few treasures of more lasting worth than the experiences of a way of life that is in itself wholly satisfying. Such, after all, are the only possessions of which no fate, no cosmic catastrophe can deprive us; nothing can alter the fact if for one moment in eternity we have really lived.

Stephen Venables
June 2010

Introduction: Eric Shipton
by Jim Perrin

Early in 1930 a young planter in Kenya unexpectedly received a letter from an ex-soldier ten years his senior, who had settled in the colony after the Great War. The letter mentioned that its writer had done some climbing in the English Lake District on his last home leave, and asked advice about visiting the East African mountains. Its immediate results were a meeting between the two men, an initial jaunt up Kilimanjaro together, and the first ascent, later that year, of the West Ridge of Mount Kenya – one of the major pre-war achievements of British alpinism.

The two men were, of course, Eric Shipton and H.W. Tilman, and their chance meeting, out in the colonies at the very beginning of the decade, led to one of the most fruitful partnerships and entrancing sagas in the history of mountain exploration. Indeed, the centrality of their role in that history throughout one of its vital phases is unarguable. The chance of their acquaintance and the magnitude of their travels aside, there is another aspect of these two men which is perhaps even more remarkable. For they were both inveterate chroniclers of their climbs and journeys, and the quality of the writings so produced places them absolutely in the forefront of mountaineering and travel literature.

For the span of their contents alone, Shipton's books are noteworthy: *Nanda Devi* (1936), his first, deals with the 1934 penetration up the Rishi Gorge into the Nanda Devi sanctuary in company with Tilman, as well as the two traverses of the Badrinath-Kedamath and Badrinath-Gangotri watersheds. From the moment of its first publication, for reasons to be examined below, it was regarded as one of the revolutionary texts of mountain literature, and it remains an enthralling story of hazardous and uncertain journeying with minimal resources through unknown country. *Blank on the Map* (1938) describes the 1937 Shaksgam survey expedition undertaken with Michael Spender, John Auden, (brothers to the poets) and Tilman – an important venture into a little-known region of the Himalayas which provided a basis for much subsequent mountaineering activity in the Karakoram. (First editions of this very rare title now command fabulous prices amongst collectors.)

From 1940 to 1942 Shipton served as British Consul-General at Kashgar, in the Chinese Province of Sinkiang. During this period he completed a first volume of memoirs, entitled *Upon That Mountain*, published in 1943. This frank, vivid polemic set out his basic mountaineering creed, whilst also describing his early Alpine and Himalayan seasons, the series of climbs on Mount Kenya, and the four attempts on Everest and two survey-trips to the Karakoram in which he took part during the thirties. His next book was very different in tone. *Mountains of Tartary* (1950) is a series of light-hearted sketches of weeks or weekends seized from official consular work – in the main during his second spell of office in Kashgar – and spent on Bogdo Ola, Mustagh Ata, Chakragil (mountains which are again coming into vogue in the eighties since China's relaxation of restrictions on travel). The *Mount Everest Reconnaissance Expedition 1951* (1952) was basically a photographic volume, prefaced by a succinct and entertaining narrative about this vital piece of mountain exploration, which cleared the path for John Hunt's successful expedition to the mountain in 1953. The final book in this series, *Land of Tempest*, written in 1963, takes for theme the period of Shipton's life from 1958 to 1962 and includes accounts of three trips to Patagonia – on the last of which he made the first crossing of the main Patagonian ice-cap – and one to Tierra del Fuego.

The above bald catalogue suggests the range, but captures little of the flavour, of this extraordinary man's life, the brief outline of which is as follows. He was born in Ceylon in 1907, his father a tea-planter who died before his son was three. Thereafter, Shipton, his sister and mother travelled extensively between Ceylon, India, France and England, before the family finally settled in the latter country for purposes of the children's schooling. Shipton's mountaineering career began in 1924 with holidays in Norway and Switzerland and was consolidated through four successive alpine seasons in 1925-1928. His first ascent of Nelion, the unclimbed twin summit of Mount Kenya, with Wyn Harris in 1929, and of the same mountain's West Ridge with Tilman the following year, brought him to the notice of the mountaineering establishment of the day and elicited an invitation to join the expedition led by Frank Smythe to Kamet, in the Garhwal region, in 1931. Shipton distinguished himself on this trip, being in the summit party on eleven of the twelve peaks climbed by the expedition, including that of Kamet itself, which at 25,447ft was the highest summit then attained. His performance in 1931 led to an invitation to join Ruttledge's 1933 Everest expedition. Thereafter the milestones slip by: Rishi Gorge 1934; Everest Reconnaissance 1935, which he led; Everest and Nanda Devi 1936; Shaksgam 1937; Everest 1938; Karakoram 1939 are the main ones amongst them, but virtually the whole decade was spent in Himalayan travel, and the extent of his exploratory achievement perhaps even now lacks full recognition.

He spent the Second World War in Government service in Sinkiang, Persia and Hungary, went back for a further spell in Kashgar from 1946 to 1948, accompanied by his wife Diana, and was Consul-General at Kunming, in Southern China, from 1949 to 1951. On his return to England he was asked to lead an expedition to reconnoitre the Southern approaches to Everest, in the course of which he and Ed Hillary first espied the eventual line of ascent up the Western Cwm to the South Col, from a vantage point on the slopes of Pumori. The following year he led a rather unsatisfactory training expedition to Cho Oyu. In the late summer of 1952, Shipton having been urged to lead a further expedition to Everest in 1953 and having accepted, the joint Himalayan Committee of the Alpine Club and the Royal Geographical Society performed an astonishing volte-face, appointing the competent and experienced but at that time virtually unknown Colonel John Hunt as leader, and accepting Shipton's consequent resignation.

This sorry episode effectively formed a watershed in Shipton's life. After the break-up of his marriage and loss of his post as Warden of the Outward Bound School at Eskdale, which occurred shortly after the events of 1952–53, he lived for a time in the rural seclusion of Shropshire, working as a forestry labourer. He was enticed back for a last trip to the Karakoram in 1957, and thereafter developed a new grand obsession with travel in the southernmost regions of South America, which absorbed most of the next decade in his life. Finally, in his sixties, he was a popular lecturer on cruises to such places as the Galapagos Islands, and leader of mild Himalayan treks. He died of liver cancer at the home of a friend in Wiltshire during the spring of 1977.

This, then, is the bare outline of an outstanding life. The man who lived it, through his involvement in the 1931 Kamet and 1933 Everest expeditions, had attained a considerable degree of national celebrity by the early thirties, yet at that time he was to all intents and purposes a professionless pauper and a kind of international tramp, whose possessions amounted to little more than the clothes in which he stood. There is an admirable passage in *Upon That Mountain* where Shipton recounts the dawning of a realisation that the way of life which most appealed to him perhaps presented a practical possibility. It happened on the way back to India from the North Side of Everest in 1933. In company with the geologist Lawrence Wager, he had made his way across a strip of unexplored country and over a new pass into Sikkim. Wager's influence shifted the emphasis of Shipton's interest away from the climbing of peaks to enthusiasm for a general mode of exploration – a fascination with geography itself. Twenty years later, this shift was to provide his detractors with an easy target. For the moment, his mind works over the ground thus:

> Why not spend the rest of my life doing this sort of thing? There
> was no way of life that I liked more, the scope appeared to be
> unlimited, others had done it, vague plans had already begun to
> take shape, why not put some of them into practice? ... The most
> obvious snag, of course, was lack of private means; but surely such
> a mundane consideration could not be decisive. In the first place I
> was convinced that expeditions could be run for a tithe of the cost
> generally considered necessary. Secondly if one could produce
> useful or interesting results one would surely find support ...

When he took into account his reactions to the milieu of the large expedition, ('The small town of tents that sprung up each evening, the noise and racket of each fresh start, the sight of a huge army invading the peaceful valleys, it was all so far removed from the light, free spirit with which we were wont to approach our peaks'), then the virtue to be made of necessity was obvious, and of it was born what came to be known as the 'Shipton/Tilman style of lightweight expedition'. I referred above to Shipton's *Nanda Devi* as a revolutionary text, and it was just that. I doubt if there has ever been a less formulaic account of an expedition. It has a magical, fresh quality, a get-through-by-the-skin-of-your-teeth spontaneity, a candour, a clear rationale, an excited commitment, an elation about the enterprise undertaken, which no previous mountaineering book had approached. From the outset the terms are made clear: five months in the Garhwal Himalaya to tackle some of its outstanding topographical problems, 'climbing peaks when opportunity occurred', on a budget of £150 each for himself and Tilman (some of Shipton's share of which is advanced by Tilman 'against uncertain security'). The scenes throughout, from the broken-toed, frock-coated setting-out from Ranikhet to the final descent from the Sunderdhunga Col to Maiktoli, are evoked in a clear and economical style. But it is the message – the simple moral that it is possible, and in terms of response to the landscape and its peoples even desirable, to travel cheap and light, to move fast and live off the land – which is the book's revolutionary charge, and which was to make Shipton and Tilman, in the words of the American writer David Roberts, 'retroactive heroes of the avant-garde'.

Two major characteristics distinguish *Nanda Devi* and were to become hallmarks of Shipton's writing. The first of these is an intense curiosity-which remains with him, his conclusions growing more authoritative with increase of experience – about natural landforms, whether they be mountains, valleys, rivers, volcanoes or glaciers. This curiosity acts as a stimulus, a fund of energy, in his explorations, continually used as a basis, a point of reference: 'It was enthralling to disentangle the geography of the region … for me, the basic reason for mountaineering'.

Alongside this drive to understand the physical make-up of a landscape there operates a more reflective principle, very close to traditional nature-mysticism, which Shipton almost invariably carries off with great poise and delicacy, sure-footedly avoiding the obvious pitfalls of bathos or inflation.

> We settled down on a comfortable bed of sand, and watched the approach of night transform the wild desert mountains into phantoms of soft unreality. How satisfying it was to be travelling with such simplicity. I lay awaiting the approach of sleep, watching the constellations swing across the sky. Did I sleep that night – or was I caught up for a moment into the ceaseless rhythm of space?
> *Blank on the Map*

A very satisfying irony lies in suggesting an affinity with mysticism of a man who claimed througout his adult life to be an agnostic, and who would probably, even if only for the sheer joy of argument, have vigorously rejected the intimation. Perhaps his disclaimer of religious belief was like that of Simone Weill, and masked a genuine sense of divine mystery within the universe. Certainly much of the interest in Shipton's writings derives from a tension between the very practical preoccupations with physical phenomena, and a frequent lapsing into a more quietistic mode of thought. (To compound the mischief, I have to say that *Nanda Devi* puts me in mind of no other text so much as one of the late poems of that most ascetic of saints, St John of the Cross, quoted here in the translation by Roy Campbell:

> The generous heart upon its quest
> Will never falter, nor go slow,
> But pushes on, and scorns to rest,
> Wherever it's most hard to go.
> It runs ahead and wearies not
> But upward hurls its fierce advance
> For it enjoys I know not what
> That is achieved by lucky chance.

Those who knew Shipton well sound a recurrent note in their reminiscences which supports the contention that there was a mystical element to his character. It concerns a quality of detachment he possessed, and invariably fastens on a specific physical detail. The following is typical:

> He had the most marvellous blue eyes, very kindly, very amused, and very wise. But there was always a sense, when you talked with him, that somehow he was not with you, was looking right through you, searching out farther and farther horizons.

In the course of researching Shipton's biography, it was remarkable and eventually almost comical how often that impression, almost word-for-word, was repeated. Without the evidence of the text it could be taken as a mannerism, but in his books there recur time and again passages which define his response to landscape as one striving towards a mystical awareness.

In this he is very different to Tilman, his most frequent companion of the thirties, and it is interesting to compare the two men. The ten-year difference in age is for once significant, for Tilman's seniority ensured that he underwent the determining influence on his character of the First World War, and it affected him profoundly. It is what made him a master of that most serious of all forms of writing, comic irony, and it is what causes him to veer dangerously close at times to a distinct misanthropy. It explains the prelapsarian vitality with which he imbues his native characters, the neglectful portrayal of his compatriots, and the isolation which identifies his authorial persona. In his personal conduct, it provides the reason for his taciturnity, his phlegmatism and unemotional responses to situations. The vulnerability of youth, its lack of circumspection and eager commitment to affection or cause were in Tilman's case the victims of war, and the survivor, psychic and physical, of that particularly obscene war had need to be encased in adamantine.

Shipton's enthusiasms, on the other hand, operate under no such constraint. He can indulge his feelings as freely as he will, the zest and gaiety of the twenties glitters around his early activities. He commits himself freely, and as equally with a climb as a journey of exploration or to one of the many women who shared his life. A couple of comments upon him from 1931 by Frank Smythe capture the temperament of the man:

> No one who climbs with Shipton can remain pessimistic, for he imparts an imperturbability and confidence into a day's work which are in themselves a guarantee of success.

Or again, about his climbing:

> I saw Shipton's eye light up, and next instant he went at the slope with the energy of a boxer who, after months of training, sees his opponent before him.

The differences in their characters probably acted as a bond between Shipton and Tilman, and account for their sharing of some of the most ambitious undertakings of their lives. For Tilman, his own youth lost, Shipton's enthusiasm and boundless energy must have been inspiriting and invigorating, whilst the fatherless Shipton may well have found that Tilman's wry, benevolent maturity fulfilled a need in him at a certain stage of his life. In mountaineering terms, the roles were reversed, and the more experienced Shipton was the leader. One very telling indication of this occurs in Tilman's diary for 30 May, 1934. After reconnoitring one of the crucial – and very tortuous – passages of the route up the Rishi Gorge, they have to hurry back to camp. The subsequent diary entry briefly states, 'Shipton's route-memory invaluable as usual, self hopeless.'

It has to be said, though, that a change occurs in Shipton's outlook, especially with regard to mountaineering, during the mid-thirties. It seems to me complex and cumulative rather than associated with specific circumstances. The influence of older companions such as Tilman and Wager would have played a part. So too, perhaps, did the relationship upon which he had

embarked with Pamela Freston. But two related events could be seen as deci-
sive in the transition from joyful mountaineering innocence to prudent
experience. These were the two avalanches which Shipton witnessed on the
slopes leading to the North Col of Everest during successive expeditions in
1935 and 1936. Of the first one, he had to say 'I am sure that no one could have
escaped from an avalanche such as that which broke away below us while we
were lying peacefully on the North Col'. The following year, as he and Wyn
Harris were climbing up the same slope, this is what happened:

> We climbed quickly over a lovely hard surface in which one
> sharp kick produced a perfect foothold. About half-way up to
> the col we started traversing to the left. Wyn anchored himself
> firmly on the lower lip of a crevasse while I led across the slope.
> I had almost reached the end of the rope and Wyn was starting
> to follow when there was a rending sound … a short way above
> me, and the whole surface of the slope I was standing on started
> to move slowly down towards the brink of an ice-cliff a couple of
> hundred feet below …

Wyn Harris managed to jump back into the crevasse and re-establish the belay,
the snow failed to gather momentum, and Shipton survived. It was the last
attempt on the mountain that year. The point is, that Shipton's faith in the material he was climbing had been undermined – just as in personal relationships,
when the trust has gone the commitment is withdrawn. Shipton's heyday as a
climber is delimited by these events. Though there are inevitably some exciting
and perilous escapades after 1936 – the climb on the Dent Blanche-like peak
above the Bostan Terek valley is a striking example – henceforwards, reading
these books, we keep company with a much more circumspect mountaineer.

This line of reasoning inevitably leads us towards a consideration of what is
generally and I think rightly regarded as one of the cruces of Shipton's life –
the circumstances surrounding the choice of leadership for the 1953 expedition
to Everest. It is very difficult to summarise in brief the main points of what is
still a controversial topic. Even Walt Unsworth's Everest book, which comes
nearest to being an authoritative history of the mountain, overlooked important material in its researches which throws a clearer light on some aspects of
this vital area. What emerges, from close examination of relevant Himalayan
Committee minutes and written submissions from its surviving members, is a
bizarre tale of fudging and mudging, falsification of official minutes, unau-
thorised invitations, and opportunistic and desperate last-minute seizures of
initiative by a particular faction. It is a perfect illustration of the cock-up rather
than the conspiracy theory of history, from which little credit redounds upon
the British mountaineering establishment of the time. The saddest fact about

the whole sorry tale is that it appeared to place in conflict two honourable and quite innocent men – Shipton and John Hunt.

There are two basic themes to be considered. The first of these is the general climate of feeling surrounding Shipton's attitude for, and interest in, the leadership of an expedition which, even in the early stages of its planning, was subject to a jingoistic insistence that Everest must be climbed by a British party. (That this was not to be achieved for a further 22 years scarcely mattered in the event, the national attachments of the first summiteers being clearly turned to the Commonwealth's greater glory.) This climate of feeling, accepting some of Shipton's own statements at face value, and drawing in other rather more questionable evidence, particularly that relating to the 1952 Cho Oyu expedition, where peculiar circumstances undoubtedly affected Shipton's leadership, had drifted towards the view that Shipton lacked the urgency, the thrust, the killer instinct which would be necessary to 'conquer' Everest.[1] It was immeasurably strengthened by Shipton's own submission to the Himalayan Committee meeting of 28 July, 1952, in which he expressed doubts about his suitability for the job on the following grounds: he had to consider his own career – with a wife and two young children to support, he was out of a job and needed to get one; he felt that new blood was needed to undertake the task; his strong preference was for smaller parties, lightly equipped.

At this juncture we need to pass over to a consideration of the second basic theme – the conduct of members of the Himalayan Committee over the matter of the leadership. The first point to be made is that the Committee was very weakly chaired. Because of this, the pro-Shipton faction carried the day at the meeting of July 28 and, chiefly through the efforts of Laurence Kirwan, Shipton was strongly prevailed upon to accept the leadership, the contention then resting with the matter of deputy leadership.

However, there also existed a pro-Hunt faction, headed by Basil Goodfellow and Colonel Tobin, who had both been absent from the July 28 meeting. These two men lobbied forcefully that the deputy – or assault – leadership should fall to Hunt, which would inevitably compromise Shipton, whose choice had been Charles Evans and to whom Hunt was therefore unacceptable in that role. The crucial committee meeting took place on 11 September. The pro-Hunt faction was present in force, determined to reverse the decision of the previous meeting. The more ardent Shiptonians – most notably Kirwan and Shipton's old friend Wager – were absent. Shipton was morally compelled to offer his resignation. The rest is history, apart from a few squalid diversions, such as the subsequent falsification of this meeting's minutes by Claude

---

1 In *Upon That Mountain*, for example, he had written that 'there are some, even among those who have themselves attempted to reach the summit, who nurse a secret hope that Mount Everest will never be climbed. I must confess to such feelings myself.'

Elliott, the chairman – in the words of one contemporary observer, 'as bad a chairman of committees as one could find; he was hopelessly indecisive and hesitant and was too easily swayed by anyone (like Kirwan) who held firm opinions, however wrong these might be'.

What the effect would have been upon Shipton had he led the successful expedition to Everest is a matter for conjecture. John Hunt was patently well-equipped to cope with the ensuing celebrity, and used it tirelessly in the public good. It could perhaps be thought doubtful that Shipton would have enjoyed, and responded so positively, to the inevitably massive public acclaim.

After 1953, his life went through a difficult period, but it emerged into a golden late summer of exploration in an area completely fresh to him. His Patagonian journeys of the late fifties and sixties were a harking-back in many ways to his great Karakoram travels of the thirties. They would have been rendered immensely more public and difficult and perhaps thus less satisfying to him, by the burden of international fame. Instead, he was able to slip quietly away, pursue his own bent amongst the unknown mountains and glaciers of a new wilderness. It is a myth fulfilled, a proper consummation in the life of this explorer-mystic, whose outlook and progress resonate so closely with those of Tennyson's 'Ulysses', from which poem he took the motto for the first part of *Blank on the Map*, and the title for his magnificent second autobiography, *That Untravelled World*.

There is a phrase of Shipton's from this latter book which gives perfect expression to one of the great lives of our century – 'a random harvest of delight'. That is exactly what the books collected together between these covers are, in general terms. But they are also an opportunity for a new generation of readers to engage with one of the most attractive personalities the sport of mountaineering has ever produced, to keep company with his spare, lithe figure loping off into the ranges, seeking out the undiscovered country, his distant blue eyes lingering on the form of a particular peak, the passage over to an unexplored glacier. If curiosity, appreciation, aspiration and delight are a form of praise – as assuredly they are – then here is one man's testament of a lifetime spent in worship of the great world around him.

> I am a part of all that I have met;
>   Yet all experience is an arch wherethrough Gleams that untra-
> velled world, whose margin fades For ever and for ever when I
> move.

It is the epitaph Shipton would have chosen for himself. No man lived out its theme more fully, nor finally more deserved its implicit tribute.

Jim Perrin
January 1985

Foreword
by Hugh Ruttledge

When Mr Shipton honoured me by an invitation to write a foreword to his book, I accepted with a particular sense of both privilege and opportunity; of privilege because the book is an epic of mountaineering exploration, of opportunity because so little is yet known of three aspects of Himalayan travel: the comparatively easy and inexpensive access to some of the wildest regions, the almost unlimited scope for small but thoroughly competent parties, and the amazing strength and capacity of the Sherpa porter.

I had the good fortune to serve for nearly five years in the section of the Central Himalayan chain with which this book deals. I climbed there with Sherpa, Gurkha, Bhotia and Kumaoni – as well as British – companions; and we made four attempts to enter the great Nanda Devi Basin, as better mountaineers had done before us. It is therefore with some knowledge of the facts that I acclaim the success gained by Messrs Shipton and Tilman and their three Sherpa comrades as one of the greatest feats in mountaineering history. Not only that: it has proved beyond doubt that, in these regions at any rate, a small homogeneous party, self-contained, able to live off the country, with no weak links and ably led, can go further and do more than the elaborate expeditions which have been thought necessary for the Himalaya. What a field of adventure and enterprise this throws open to young mountaineers, now that most of the other great mountain ranges of the world are but too well known.

One word of warning is perhaps necessary: work of this kind should be undertaken only by those who have attained the highest degree of mountaineering skill, judgment and endurance. Those who read this book with understanding will realise the number of tight places this party got into, where nothing but the most brilliant technical competence could have got them out alive. It is not a game for the beginner, or for the lover of flesh-pots.

The greatest feat was the successful entry into, and departure from, the 'inner sanctuary' of the Nanda Devi Basin – a place only about seventy-five miles from Almora, yet hitherto more inaccessible than the North Pole. At last men have set foot upon the slopes of the greatest mountain in the British Empire; and to them will be extended the admiration of those who have struggled and fought for it – notably Dr T. G. Longstaff, who so nearly succeeded in 1907.

Less spectacular perhaps, but hardly less exacting, were the two great traverses of the Badrinath–Gangotri and the Badrinath–Kedarnath watershed, along lines famous in Hindu mythology. These were replete with all the misery that mountaineering in the monsoon season can entail, but the climbers have their reward in the completion of a task that was well worth accomplishment, and in the regard of good Hindus, in whose eyes this would be a pilgrimage of superabundant merit.

Mr Shipton has paid generous and well-deserved tribute to the three Sherpa porters who accompanied him. It is no exaggeration to say that, without men of this type, climbing the higher Himalaya would be impossible. On them are based our hopes of climbing Mount Everest, and for years to come there will be none among the Himalayan peoples to equal them as mountaineers, porters, and loyal, unselfish companions. They are well on their way to become a corps of guides as famous as the men of the Alps. In time there may be others as good – there is splendid material in Kumaon, in Hunza or in Baltistan, to name a few Himalayan regions; and the humble Nepalese Dotials who served Mr Shipton so faithfully in the Rishiganga are worth their salt. At present the Sherpa holds pride of place, and his morale and *esprit-de-corps* are tremendous assets. Given the right leaders – and they must be of the best – he is unbeatable. The description of him in this book is the most understanding and delightful that has ever been written.

The lists are now set for great deeds in the Himalayan snowfields. Messrs Shipton and Tilman have shown the way; let us hope that many will follow.

Hugh Ruttledge

Part 1

Innocents from Nepal – and London

1 Chapter 1

In the exploration of a continent the mountainous areas are generally the last strongholds of mystery to fall before the onslaught of man, be that onslaught brutal, scientific or merely inquisitive. The difficulties of transport are so great; the physical hardships so heavy; the reward so small – for glacier regions are materially useless. For these reasons then the high places of the earth remain remote and inaccessible until man, having explored all fertile regions of a particular country, finds himself dwelling under the very shadow of the mountains and becomes aware of an overwhelming desire to conquer them. This feeling doubtless owes its force partly to the attraction of the unknown and partly to the natural beauty and sublime grandeur of mountainous districts; but I like to think that it goes deeper; that the wish to explore springs from a delight in the purely aesthetic nature of the quest.

When man is conscious of the urge to explore, not all the arduous journeyings, the troubles that will beset him and the lack of material gain from his investigations will stop him. As a famous Arctic explorer remarked many years ago: 'The great majority of men who visit the Arctic *do so because they want* to, a large number do so for publicity, while it is possible that one or two have gone there for purely scientific purposes.'

The italics are mine. What was true of the Arctic then is equally true of the little-known mountain country of today, and of the Alps before they became 'the playground of Europe'. To the early explorer fighting his way across the passes of *Haute Savoie* and to people who, like myself, have come under the spell of the high Himalaya the reason for exploration remains the same – *we do so because we want to*.

It was my good fortune to visit the mighty ranges of South Central Asia, which stretch from east to west without a break for over 1,500 miles, as a member of F. S. Smythe's Kamet expedition in 1931. Then, for the first time, I saw mountains whose rugged splendour baffles description and whose complex structure probably renders them inaccessible even to the most advanced mountaineering technique. With this vision before me, surpassing all the wildest dreams of my early mountaineering apprenticeship, I welcomed the opportunity, some two years later, of joining the fourth expedition to Mount Everest, where I saw the harsher and less lovely aspect of the Tibetan side of the range.

The Kamet and Everest expeditions had, as their main objective, the climbing of a single lofty peak. In the one case we succeeded: in the other we failed. But on each occasion I had a mighty longing to detach myself from the big and cumbersome organisation which for some reason had been thought to be necessary for an attack on the more lofty summits of the earth, and to wander with a small, self-contained party through the labyrinth of unexplored valleys, forming our plans to suit the circumstances, climbing peaks when opportunity occurred, following up our own topographical clues and crossing passes into unknown territory. This desire held me captive even before I left the Everest base camp in July 1933, and I resolved to carry out some such scheme before age, marriage or other considerations made it impossible of accomplishment.

During the winter of 1933–34 I began to form plans. The primary choice of district was not difficult. There can be few regions of the Himalaya providing topographical problems of more absorbing interest than that lying in the Almora and Garhwal districts of the United Provinces. Here there are no political obstacles (the bugbear of the Asiatic explorer) to be overcome as the region lies almost entirely in British India. Moreover, the transport of supplies and equipment to a suitable base is a simple matter, the organisation of which does not require any vast experience of the country or knowledge of the language. Brief acquaintance, while with the Kamet expedition, had given me some first-hand information on a number of problems and I felt confident that, with the modest resources at my disposal, I should be able to carry out my proposed campaign with some fair chance of achieving useful results. Therefore I plumped for Almora and Garhwal.

The question of companionship did not worry me. There were a number of people who would be quite prepared – and suitably qualified – to take part in such an enterprise, and my association with the Nepalese and Tibetan porters of the 1933 Everest expedition had convinced me that their natural, if undeveloped, mountaineering ability, their constant cheerfulness and their wonderful sense of loyalty, would make them ideal comrades. So I got into touch with Karma Paul, the Tibetan interpreter to the Everest expeditions, and requested him to send word to Angtharkay, Pasang Bhotia, and Rinzing, three men for whom I felt particular liking since they were among the eight porters who had placed our Camp VI at the enormous altitude of 27,400 feet the previous summer. Rinzing, however, was not available, and at the last moment Angtharkay brought forward his cousin, Kusang Namgir, a man of extraordinary toughness and ability.

In January '34 I had my best stroke of luck, in a letter from my old friend H. W. Tilman, who had been my companion on three expeditions to the mountains of east and central Africa. This letter announced that, since he had long leave from Kenya, he had bought a second-hand bicycle and had ridden it across the continent alone, through Uganda, Belgian Congo and French

Equatorial Territory, finally emerging on the west coast where he sold the bicycle and boarded a cargo steamer bound for England. The letter said further that this had proved a most cheap and efficacious method of reaching home and that the writer, during his cycling travels, had existed entirely on native food, keeping pretty fit except for a few bouts of fever.

Here indeed was a kindred spirit. When I told him of my plans he at once offered to put up his share of the expenses. This, I estimated, would amount to £150 all told: that is, the whole expedition would not cost more than £300. Actually, we managed on less than that.

Our party was now complete and numbered four besides myself: Tilman, Angtharkay, Pasang and Kusang. Nobody could have had four more loyal, determined and unselfish comrades and there remained now only the choice of a main objective.

Now, nobody attempting mountain exploration in the Himalaya (or anywhere else, for that matter) can afford to miss an opportunity of discussing his plans with Dr T. G. Longstaff. When he gave me that opportunity, therefore, I accepted with alacrity and, as a result of long discussions with him, I determined to make an attempt to force the hitherto inviolate sanctuary of the Nanda Devi Basin.

At first this seemed as if we were flying too high. Here was a mountain whose summit was the highest in the British Empire. For centuries it had inspired worship and propitiatory sacrifice as the 'Blessed Goddess' of Hindu philosophers and scribes. For more than fifty years it had been the inaccessible goal of explorers who, attracted by the impregnability of its surroundings, had failed in repeated attempts to reach even its foot, the reason being that around the 25,660-foot mountain itself stretched a huge ring of peaks, more than thirty of them over 21,000 feet high, that constituted themselves unrelenting guardians of the great mountain and defeated any penetration.

And we, with light equipment, few stores, and a joint capital of £300, were setting forth to reach this goal. That we eventually succeeded was largely due to the unremitting labour of those who preceded us. To explorers in general and to mountaineers in particular, it is a well-known fact that each successive attempt at the solving of a problem makes that problem easier of solution. Few great mountains have been climbed, and few passes crossed, at first, second or even third essay. The man who eventually reaches the summit of Mount Everest will have done so, not by his own efforts alone, but over the shoulders of the pioneers – Mallory, Norton, Somervell – without whose hard-won experience he would have stood no chance. So with our own – seemingly fantastic – expedition. That measure of success met with in our enterprise, we owe primarily to those who went before us.

The days went on, passed swiftly in discussion of our base, our transport, our food – enthralling, this business of arranging an expedition that might well have been formulated on that classic statement of the great Duke of Wellington when comparing the organisation of the French tactical scheme in the Peninsular War with that of his own. Of Napoleon's generals he said that their plans were laid with such thoroughness that, at a single slight hitch, their whole structure was liable to collapse; whereas, if anything went wrong with his (Wellington's) less complex arrangements, all he had to do was 'to tie it up with string' and so carry on … a moral that applies to exploration as well as to war, and is probably the reason why a small expedition, such as our own, almost invariably achieves far more than does a large and elaborate one when proportionate costs are taken into consideration.

So, on April 6th, 1934, after a short period of preparation we left Liverpool for Calcutta in the Brocklebank cargo ship *Mahsud*.

2 Chapter 2

During the long hot days of the four weeks' voyage we discussed and re-discussed our plans, and made ourselves familiar with the history and geography of Garhwal; and in order to present the reader with a simple picture of the country, I cannot do better than to revert for the moment to geographical data.

'The Himalaya' is the rather loose name given to those mountains which extend, in an unbroken chain, for some 1,500 miles across the north of India. The word itself is a combination of two Sanskrit words, *him* meaning snow, and *alaya* abode. Modern geographers restrict the name to the range enclosed within the arms of the Indus river on the north-west, and the Brahmaputra on the south-east; but one must remember that the Karakoram and Hindu Kush ranges north and west of the Indus, and the mountains of northern Burmah and western China are all part of the same system.

Behind the chain to the north lies the plateau of Tibet at a general altitude of 15,000 feet. Here, at a point almost opposite the centre of the chain and within 100 miles of each other, rise those two great rivers, Indus and Brahmaputra, which flow, in opposite directions to each other and parallel to the Himalaya, until they bend south and cut a way through the mountain barrier practically at its two extremities.

It might be expected, therefore, that the highest part of the Himalaya would form a watershed, but this is not so, and the Ganges, the Sutlej and numerous tributaries which between them constitute the system, rise on the north side of the axes of highest elevation. Two explanations are given of this: (a) that the rivers are gradually 'cutting back' (that is, that the heads of the streams are eating their way northwards owing to the greater rainfall on the southern rather than the northern slopes); (b) that the line of drainage was formed antecedent to the elevation and has, by erosion, maintained its original course during a slow process of upheaval which is supposed to be still going on at the rate of a fraction of an inch a year.

Such geographical explanation may be dull, but it is intensely difficult to appreciate the Himalaya as it now is without indulging in these lofty speculations as to how or why. The extent of such a vast range is not easily realised, and many picture to themselves an area about the size of that of the Alps, with Everest towering in the centre and all the lesser satellites grouped round him.

Some better notion may be gained if we visualise a mountain chain running from London to the Black Sea with Everest somewhere near Belgrade and Nanga Parbat somewhere near London.

Having these relative distances in mind it may be of further assistance to consider the range in its artificial or political divisions. Starting from the Indus valley, over which looms the Nanga Parbat massif, the chain runs for 200 miles through Kashmir, and in the same state, but across the Indus to the north, lies the parallel range of the Karakoram and Mount Godwin Austen (K2), second in height only to Everest.

Continuing south-east for another 200 miles through a number of small states known collectively as the Simla Hill States, the range enters Garhwal. East of this it runs for nearly 600 miles through the independent state of Nepal which contains the highest crest-line, all the southern slopes and, in its extreme north-east corner, Everest itself, the main watershed following the Nepal–Tibet border.

Two more independent states follow, Sikkim and Bhutan, which together account for another 200 miles of the Himalaya. These states approximate in language, religion and custom to Tibet, and have both a spiritual and a temporal ruler. Finally, between Bhutan and the Brahmaputra are 300 miles of wild and mountainous country, nominally Chinese, about which even now our knowledge is very imperfect.

The districts of British Garhwal and Almora, with which Tilman and I were chiefly concerned, lie almost in the centre of the Himalayan range and are, moreover, the only place where our border marches with that of Tibet. Garhwal has had a chequered history. In early days it was divided amongst no less than fifty-two petty chieftains, each with his own fortress, a state of affairs to which the name itself is a description, since the word garh means castle. Five hundred years ago the strongest chieftain brought the other fifty-one under his dominion and ruled as Prince of Garhwal, and from then down to the close of the eighteenth century there was constant warfare between his descendants and the rulers of the neighbouring state of Kumaon. But the Gurkhas of Nepal (it is worthy of note that even now Nepal, which contains at least forty-eight peaks known to exceed 25,000 feet, is strictly closed to European exploration), failing to extend their conquests in the direction of China, turned their attention to the west and overran both Garhwal and Kumaon as far west as the Sutlej. Garhwal they ruled with a rod of iron, and from this mountain stronghold they began to make raids into the plains – at the expense of subjects of the British Raj. As a consequence there followed the Nepalese War of 1814–15, which, after the usual disastrous start, finally resulted in the Gurkhas being driven back within their present boundaries. Western Garhwal was restored to its native ruler, and the rest of the state, plus its neighbour, Almora, became part of British India.

The first commissioner was G. W. Traill, who reduced the country to order and laid a secure foundation for its future peace and prosperity. A worthy memorial to his work and the goodwill he earned as heritage for his successors is the well-known pass which he was the first to cross and which is named after him.

Garhwal covers about 100 miles from east to west and some fifty from north to south. The natives are short and sturdy, and fairer in colour than the inhabitants of the plains. Blue eyes and cheeks tinged with red are not uncommon and some of the women are very beautiful although here, as in most mountainous regions, goitre is very prevalent. Approaching the Tibetan border the people are Bhotias of Tibetan origin, speaking a Tibetan-Burman dialect. They have few traces of Buddhism and profess to be Hindus, but not of a strictly orthodox type. For instance, they are quite ready to eat with Tibetans, a fact which helps them considerably in their trade with that country. Indeed, they hold a monopoly of such trade and use goats and sheep to carry rice and wheat over the high passes, returning with borax, salt, and yaks' tails.

A broad outline of the topography of Garhwal is best understood by looking at the three or, if the Tehri State is included, the four great river valleys which run right up into the heart of the country, forming the trade routes and attracting populous centres. These valleys are of great depth and within ten miles of 20,000 feet snow peaks the valley floor may be but 4,000 feet above sea level and clothed in tropical vegetation.

All these rivers rise to the north of the main axis of elevation and have cut their way through the east-west range almost at right angles so that the containing walls of the valleys, on which are grouped the highest peaks, run roughly north and south. There are three such main ridges, each possessing many minor features of distinction: on the east that on which stands Nanda Devi, 25,660 feet, the highest peak in Garhwal; in the middle that of Kamet, 25,447, the second highest peak; and on the west that of the Badrinath–Kedernath group of peaks, in formation much more complex than that of the other two.

The Gori river, rising on the Tibetan border in the depression which forms the Untadhura Pass, for the first twenty miles of its course separates the eastern (or Nanda Devi) group from the tangle of snow peaks in western Nepal. Beyond this point the Gori bends away to the south-east to fix the political boundary of Nepal and concerns us no more, but its place is taken by the Pindar river which rises on the south-eastern extremities of the Nanda Devi group and, curling round it to the west, marks the termination of the regions of ice and snow in the south.

Before passing on to mention of the third river there are some interesting features to note about the valley of the Gori river, known as the Milam Valley. It forms the main highway between India and western Tibet and from it three routes lead to the Tibetan market of Gyanima and Taklakot. All involve the crossing of several high passes, the easiest of which is 16,750 feet high and can only be negotiated eight months of the year. The Bhotias have an amusing legend of the way these routes were pioneered: it seems that the first inhabitants of the Milam Valley were, like Esau, hairy – even to their tongues – and on the Gori Glacier there lived a bird of prey whose sole diet was these hairy ones. To free the people from this predatory fowl a Tibetan Lama sent his servant to kill it, and gave him as guide a man who was for ever changing his form, first into a dog at the pass which is now called Kingribingri, then into a stag, which gave the name to the Dol Dunga Pass, then into a bear at the Topi Dunga Pass, a camel at the Unta Dhura, a tiger at the Dung Udiyar, and finally a hare at Samgoan. Thus the route to India was first shown and the bird of prey eventually killed – but not before it had eaten all the hairy ones. And the servant liked the valley so much that he expressed a desire to live in it but complained that there was no salt, so the kindly Lama took salt and sowed it like grain, with the result that there is today a salty grass on which the Bhotia flocks feed, and even yet Buddhist priests entering the valley ask for alms in the name of the Lama who sowed the salt, and Tibetans bring their herds over the border for the sake of the salty grass.

I digress. It is high time we followed the Pindar river westwards to where it flows into the Alaknanda some thirty miles away. Above this junction the Alaknanda bends to the north and receives from the north-east a large tributary, the Dhauli, whose valley lies between the Nanda Devi and the Kamet groups. At the head of this valley thirty miles further to the north is the Niti Pass, also leading to Tibet, and the river itself rises from the glaciers to the east and slightly north of Kamet. From this mountain near the Tibetan border the massif runs almost due south very nearly to the Dhauli-Alaknanda junction.

The main Alaknanda Valley which, as we saw, continues due north, separates the Kamet range from the Badrinath-Kedarnath group. The river rises near the Mana Pass and, passing under the western flanks of Kamet, receives large tributaries from the Badrinath peaks. This latter range does not extend so far south as its companion ranges but turns sharply back to the north-west, forming an acute angle in which lies the Gangotri glacier, the largest in these parts and the source of the Bhagirathi River, the main tributary of the Ganges.

The Nanda Devi group itself, around which the interest of Tilman and myself gyrated throughout our voyage to Calcutta, presents unusual features. Imagine a main ridge running from north to south and in the southern half three arms projecting to the west. At the southern extremity a long one leads up to Trisul, 23,360 feet, and terminates ten miles to the west in Nandakna, 20,700 feet. Several miles north is a shorter arm on which is Dunagiri, 23,184 feet, and between the two lies the shortest arm of all which ends abruptly at Nanda Devi itself. From Trisul and from Dunagiri two spurs project towards each other to form the fourth side of the wall, nowhere less than 18,000 feet high, which surrounds Nanda Devi. The only breach in this formidable barrier is between these spurs where the Rishi Ganga, the river which drains the glaciers around Nanda Devi, breaks through by way of a deep gorge.

And it was by following the Rishi Ganga that we hoped to reach the shrine of the 'Blessed Goddess'.

3   Chapter 3

Himalayan travel is of course full of complexities. The shortness of the season during which expeditions are possible, the uncertainty of the monsoon, the danger of land-slips, endemic cholera and other diseases of the lower valleys, leeches and insect pests, extremes of heat and cold, altitude, local superstitions and the consequent difficulty in obtaining help from the natives – these are but a few of the obstacles to be overcome by the traveller.

And in the case of Nanda Devi one tremendous problem was added, the fact that the peak is encircled by a huge amphitheatre that must surely be unique. It is hard for anyone who has not studied this phenomenon at close quarters to form an adequate conception of a gigantic rampart, in places over 23,000 feet high, enclosing a bit of country itself not above the limits of dwarf trees, from the centre of which rises a stupendous peak 25,600 feet in height. Small wonder that this grim seventy-mile ring of mountains had repulsed all assaults, and that the sanctuary of the inner basin had remained inviolate.

Mr Hugh Ruttledge wrote in an article published in *The Times* of 22 August 1932, soon after his attempt of that year: 'Nanda Devi imposes upon her votaries an admission test as yet beyond their skill and endurance; a seventy-mile barrier ring, on which stand twelve measured peaks over 21,000 feet high, which has no depression lower than 17,000 feet – except in the west, where the Rishi Ganga river, rising at the foot of Nanda Devi, and draining an area of some 250 square miles of snow and ice has carved for itself what must be one of the most terrific gorges in the world. Two internal ridges, converging from north and south respectively upon this river form, as it were, the curtains of an inner sanctuary, within which the great mountain soars up to 25,600 feet. So tremendous is the aspect of the Rishi Ganga gorge that Hindu mythology described it as the last earthly home of the Seven Rishis. Here, if anywhere, their meditations might be undisturbed.'

As I mentioned earlier, it was our intention to attempt to force our way up this gorge into the basin beyond. Naturally, therefore, we made an intensive study of all previous exploits of mountaineers and explorers who had tried to gain access to what Mr Hugh Ruttledge calls, so aptly, 'the inner sanctuary'.

Most of the early explorers of the Nanda Devi group approached it from the east. As long ago as 1830 G. W. Traill, who was first commissioner of Garhwal and Kumaon, ascended the Pindari Glacier and crossed a pass at its head into the Milam Valley. The object of this exploit was probably rather to find a short cut to Milam than to explore mountains. The fact that Traill suffered severely from snow-blindness was regarded by the natives as a sign that the Goddess had visited her wrath upon him and this belief had such effect that in 1855, when Adolf Schlagintweit, that remarkable Himalayan traveller, attempted to cross the range by the same route he took the precaution of making a handsome offering at the temple of Nanda Devi in Almora before he started. This inspired his coolies with much confidence and even when, on the glaciers, two of his strongest men were seized with epileptic fits, he was able to point out to the rest that it could be none of the goddess's doing and so persuade them to carry on. Later he was joined by his brother Robert, and together they explored the great Milam Glacier and crossed another pass which led them into Tibet. Travelling to the west they reached Kamet and climbed to an altitude of 22,239 feet on its Tibetan side, thus reaching the greatest height which had been so far attained.

In 1861 Traill's pass was again crossed by Colonel Edmund Smyth in the course of a memorable journey in those parts, while in 1883 Mr T. S. Kennedy, the celebrated Alpine climber, carried out some further work on the Milam side of the range.

In that same year, on the western side of the group, was undertaken a portion of what Dr T. G. Longstaff in 1906 described as 'the greatest Himalayan expedition that has yet been made'. The party was a small one and consisted of that redoubtable Himalayan explorer, W. W. Graham; the famous Swiss guide, Emil Boss, of whom Graham wrote: 'One of the best mountaineers living, extremely well-educated, speaking seven languages equally fluently ; a captain in the Swiss Army he is a splendid companion and I deemed myself fortunate to have his company.' And lastly another first-rate guide, Ulrich Kauffmann, of Grindelwald. (Boss and Kauffmann are well remembered for their work on the Southern Alps of New Zealand for which, in conjunction with his Indian achievements, Boss received the Black Grant from the Royal Geographical Society.)

Dr Longstaff writes (*Alpine Journal*, 1906, Vol. XXIII, pp. 203–204): 'No one who reads the short and modest description of his (Graham's) Garhwal trip can fail to be fired with longing to revisit the scenes of his struggles, and no one who has not been lucky enough to have been there can realise what he went through, and what a strenuous pioneer and splendid climber he must have been. We can only lament that he did not give us as detailed an account we have since come to expect from the returning wanderer.'

Graham's principal objective was to force a route up the Rishi Ganga gorge to the western base of Nanda Devi. Travel among the foothills must have been a very different proposition from what it is now, and only after several weeks of hard going did his little party reach the tiny hamlet of Rini, where the Rishi Ganga, issuing from the mouth of its lower gorge, bursts into the Dhaoli River.

'On the next day, 6 July,' (he writes in *Good Words*, January, 1885) 'we wished to start for Nanda Devi. As the crow flies, it was some twenty miles but, seeing the nature of the ground, we decided to allow at least a week to reach the foot of the peak. On inquiring for a guide we were told that the valley was impassable, that no sahib had ever been up it … etcetera, etcetera. We took most of this *cum grano*, but found, alas, that it was only too true! After getting up four miles we came to an unexpected obstacle. A glacier had once run due north from Trisul to the river; it had now retreated, leaving a bed with sheer perpendicular walls some 400 feet in depth. We tried up and down to find a place where we could cross. Below, it fell sheer some 1,500 feet into the river: above, it only got deeper and deeper. It was a mighty moat of nature's own digging to guard her virgin fortresses. We gave it up and returned rather disconsolately to Rini.'

After this the party moved round to the north and continued their explorations in that direction. In the course of this journey they made a determined but unsuccessful attempt to climb the giant peak of Dunagiri, which stands on the outer rim of the Nanda Devi Basin. Later they learnt from the shepherds of the Dhaoli Valley that a way was known across the ridge that formed the northern retaining wall of the Rishi Nala.

Once more they started for Nanda Devi. 'On 15 July,' so the record goes, 'we began to make our way up the northern side of the Rishi Ganga. The climb was sufficiently steep, there being no path, and we having pouring rain the whole time. On the evening of the second day we reached a lovely little tableland called Dunassau (Durashi). The last day's route had been extremely wild, running along the southern face of the ridge, sometimes with a sheer drop to the river below – some 7,000 to 8,000 feet. Such wild rocks and broken gullies I had never met with before.'

At Durashi, Graham and his companions were held up by heavy falls of snow and were deserted by most of their terror-stricken coolies. These men had been recruited from the Dhaoli Valley and shared the local superstition that their route was infested with devils. Carrying double loads, the three Europeans and the few local people who remained faithful to them, struggled on. 'Our progress,' writes Graham, 'was very slow, partly because we had to carry fifteen loads between nine of us, partly owing to the nature of the ground, which was not only very broken and precipitous but quite *terra incognita* to the whole party … Guiding in its strict Alpine sense was wanted here; sharp rocky ridges ran down from the peaks on our north, and fell, with high precipices, sheer into the stream some five thousand feet below. Occasionally we had to hang on by a tuft of grass, or a bunch of alpine roses, and I do not exaggerate when I say that for half the total day's work hand-hold was as necessary as foot-hold. By nightfall, after twelve hours' work, we had gained some three miles in absolute distance, and this, perhaps, better than anything will give an idea of the labour involved in working along these slopes.'

And after several days of this sort of work Graham writes further:

'We camped on a little space, the only one we could find which was not so steep as the rest and, after building a wall of stones to prevent us from rolling into the river, we turned in. I found, however, that sleeping at an angle of thirty degrees is not conducive to comfort. Time after time did I dream that I was rolling over the edge, and woke to find myself at the bottom of the tent on top of Boss, or vice versa. (We took it in turns in a most impartial manner to roll down first and made a bed for the other, who speedily followed.) On the morrow Kauffmann took the coolies back to bring up the other loads, and Boss went forward to explore the route. I lay, an interesting invalid in the tent, my foot giving me great pain, and being quite unable to wear a boot.

'Next day we worked along the spur, following Boss, who had seen a place where he thought we could cross the river. When above this we descended to it, the hill being very steep and covered with thorny jungle. Rain began again and we found ourselves on the bank of the stream shivering and waiting for Boss, who had gone after some pheasants. This little delay effectually settled our chances of crossing. The stream rose several feet in an hour, and though we tried very hard to bridge the flood, everything was washed away as soon as laid in position. Boss stood up to his knees on a slippery rock, with the water rushing by at some twenty miles an hour and worked like a horse, but it was of no avail. Once, indeed, I thought that he was gone as he slipped and nearly fell. Needless to say, to fall into that torrent would have been certain death, battered to pieces against the tremendous rocks that blocked the way. At last, soaked to the skin and very tired, we gave it up and pitched camp under an overhanging boulder.

'Next day, Kauffmann and the coolies returned to fetch up the rest of the provisions, while Boss and I worked along the river to see if we could find a crossing. About half a mile up we came to a most magnificent gorge, one of the finest specimens of water erosion ever seen. Two hundred feet above, the rocks nearly met, their smooth, black, shiny sides overhanging considerably. Through this tunnel roared and raved the torrent, here pent within very narrow limits, raging with a sound as of thunder. Yet in this fearful din and turmoil we saw a curious thing. On a tiny ledge, just above the dashing waves, a pigeon had built her nest and therein lay the two white shining eggs in perfect security: no enemy could touch them there. We carefully examined the stream up to the point where it descended the cliff in a grand fall, and found that nowhere in its present state could a crossing be effected.

'It was provoking: we were halted high under the great cliffs of Nanda Devi, which rose almost perpendicularly above us, and we could see, so near and yet so far, the spur by which we had hoped to climb. To cross, however, was out of the question with our limited appliances, and we reluctantly decided to return.'

They camped where they were: 'Suddenly there entered Kauffmann and the shikari (hunter).

'"Well, Kauffmann, when are the others coming?"

'"*Hélas, Monsieur, ils sont tous partis!*"'

That remark, uttered under the very shadow of the mountain for which these few men had dared so much, was the death-knell to the expedition. Yet Graham's reaction to it was wholly admirable. 'It was only too true,' he writes. 'The coolies had evidently planned the affair and, as soon as they had got out of sight of camp, had fairly bolted. Kauffmann's face was so lugubrious that, serious as the matter was, I couldn't help bursting out into laughter. However, this settled what we had previously almost decided.'

To go on without native help was impossible. Graham and his party abandoned everything that was not absolutely necessary and fought their way back down the gorge. A heart-breaking journey that must have been, unrelieved by knowledge of happenings yet in the future which were to show the true value of Graham's achievement, since further attempts to penetrate the upper gorge of the Rishi Ganga met with but small success and it was not until 1907 that any other noteworthy exploration was carried out on this side of the range.

In July, 1893, Dr Kurt Boeckh attacked the eastern side of the range and made his way up the Milam Glacier with the idea of forcing a passage across the eastern portion of the barrier wall surrounding the Nanda Devi Basin. He had with him the Austrian guide, Hans Kerer, but when the coolies realised his intention they refused to advance and Boeckh was obliged to abandon his project before he had got very far. (Even if the coolies had agreed to accompany him it is doubtful if he would ever have been able to lead them safely over the range; such a route entailing work of a tremendously high standard of mountaineering.) Unwilling to return by the way he had come Boeckh carried out a fine journey to the north, crossing the Untadhura Pass in the middle of September and descending the very difficult gorge of the Girthi to Malari in the Dhaoli Valley.

But early in the present century, the district attracted the attention of Dr T. G. Longstaff, whose record as a mountain explorer is assuredly in a class by itself. In 1905 he came out with the Italian guides, Alexis and Henri Brocherel, with the intention of continuing the work which Graham had started on the western side of the group. The opportunity of accompanying Mr C. A. Sherring on a political mission into western Tibet, however, caused him to alter his plans and to spend the period before the breaking of the monsoon in exploring the valleys east of Nanda Devi. After several marches through the fern-clad cliff country of the Gori defile and up into the bare, wind-swept valley of Milam, they pitched camp on 27 May near the hamlet of Ganaghar, on the right bank of the Gori, at a height of 11,100 feet. From here they pushed their way up the Panchu Glacier and eventually crossed a difficult snow pass at its head. This brought them on to the Lwanl Glacier, running parallel with the Panchu and not into the Nanda Devi Basin as their map had led them to expect. They descended to the main valley for supplies and shortly afterwards returned to the Lwanl. After three days climbing they gained the Almora-Garhwal water-parting which forms at this point part of the rim of the Nanda Devi Basin and from here, for the first time in history, did man gaze down upon the glaciers at the southern foot of the great mountain.

A descent on the other side of the ridge was found to be impracticable and after an unsuccessful attempt to climb the great peak of Nanda Kot the party continued their explorations to the south and succeeded before they were overtaken by the monsoon, in crossing a pass from the head of the Salung Gadh to Baughdiar, a remarkable piece of mountaineering.

But the lure of Nanda Devi stayed and 1907 again found Dr Longstaff in the vicinity, this time concentrating on his old plan of continuing Graham's work on the country around the Rishi Ganga. He brought with him a very strong mountaineering party, including Major (now Brigadier-General) the Hon. C. G. Bruce – the most experienced Himalayan mountaineer of his time – Mr A. L. Mumm, and three Alpine guides, the two brothers Brocherel again and Moritz Inderbinnen of Zermatt, who had been Mumm's companion for over twenty years.

Their first objective was the Rishi Valley and examination of the lower gorge decided them to attempt Graham's route, the first part of which was known to the Tolma and Lata shepherds of the Dhaoli Valley. But they were too early in the year and found too much snow to allow them to make the passage of the Durashi Pass so they moved round to the Bagini Glacier, in the hope that if they were able to cross a certain pass at its head they would find themselves in the Nanda Devi Basin. They made their way up the glacier on 20 May and came in sight of a gap ahead of them. 'All who were bound for the pass,' writes Dr Longstaff (*Alpine Journal*, Vol. XXIV), 'were heavily loaded as we had to carry Primus stoves, petroleum, cooking pots, tents, sleeping bags, instruments, rifles and ammunition, a large supply of ropes, and provisions sufficient to last our party of eight for ten days. For, having got into the Rishi Valley, we intended to get out of it some time. In the interval we must be self-supporting. The sun was so oppressive that after tramping over the snow for five hours, we stopped, at 11 a.m. (21 May), under the shade of some huge blocks, which formed part of an irregular medial moraine (18,300 feet).

'Instead of making for the pass directly under Changabang, we had now decided to go right up to the head of this arm of the glacier, more directly under the great easterly spur of Dunagiri. Mumm, who was not very fit, did not intend to cross the pass with us, and returned to the camp above Dunagiri (grazing ground) with Inderbinnen and Damar Sing, leaving us a party of four Europeans and four Gurkhas. He rejoined us later at Surai Thota.

'On 22 May we started at 4.30 a.m., but Bruce and I had very soon to stop with cold feet; and it was probable at this time that Karbir got his frostbite.

We had to rope over the last slopes, and the guides cut many steps. Our loads seemed to grow inordinately heavy, but at 10 a.m. we stood on the crest of the pass. Its height comes out at 20,100 feet, and the name Bagini Pass would most naturally belong to it. From the pass we looked down to a vast firn (snow field), shut in by snow-clad peaks, while 3,000 feet above us on the west towered the icy crest of Dunagiri. But the descent of the south side looked so bad that we had to set about it at once. The Brocherels had brought a good supply of pitons (iron stakes) from Courmayeur, and by means of these we were able to lower our loads down the snow-draped cliffs below us. It really was a difficult bit of mountaineering, the descent of about 1,000 feet occupying over five hours; and the two Brocherels were in their element. This was a very fine performance on the part of the Gurkhas, and a striking testimony both to their inherently resolute character, and to the excellence of their military training. Remember that they were called upon to perform a feat which was quite beyond the powers of any of the local men … We were very glad to camp about 4 p.m. on the snow-field directly at the southern foot of the pass (18,800 feet) … We had fondly hoped to find ourselves on the great glaciers at the foot of Nanda Devi itself.'

But on descending from the snow field they were on, they found themselves in the Rishi Nala, at a point below that which Graham had reached in 1883. They were able to shoot some bharal (wild sheep), which provided them with sufficient food to enable them to force their way down the valley to Durashi, and so to reach their main base at Surai Thota, in the Dhaoli Valley, after nearly a fortnight of very difficult mountaineering.

Later the party came back up the Rishi Valley, and it was then that Dr Longstaff made his famous ascent of Trisul (23,406 feet), which for twenty-three years remained the highest summit reached by man. After this he and two of the Gurkhas pushed their way further up the valley. 'With considerable difficulty we reached the junction of the Rhamani torrent with the Rishi Ganga, where we crossed the latter to the northern bank by a snow bridge (11,790 feet), as we could get no further along the southern bank, and the current was too strong for wading. Here we camped under an overhanging rock amongst the birch trees. That morning we climbed straight up to about 13,500 feet, and in the intervening 1,700 feet of cliffs between this and the Rishi Ganga, saw no practicable route up the valley, though we obtained a most wonderful view of Nanda Devi, the "Blessed Goddess", that queen of mountains fit to rank with the Matterhorn and Ushba. I think that we were just beyond Graham's furthest point in this direction … Though no one, native or European, has yet succeeded in forcing his way up the gorge to the western base of Nanda Devi, yet I feel convinced that it is possible to do so. I can think of no more interesting or arduous task for a party composed of mountaineers, than to follow up the great glacier under the southern face of Nanda Devi, and to cross the ridge on which I camped in 1905, over into the Milam Valley. The height of the pass is about 19,000 feet, and as we stood on its crest it appeared quite possible to climb up to it from the Nanda Devi Glacier on the west. But this expedition would involve the abandonment of the base camp and all impedimenta in the Dhaoli Valley, for at least a month. The return could be made most quickly by the Untadhura Pass, and the difficult Girthi Valley to Malari, for I do not think anyone would be likely to return by the same route.'

Since then, until last year, 1934, the upper gorge of the Rishi Valley was left severely alone.

During the monsoon of 1907, Dr Longstaff proceeded to explore the Nandagini and Sunderdhunga valleys, both of which lead up to the wall of the basin from the south. Only those who have travelled amongst the unexplored valleys of those parts in the monsoon can appreciate the appalling conditions which rendered these two reconnaissances inconclusive.

No fewer than twenty years later Dr Longstaff returned to the Nandagini with Mr Hugh Ruttledge, and reached the crest of the wall at its lowest point, 17,000 feet. Bad weather prevented further progress, but in any case this approach would have led them down to a point in the Rishi Nala below that reached in 1907.

In 1926 a further attempt was made to reach the great mountain from the east by a strong party, consisting of Mr Hugh Ruttledge, Dr Howard Somervell, who accompanied Mallory and Norton on the two highest climbs on Everest in the years 1922 and 1924, and Colonel Commandant (now Major-General) R. C. Wilson. Though the attack was not pushed home, enough was done to warrant a conclusion that the defences on this side are even more elaborate than on the south or west.

May 1932 saw Mr Ruttledge coming again to the attack, this time with the Italian guide, Emil Rey, of Courmayeur, grandson of his famous namesake, and six of the Everest Sherpas. His plan was to attempt to cross a gap at the head of the Sunderdhunga Valley, which had been tentatively reconnoitred by Dr Longstaff in 1907. If the gap could be crossed it must lead into the inner sanctuary of Nanda Devi.

In an article published in *The Times* (22 August 1932), Mr Ruttledge writes: 'In a mood of hopeful anticipation our party, on 25 May, trudged up the narrow glacier which leads from Sunderhunga itself to the base of the wall, of which the greater part is invisible from a distance. The Sherpas cheered derisively as a little avalanche had an ineffective shot at us from the cliffs above; and raced round the last corner. One step round it, and we were brought up all standing by a sight which almost took our remaining breath away. Six thousand feet of the steepest rock and ice. '*Nom de nom!*' said Emil, while Nima exclaimed that this looked as bad as the north-west face of Kangchenjunga in 1930. However we had come a long way to see this, so we advanced across the stony slopes to a point from which we hoped, by detailed examination, to reduce terrific appearances to milder reality. But the first impressions were accurate. Near the top of the wall, for about a mile and a half, runs a terrace of ice some 200 feet thick; in fact the lower edge of a hanging glacier. Under the pull of gravity large masses constantly break off from this terrace, and thunder down to the valley below, polishing in their fall the successive bands of limestone precipice of which the face is composed. Even supposing the precipice to be climbable, an intelligent mountaineer may be acquitted on a charge of lack of enterprise if he declines to spend at least three days and two nights under fire from this artillery. As alternative, there is a choice of three knife-edge arêtes, excessively steep, sometimes overhanging in the middle and lower sections, on which even the eye of faith, assisted by binoculars, fails to see one single platform large enough to accommodate the most modest of climbing tents.

'The jury's verdict was unanimous; and so, with a homely vernacular *non possumus* from Emil, vanished the last hope of a straightforward approach to Nanda Devi; and the goddess keeps her secret.'

Would the goddess, who had so protected herself from human intrusion throughout the centuries, reveal her secret to us, with an expedition absurd in its smallness? As we neared Calcutta both Tilman and I realised more and more the size of our task and the unlikelihood of success. But if our resources were small, we had at least the 'eyes of faith' and the knowledge of the experience of our predecessors to help us to reach our goal.

4   Chapter 4

Before leaving England we had arranged to send a wire to Karma Paul in Darjeeling as soon as we knew the date of our arrival in Calcutta and he was then to send our porters to meet us there, but, as Tilman and I rehearsed for the fiftieth time the programme we had so carefully mapped out and we steamed ever nearer to our goal, we grew impatient and debated the advisability of disembarking at Visagapatam, the last port of call before Calcutta, which lies three days ahead. By taking the train from Visagapatam we could save two precious days. This idea, however, had to be turned down on the score of expense and we went ashore there merely to send a wire requesting that the three Sherpas should be sent down to Calcutta, to arrive there the same day as ourselves. Although the homes of these men lay far from Darjeeling, it was there that they spent most of their time working as rickshaw coolies, and the hill-station was all they knew of civilisation. To our knowledge they had never even travelled by train before and to avoid the risk of their wandering alone in Calcutta, Karma Paul was instructed to impress upon them most strongly the necessity of not stirring a yard from the station until met by us.

These arrangements made we had a further three days in which to ponder the mischances that might befall our innocents before we met them. Another problem was whether, on the day of our arrival, we could possibly do some shopping, dispatch business at a bank, interview several people and transport half a ton of stores from the ship to the Howrah Station in time for the nine o'clock train that night. Such was our impatience to reach the mountains that the possibility of an enforced week end in Calcutta seemed to jeopardise the success of the whole expedition.

We landed in good time on a Saturday, got the most important jobs done and then hastened to our hotel, expecting to find a telegram advising us of the dispatch of the Sherpas. Sure enough, there was the wire, but it merely said that on receipt of journey-money and an advance of pay, the men would be put in the train.

We were annoyed, to say the least! Our invective must surely have made Karma Paul's ears tingle up in Darjeeling but a little reflection showed us that the demand was perfectly reasonable and that we had been exceedingly stupid not to think of its necessity earlier. I smile even now to think of the unnecessary stew into which we worked ourselves.

Well, the money had to be sent, and quickly, or the post office would be closed until Monday, so off we raced only to find that there exists in Calcutta the most exasperating arrangement whereby the wire is handed in at one office and the money paid over at another about half a mile away. To our harassed minds it seemed that the greater part of India's three hundred million inhabitants were assembled for the purpose of sending telegrams – and that five minutes before closing time – but eventually we got the money off.

This delay was a severe blow but it was softened when we obtained permission to live on the ship over the week end, so that our somewhat slender financial resources were not depleted by extra hotel bills. We were now 'sweating' on getting away by Monday and this war-time expression most adequately describes our condition, physical and mental. Even departure on Monday was expecting a lot, because were Karma Paul on the spot to receive the wire, he would have but Sunday morning in which to round up the men, give them time to make their arrangements, and shepherd them to the train.

No further news arrived and, assuming all was well, we made our way to the Sealdah Station at seven on the Monday morning. We reached the platform when the train was already in and disgorging its passengers. I, from my previous acquaintance with the Sherpas, knew the men we were looking for, and Tilman, who had never seen a Sherpa, observed that 'Three men from the wilds of Nepal, shrinking from the noise and bustle and wearing a sort of 'Bing Boys on Broadway' air, should be easy enough to spot'.

When most of the crowd had passed the barriers with no sign of our men, we began to search the platform, and soon our choice was reduced to some station coolies fast asleep, a sweetmeat seller, and a one-legged beggar – whom even Tilman, inexperienced as he was, rejected as a candidate. Doubtful now, we cast our net wider, taking in all eight platforms, the booking-hall, the first, second and third-class waiting-rooms for men and women, the refreshment-rooms for Europeans, Hindus, and Mohammedans, and all other likely and unlikely places in which three affrighted innocents abroad might seek refuge from the confusion around them.

Doubt became fear. Tilman was convinced they had not come: I had more faith in Karma Paul and our luck, and began to cross-question every official I could persuade to listen to our story. It was a shade too early to get hold of any of the directors or the general manager, but having catechised the higher ranks – as personified by traffic manager and station-master, we descended grade by grade to humble ticket-collectors. One of these proved more observant than seemed possible – or else something passing strange had arrived by the Darjeeling Mail – for his attention had been excited by 'three exotic figures', apparently from the remoter parts of Asia. Here was a gleam of light, but, on thinking matters over we realised that the exotic three (whoever they might be) were now at large in the City of Calcutta and probably untraceable.

Before enlisting the aid of the Police we decided that it would be as well to ring up our hotel to see if there were any news from Darjeeling.

'There is no telegram,' came the reply, 'but can you throw any light on three very rum-looking birds who drove up here in a taxi an hour ago?'

'Are they from Darjeeling?' I asked excitedly.

'Well, they seem to talk Chinese,' was the answer, 'and I don't know enough of the language to ask them where they come from but they are in search of two sahibs, so you had better come along and see them – and the sooner the better. They're no advertisement for my hotel!'

We drove back in silence, conflicting emotions rendering us speechless. Swift decision followed by swift action seemed to be the habit of these three and we wondered if they would wait or set off on a wild goose-chase around the city looking for us.

They *had* waited. Not in the lounge (as we had been half afraid they would do) and they *were* our Sherpas! We found them sitting patiently in the back regions and realised immediately the true meaning of the ticket-collector's description. Indeed, 'exotic' was a mild adjective. Clad in shirts and shorts, and crowned with billycock hats from under which glossy black pig-tails descended, the three were distinctive enough, but when one took into consideration that their shirts were a blinding purple in colour and that this crude shade was matched in their lips and teeth (the result of much betel-chewing) one understood how even the most myopic ticket-collector would notice them.

They greeted us gravely, apparently completely unconcerned. In the face of such oriental calm Tilman and I restrained ourselves, although our relief at finding them after our mad chase had induced a mild form of hysteria in us both, and we carefully avoided mention of the events at the station. Soon we were all down at the docks, hard at work getting our gear on shore. The astonishment of the ship's company was considerable, but the Sherpas went about their work in a matter-of-fact way, as little impressed by an 11,000 ton ship and the busy traffic of the Hooghly as with a bullock-cart in the Darjeeling bazaar.

This attitude should not have been a surprise to either of us who were both well acquainted with African natives. When the savage sees a train or a motor car for the first time in his life he does not, as one would expect, show either excitement or fear; nor does he behave like the old lady, who, when confronted for the first time with a giraffe, said that she didn't believe it. Tilman has told me that in East Africa the inauguration of the Air Mail caused no sensation whatever. An aeroplane passing overhead was regarded merely as an excuse to stop work for a moment – if the native was not working he simply did not bother to look up! Similarly, a native boy who accompanied a friend of his to England was impressed only by the meat hanging in the English butchers' shops, and although the Sherpas have little in common with the African native they are certainly alike on this one point – their attitude to the modern amenities of civilisation.

Having somehow got all our baggage to Howrah Station we sent the Sherpas off to see the sights of Calcutta in charge of a friend's servant, a man well fitted to be their cicerone since he acted in the same capacity to the seventy porters of the German Nanga Parbat expedition. Afterwards he informed us that the zoo alone had excited any interest!

Meantime Tilman and I went off to arrange for seats on the train and met with an unexpected difficulty. The 9 p.m. train was the Bombay Mail, which took no third-class passengers but allowed other passengers one bearer apiece; at 10 p.m. there was another train which boasted third-class accommodation but on this we could not go since all second-class seats had been reserved. Very unwillingly we decided to split our party, taking one man with us and leaving the other two to follow on the later train. Their morning's work had shown us they were not quite the simpletons we had imagined – but it was tempting providence to let them travel to an unknown destination with but a smattering of Hindustani between them. Still, the only alternative was to wait yet another day – and another day of Calcutta would have worn what small patience we had left to tatters.

As it was we did not depart without further strain on our frayed nerves, for the friend with whom we had a farewell dinner insisted that ten minutes was ample time in which to weigh, book and load our 1,000 pounds. of luggage. Personally I felt that a full hour would be all too short and endured torment (with both eyes on the clock) while he ordered beer – and yet more beer. In the end we only reached our carriage with a second or two to spare, followed by the two Sherpas who were to take the later train loudly bemoaning their lot until our friend, who was thoroughly enjoying the whirl of our departure, forcibly restrained them from climbing in beside us and promised to see them off safely at ten o'clock.

With us travelled Angtharkay, short, sturdy and self-possessed, and despite all our arguments he flatly refused to occupy the small cupboard thoughtfully provided by the railway for bearers, and insisted upon sleeping on the floor of our compartment – much to the disgust of our fellow passengers. It was a stifling night and Angtharkay, who felt the heat, recklessly squandered his money on beakers of tea at one anna a time. Tilman and I fumed and fretted about our abandoned Sherpas, whom we were to pick up some twenty-four hours later at Bareilly so that we could all take the Kathgodam train together.

At last we steamed into Bareilly Station, ill-tempered, dusty and exhausted. Fortunately we had time to wash off the outer layer of dust, stow our baggage in the Kathgodam train and have some food before meeting the Calcutta train bearing our precious freight. We were not feeling too happy – remembering our hectic time in Calcutta. True, our friend had had the strictest instructions to tell the Sherpas to sit tight until pulled out by us, since the name Bareilly conveyed no more to them than did Bombay, but twenty-four hours of sweltering heat might well have exhausted their patience and, if they thought we had missed them, they were perfectly capable of getting out where they thought fit. Moreover, the train only stopped for ten minutes, the platform was abominably lit, and most third-class passengers were certain to be asleep.

When the train arrived our hearts descended into our boots. It seemed twice as long as any train ought to be, its carriages were of vast size, very dark and over-crowded with natives lying asleep on top of each other, all with their faces covered. Packed like sardines is a poor simile, for packing denotes order and here was chaos. To search thirty-odd 'black holes of Calcutta' in a few moments was an impossible task, so I shouted orders to Tilman and Angtharkay and we all began to dash frenziedly up and down, bawling the names of our two men through the open windows. Yells of 'Kusang!!' ... 'Pasang!!' rose above the hiss of the engine and the few passengers who were sufficiently awake to take any notice scrambled to their feet and eyed us askance. But all our clamour utterly failed to upset traffic arrangements and after its allotted time the train pulled out, several occupants shaking their heads from the windows as though in relief that the three madmen were being left behind.

Here was a pretty mess. Blank-faced and sore-throated we stood miserably and debated our next move. Should we go or should we camp out on Bareilly platform, giving a rendering of our bawling performance to every train from Calcutta? Just as we began to debate this dismal question a warning toot sounded from the Kathgodam train and we sprinted towards it, fearful of losing luggage as well as men.

As we ran we glanced rapidly into each carriage trying to spot our gear and, of a sudden, Tilman gripped me by the arm. There, comfortably established among their possessions and eating oranges with every evidence of serene enjoyment, were Kusang and Pasang! It seemed a pity to disturb them. We crept quietly past to our own carriage, horribly conscious that Angtharkay's account of our antics would lose nothing in the telling.

But far into the night we argued about the mystery. The most experienced traveller who had to effect a change of trains at midnight in a country whose language he did not know, might be very pleased with himself if he managed without mishap. Yet two Sherpas, neither of whom had ever travelled by rail, neither of whom even knew the name of their destination, had contrived to get out at the right station and into the right train.

Part 2

The Secret Shrine

5 Chapter 5

The remainder of our journey to Kathgodam was a peaceful one. The Sherpas were (presumably) behaving themselves in their compartment and the countless irritations of the past few days faded from our minds. Our spirits rose as we left the train at last and packed ourselves and our belongings into a somewhat decrepit lorry and began the last fifty-mile stage of our road to Ranikhet, one of the loveliest of Indian hill-stations. Jolting along the broad motor-road that winds its way amongst the steep, forest-clad foothills rising abruptly from the plains, we took great gulps of the cool, pine-scented air, deliciously sweet after two days of travel in the appalling heat and dust of pre-monsoon India.

Up and up the lorry circled to Ranikhet, from the crest of whose pine-clad ridge there is to be seen a vast panorama of the Snows. The place was full of troops and all the usual pleasures of a hill-station were in full swing but these, however, were not for us, as we hoped to get away on our first march to Joshimath in two days' time if all necessary arrangements could be completed.

We were lucky to find ourselves sole occupants of a spacious rest-house, where we could spread ourselves as much as we liked. We arrived at midday on 9 May and straight away before lunch we went down to recruit coolies. We only required a dozen men and within an hour all was settled and twelve lusty Dotials had promised to leave at once and meet us two days later at Baijnath, a little village fifty miles to the north at the end of the motor-road. These coolies were not beautiful, but they were a likely looking lot and inspired us with confidence, for we gave them a substantial advance of pay and never had the slightest doubts about their failing to keep the rendezvous!

The next thirty-six hours were very fully occupied in making preparations for departure. A ration of kit was allotted to each member of the party, and all the surplus clothing which convention had thus far imposed upon us had to be packed away and handed over for safe custody. Each man was issued with a suit of light, wind-proof material, under which he might wear quite a quantity of garments. (I may say that this 'underclothing' consisted of a heterogeneous mixture collected from various friends and included long-forgotten shirts, pyjamas, tail-coats, etcetera, which I had unearthed when turning out a box-room before leaving home. Later, Kusang became firmly attached to a pair of my dress trousers, while Pasang, considering that an ancient dinner-jacket I gave him would be wasted in Garhwal, proudly carried it back to his native

Tibet when the expedition was over.) Then boots – the most important item of all – had to be attended to; and finally a careful estimate of the cash which would be required over the next five months had to be worked out and the amount obtained, almost entirely in coin, from the local native bank. Since this was not a correspondent of our Calcutta bank we had been compelled to draw all our money from there in notes and travel up with them in our pockets, a proceeding we had found very wearing indeed, and we now discovered that the process of exchanging these for silver was a lengthy one owing to the many spurious rupees in circulation in India. The Sherpas willingly assisted at this business, and were far quicker at spotting duds than we were, rejecting all doubtful ones without ado. At first our feelings were hurt at seeing any money we tendered being scrutinised, rung on a stone, bitten or otherwise tested, but we soon found it paid us to do the same.

We took one large Meade tent for the Sherpas and a smaller one for ourselves. We also had a very small tent weighing about six pounds. in all, but we soon realised that the weight saved in carrying it was not worth the discomfort of sleeping in it! We had the usual down sleeping bags – though real eiderdown ones would have been worth the extra expense; and for the purposes of cooking above the limits of firewood, we took a small Primus stove and about four dozen 'Tommy's Cookers' for use when Tilman and I were separated from the Sherpas. We had brought with us about 250 pounds of foodstuffs to help us out while we were getting accustomed to local food (which consisted almost entirely of coarse flour) and for use at high camps. Various last-minute purchases were made in the Ranikhet bazaar and then everything had to be packed in one-man loads, eighty pounds each, for the first stage of our journey.

In the early hours of the morning of 11 May we piled our stuff on to the waiting lorry, starting off at 7 a.m. Passing through the bazaar we suddenly remembered vegetables, lemons and eggs – and well it was that we did so. As I have mentioned before it was our aim to live on the country as far as possible, not only to save transport but because any fresh food, plain or dull though it may be, is preferable to things embalmed in tins be they ever so skilfully disguised; but though, throughout our travels, we were to find ourselves able to obtain staple foods, flour, potatoes and occasionally milk, how succulent were additional fruits, vegetables and eggs. And of these last the three dozen we bought in Ranikhet were, with one exception, the only eggs we tasted until our return.

Our lorry rolled into Baijnath at one o'clock and there we found our Dotials, who lost no time in making up their loads and starting for Gwaldam, the first stage of our ten-day march to Joshimath. 'March,' with its associations of discipline, timetables and the hard, high road, is scarcely applicable to the next lazy, carefree days. Beyond setting a time limit we had no set plan, and pace had, fortunately for me, to conform to that of the heavily-laden Dotials. I say fortunately, because I was, at the moment, far from fit. Besides a heavy cold and an inside the reverse of happy, I had broken a toe on the voyage out soon after leaving Aden which had not yet mended and which caused much pain. In consequence I was obliged to walk in a tennis shoe with a piece cut out of the side. On the ship this had not mattered, but in Calcutta it had looked a bit odd until we had joined forces with the Sherpas, who looked so amazing that had I gone about barefoot nobody would have noticed me. Even now a boot was out of the question and we discussed the hire of a pony, but in the end my journey to Joshimath was done in a pair of tennis shoes – or rather in one and a half.

So we ambled leisurely through a world of exquisite beauty. We rested when we felt inclined (which was frequently), bathed if the opportunity offered, and slept wherever seemed good to us. Until Ranikhet, Tilman and I had flattered ourselves upon our astuteness in steering three timid followers amidst the manifold difficulties and dangers of modern travel. But now that we had cast off the trammels of civilisation the boot was on the other leg, and in camp or on the march they devoted all their care to our welfare without a thought for themselves.

For the next five months we were to live and climb together, and the more we saw of the Sherpas the more we grew to like them. Porters all the time, they were also fellow mountaineers and companions, in turn playing the parts of housekeeper, cook, butler, pantryman, valet, interpreter and, on occasion, entertainer. Angtharkay was the eldest, a more sophisticated man than his brethren and possessed of Hindustani which could be understood by us and by other natives. When we had to employ them, he acted as buffer between us and the local coolies, and could generally tell us what they were thinking or feeling before they knew themselves. We could also delegate to him the very unpleasant business of bargaining, for he was a Hotspur who would 'cavil on the ninth part of a hair,' sometimes carrying this to excess and depriving us of a thing we really wanted rather than let us be 'done.' He was the soundest, too, on a mountain, both in movement and judgment, and as a route-finder we had many occasions on which to bless him.

Pasang was the most presentable of the party, taller than the other two and a bit of a dandy. He was a most graceful mover and quite brilliant on rocks, but he was exceedingly temperamental and required tactful handling. He acted as my batman – and a full-time job that was – I being the most careless of men and wont to drop my belongings all over the place. Poor Pasang was then expected to retrieve anything I suddenly asked for. Worse, he had to cope with a very bad habit of mine which was disconcerting, to say the least. No sooner was everything packed up than I would discover I *must* have something for the march, a spare woollie, a film, or a pencil. Whatever I wanted was sure to be at the very bottom of the great sack which was Pasang's load and the wretched man would have to turn it all out again. But he never seemed flustered or angered and the more work I gave him the better he liked it.

He was more Tibetan than the others and more religious. He carried a private stock of prayer-flags on which was printed the usual formula: '*Om Mane Padme Hung*' ... 'Hail, the Jewel in the Lotus Flower!' ... and one of these would be left fluttering on the top of a pass or to mark some campsite. In addition he hoarded mysterious little squares of adhesive yellow cloth which he stuck on his face just behind the corner of each eye, (after the manner of the patches of the eighteenth-century ladies of fashion), but the meaning of these we never discovered. Another of his customs was to throw a little of his food into the air before eating in order to propitiate the spirits; a rite which I regret to say was sometimes neglected, either through stress of hunger or dissatisfaction with the way the gods were treating us in the matter of weather. He was also an inveterate builder of cairns, as were his companions, particularly Kusang, in whom this building amounted to a passion. I believe this stone-posing is a favourite devotion of all Buddhists, and they like to choose the most difficult stones and perform remarkable feats of equilibrium with them. Long practice has made them very quick and skilful, and before we had found a suitable foundation stone for our cairn, they would have built one four or five feet high, surmounted by a long slab cleverly balanced on end.

Kusang was the youngest and least experienced of the three, and I fear he was rather put upon in the way of work, just as a recruit must do the chores for an old soldier. But Kusang was a lad who thrived on work, and from the time we got into camp until the time we left, he willingly became a sort of general servant. Almost before we had our loads off, if there was any firewood to be had he would stagger in half-hidden under a great load of it, and would then trot off again to fetch water or to collect snow for melting. By the time he returned the fire would be started but if, as usually happened, it was stubborn, his were the powerful lungs that supplied most of the forced draught. This bellows business became a kind of subconscious habit, for except when his mouth was full (and he ate in the wholehearted way he did everything) he directed a gentle but persistent zephyr towards the fire from wherever he happened to be sitting, with remarkable results. Indeed, when he got his head down and blew in earnest, an almost extinct fire became an inferno, and on a wet morning the first thing of which one became aware was the blast of Kusang's bellows and a comforting sound it was since it meant that tea would not long be delayed.

Washing up, that bugbear of camp life, was to Kusang a pet hobby, second only to cairn-building in his affections. To save time and trouble Tilman and I preferred to use a single plate with no washing between courses, but this Kusang seldom allowed and if, as was often the case, we were dependent on snow and the Primus for our water, his misguided enthusiasm for cleanliness in the home had to be restrained.

On the march he had a singular habit of crooning a mournful dirge, a repetition of three words and two notes, at all times and seasons. The stiffest slope or the most perilous place had no power to still him, but if we had to ford some swift, ice-cold torrent the voice would gradually die away. The habit was maddening at times and I confess to having suffered many moments when my one desire was to silence Kusang forever with an ice axe, but in places of difficulty one liked to hear him and thus be assured that the equanimity of at least one of the party was undisturbed.

We boasted no cook, and since the food we ate called for no vast display of culinary achievement, all took a hand at preparing it in turn. If more advanced treatment than boiling was required, Angtharkay, who had a light hand with a frying pan, would take charge, and we deferred to his judgment in the all-important matter of food and its cooking, for he was something of a gourmet. Further he had an extensive knowledge of edible plants which, as will appear later, proved of great value.

The Sherpas always used a very hot sauce of some kind to help down their rice, satu, or chupatties, and carried numerous condiments tied up in bits of rag, of which chillies was the most important. They assumed our tastes were similar, and to avoid blistered mouths we kept in our own hands the delicate business of seasoning our 'hoosh'.

They had an ingenious system of allotting the food when divided into three approximately equal parts; two of them would take three different sized bits of twig or grass and name one of each of them; these were then handed to the third, who did not know to whom the pieces belonged, and he placed one on each of the three portions. But they were very unselfish about food, and even when it was short were always pressing bits on each other and on us.

The making of edible chupatties is supposed to require some skill, but it is also a fairly laborious process. It devolved therefore on Kusang, and his results were not much more leathery than the professional article. It is fine exercise for the arms, and sometimes Tilman and I would take a hand, to warm ourselves and to afford the Sherpas a little harmless amusement; the sight of a chupattie in the making, curling itself round our wrists or disintegrating through too vigorous smacking, never failed to convulse them.

Their readiness to laugh was characteristic, but they had an odd sense of humour. Any minor misfortune, such as breaking a pipe or burning a hole in drying socks, would bring the house down, and once when I sat on my snow glasses and held up the result for Pasang's inspection, I thought he would have hysterics.

At one mishap which they, no doubt, considered the cream of all, they exercised commendable restraint. We were moving on very steep rock and had sat down on a narrow ledge for a rest, and taken off our sacks. Mine was put down with inexcusable carelessness and on getting up to go on, I happened to touch it with my foot, and thirty pounds of rice, lentils, and cheese went over the edge to burst like a bomb 200 feet below. The dismay on my face, great though it was, might not have restrained them, but the fact that it was food lent gravity to the affair, and they managed to control themselves. I recovered the sack, but not the contents, and the mangled remains, spilt in all directions, proved too much for them; for a month afterwards, while it yet hung together, the sight of it always fetched a laugh.

The extent of cultivation near the villages seemed out of proportion to the few people, and herds of cows and water buffaloes, and flocks of goats and sheep, gave promise of a fruitful land. Nevertheless flour was dispensed, if at all, by the cupful, and the livestock was apparently non-milk-producing; the hen and its product a legend; and fruit and vegetables unknown.

In these circumstances there was small scope for Angtharkay's talent for haggling, and on the rare occasions that an egg or a cup of milk appeared on the market, we were too eager to have it to worry about the price.

The scarcity of eggs was to be expected, because hens were seldom kept, but the milk shortage we never understood; the cows, so the story went, had just gone dry, the goats were all in a distant pasture, or there might be some milk tomorrow, if we did not leave too early. Flour was never on hand, each family grinding enough for the next meal and no more, and the promise of fruit was represented by a few unhappy apricot trees. With these last, I am willing to admit, the owners were generous and allowed the Sherpas to climb all over them, taking what they would without thought of payment. True, they were not giving away much, for I never saw a ripe one, but ripe or raw was of no importance to our hungry followers, and after they had finished, the trees appeared to have been attacked by a swarm of locusts.

The willingness of the villagers to supply us with anything they did happen to possess varied from place to place in a puzzling way. Sex seemed to have something to do with success or failure; if all the men were out in the fields and the village fort was held by a few old dames, stony indifference or harsh words were usually our portion. On these occasions we used to arm Angtharkay with some rupees and send him to bell the cat, and as he had pertinacity and a thick skin he seldom came away empty-handed. Kusang, though possessing a more ingratiating manner, would have wilted under the first torrent of abuse, while Pasang might have started throwing things. Most of these villages were on, or near, a 'Pilgrim Route' and my theory was that the traditional hospitality ascribed to mountain villages had been soured by the importunities of the many beggars, and doubtless our appearance justified them in placing us in the same category!

6   Chapter 6

The first march of our ten-day programme, an afternoon one to Gwaldam, was certainly the least pleasant of any. The road had dropped perversely, as such things do, 4,000 feet since Ranikhet, and now most of this had to be made good by untrained legs on a desperately hot day. Our Dotials must have been out of work for some time as they seemed no happier than we were, and it was late in the evening before a procession of cripples crawled painfully up the last steep rise to the forest bungalow. This was beautifully situated on the slopes overlooking the valley of the Pindar and surrounded by abandoned tea gardens, and once we had established ourselves on the veranda in long cane chairs and procured a vast bowl of milk, our toils were soon forgotten. Tonight we felt we had really started, and though still under a roof the link with civilisation was wearing thin.

The view beyond the Pindar which we had hoped morning would reveal, was hidden in mist and cloud which later turned to rain. Our way lay first down to the valley of the Pindar river, past many villages and well-cultivated fields. The flats near the river were irrigated and were used for growing rice, and great skill and industry was shown in the extensive terracing of the hillsides, a crop of winter wheat already being reaped. Later we left this smiling valley and turned north up a lateral branch, camping amongst some oaks on a high col in a drizzle of rain. At sundown the clouds lifted and from our vantage point 9,000 feet up we had a brief but satisfying vision of Nanda Ghunti.

We were now travelling across higher country between two main valleys, and villages were few and far between, a matter of indifference to us but of much interest to the porters who had to buy their daily rations from the hamlets we did pass. It was not always easy to find thirty or forty pounds of rice or of wheat flour; near the larger villages there was usually a mill turned by water, but in most of the smaller the flour was ground by hand on a flat stone, and no more done at a time than would suffice for the next meal – a really literal hand-to-mouth existence. At last, at a village called Wan, the porters got what they needed and we camped here on a little plateau above the village, under some huge Deodars.

We were now about to cross the watershed between the Pindar and Nandakganga Rivers, a long ridge, here 11,000 feet high, which leads up to the mighty Trisul ten miles away to the south-east. Our start was delayed while we waited for the Sherpas who, having only breakfasted lightly off several dou-ble-handfuls of satu, now proceeded to fill up with three of the biggest mountains of rice that plates have ever held. Two hours' steady climb through shady forests of oak and chestnut brought us to the col, and from there we climbed for another 2,000 feet up a hill west of it, for the sake of the view. The lower slopes were clothed in rhododendron forest, at this altitude still in flower and presenting a beautifully varied show of colour from white to pink and deep crimson. As we gained height, passing from forest to springy turf and then to rock, the mountains which we had been glimpsing through gaps in the trees now rose before us as a distant and broken wall of dazzling whiteness. Nearly all the giants of the Central Himalaya were there to welcome us, from the Kedarnath peaks and Kamet in the north round to Trisul in the east.

Despite a fierce sun it was very cold and snow was still lying in the gullies, so we tore ourselves away from the feast of beauty and hurried back to the col, and so down into the valley to Kanol. Against this name in my diary there is the laconic entry 'flies and bulls,' nor is more needed, for the recollection of being driven out of the camp by the one and flying naked before the other, which attacked us as we were about to bathe, is still very vivid. But Kanol is also memorable for the opening of the first of four big 'Farmhouse' cheddars we had brought with us; this somewhat premature attack on our luxuries being brought about partly by the difficulty of buying anything, already noted, and by some concern for its health. It had somehow got into my rucksack and so drew attention to itself, and we were anxious to know what effect the damp heat of Calcutta had had on it. Great was our relief to find it had suffered no serious harm. Certainly it had wilted a little but now the cool mountain air was having as bracing an effect upon the cheese as upon us.

Next day the Nandakganga was crossed and we embarked upon a succes-sion of ups and downs over a country almost bare of trees, in the full glare of a hot sun. Plodding up the dusty bridle-path, we met coming down a porten-tous cavalcade of over twenty mules, a like number of coolies, and a cloud of followers and servants, no doubt the advance-guard of some Great Personage, and we felt uneasy at the threatened meeting, because we had given up shav-ing since leaving Ranikhet. However it proved to be only a forest officer making a tour of his district, the last European we were to meet for another three months.

The magnificent forests which are such a feature of the foothills are at pres-ent safe from exploitation for timber or for paper owing to transport difficulties, the rivers being quite useless for that purpose. There is something to be said for illiteracy, and for some time India's three hundred and fifty millions and these noble forests are safe from the devastating effects of a daily Press. The only product at present is resin, the collection of which is under the forest department.

We had barely recovered from the apprehension aroused by the cavalcade and the subsequent reaction, when another passing wayfarer stretched our minds once more upon the rack of anticipation. This time the trouble was caused by an old chap who sported a row of war decorations, as many of these Garhwalis do since the Garhwal Rifles, which greatly distinguished itself in Flanders and Mesopotamia, is recruited solely from them. He saluted us with vigour and we propounded our usual question about eggs and chickens, a question we now put by way of a conversational gambit rather than as a serious inquiry, but the veteran startled us by hinting that he knew where a chicken might be got. He accompanied us to the next village talking all the time, but our replies were short as we were busy arguing the respective merits of roast and boiled chicken, finally deciding in favour of the latter because we wanted to eat it that night. Arrived at the village our friend disappeared into a house to find the victim. Returning presently with an air of self-satisfaction which told us he had been successful, he proudly produced, with the flourish of a conjurer, a rather ill-nourished fledgling whose feathers were barely visible. As a joke we thought it in rather bad taste, but we had to acquit him of that intention for when we refused to treat he became quite indignant.

The weather was now so fine and settled that every night we abandoned our stuffy tent in favour of the open, and that night we had a glorious camp on a smooth grass terrace under some pines. Shaken though we had been by the affair of the chicken, our peace and content was almost perfect as we lay round a fire of pinewood which blazed like a torch and gave off an oily smoke smelling pleasantly of turpentine. The only discordant note was provided by the Sherpas who industriously held their caps in the smoke and then suddenly clapped them on their heads, an operation which suggested, quite wrongly I believe, a very disturbing train of thought. The true explanation of this curious rite we never discovered.

In front of us now was another high ridge projecting far to the west from the slopes of Nanda Ghunti. We started early for the ascent of this, and the freshness of the morning, the oaks, the hollies, and the chestnuts, the tapping of woodpeckers and the distant note of a cuckoo, made it seem like a spring morning in England. From the col at 10,000 feet Trisul and Nanda Ghunti again showed up prominently, and then we dropped quickly down to the valley of the Bireh Ganga, and camped in a pretty dell, carpeted with big white flowers which smelt like lilies. Pleasant enough it was, but no longer reminiscent of spring at home, plagued as we were by myriads of flies and amused by a school of grey monkeys who were equally interested in us.

Early next day we crossed the river with that thirst-provoking name, the Bireh Ganga, a name, alas! and nothing more for we bathed in it in order to make quite sure. The northern slopes were steep bare hillsides up which the track wound in narrow zigzags, and at the steepest and narrowest part we were almost swept away by a flood of goats, all carrying little saddle-bags of grain. The photo I tried to take was not a success, and several goats were nearly frightened over the cliff much to the wrath of their owner. We experienced the same difficulty in taking pictures of some of the very picturesque-looking women we passed, festooned with necklaces and strings of coins, and wearing handsome jewelled nose-rings. They either fled at sight, turned their backs on us, or covered their heads.

Looking down the Bireh Ganga, a very prominent landmark is a great scar on the hillside and below it a lake of some size. This is the mark left by the great landslip of 1893 which dammed the river and formed the Gohna Lake beneath. The lake has dwindled now; at first it was much larger and the breaking of the dam caused great havoc lower down. Still mounting we finally camped amongst some large boulders near the village of Khaliaghat. By now we should have become indifferent to rebuffs in the matter of eggs and milk, annoying as it was to go without the second-named when one could hardly throw a stone without hitting a cow, a water buffalo, or a goat. But at Khaliaghat it seems to have rankled for there is something malicious about the entry in my diary, to the effect that the peasants here were of a very low type. So far as I remember we made no anthropological investigations to establish this; certainly cases of goitre were very frequent but so they were in all the higher valleys.

Next day's march, which was to bring us to the foot of the Kuari Pass, was a long one for which we made an early start on a raw, wet morning. It was so cold that at the first halt we lit a fire and sat round it for some time, baking and eating potatoes. Later it faired up and became hot enough to make a bathe in the Kuari glen a pleasant interlude.

The approach to the Kuari was up a steep, wooded glen down which a stream rushed, by gorge and waterfall, from near the pass. After a very long and steep grind the slope began to ease off, and crossing the glen we emerged on to grass downs, bare of trees but brilliant with dwarf iris and potentillas (or red buttercups, if that is not a contradiction in terms). The tinkle of sheep bells and the plaintive notes of a shepherd's pipe drew us towards a shepherd encampment, and here we spent the night, a thousand feet below the pass. There was not the savoury pot of goat's meat and the capacious goat-skin-bag full of wine which readers of Cervantes will remember almost reconciled Sancho to a shepherd's life, but for all that we were hospitably received. Like ourselves they were bound for the pass and the little bags carried by their flocks were full of grain. This is not such a contemptible form of transport as it may sound, as each animal will carry some twenty pounds, so that a flock of a hundred, which is a small one for these parts, can move a ton of stuff. When in camp the shepherds build these bags into a wall forming an admirable wind-break and as the tree line was not too far below to get fuel, we enjoyed a very snug billet.

The Kuari Pass was known to be a remarkably fine view point so we prayed for a fine morning and made a resolution to be up there early. Before turning in it began to rain, thus offering an excellent excuse for reconsidering this rash resolve, but we hardened our hearts and were duly rewarded. The top of the pass was reached by seven o'clock of a clear, cold morning and we were privileged to see what must be one of the grandest mountain views in the world. As we raised our heads above the top of the pass a gigantic sweep of icy peaks confronted us, and it was difficult to refrain from gasping at the vastness of the scene. The serrated line of the Kedarnath and Badrinath peaks, Kamet, Hathi Parbat, and the great cleft of the Dhauli Valley were easily recognised, but the glittering array of snowy peaks of all shapes and sizes which filled the gaps were easier to admire and wonder at than to identify. South of the Dhauli towered the graceful Dunagiri, but a sight of Nanda Devi, so soon to be our lodestone, was denied us.

There was some snow on the pass but not enough to trouble the porters, and presently we were down again amongst pines and grassy meadows. Here we had to stop repeatedly as fresh visions of mountain beauty, framed in vistas of pines, delighted our eyes, and film after film was exposed as we endeavoured to capture them. At the first village we came to, still high above the Dhauli, we were directed along a high-level route leading over the southern slopes to Joshimath. The porters who were behind followed the more usual route straight down to Tapoban in the valley, and then by the main track which ran close to the river. For them it was a long day and they did not get in till late and one, who subsequently quitted, not until the next day. We had reason to bless our high-level route in spite of the temporary separation from our porters, for happening to look back at a bend in the path, we found we were looking up part of the Rishi Ganga Valley and at the pyramid-like summit of Nanda Devi floating serenely in the background. It did not look to be ten miles away but was in fact at least thirty.

We ourselves reached Joshimath at three o'clock and the same evening opened negotiations for porters, and porters' food, to accompany us on our attempt on the Rishi Gorge. We wanted twenty porters and about 400 pounds of food for them, but luckily flour was not ground by hand at Joshimath or we might be there still. Some of it, however, was wanted in the form of 'satu' which takes a day or two to prepare, being made by first slightly roasting the wheat or barley (or a mixture of both) in iron pans and then grinding it. The advantage of 'satu' is that it requires no cooking and can be eaten dry (not recommended), moistened with cold water, or as a porridge; we found it went down best in tea with plenty of sugar, and was then very good.

The problem of porters was unexpectedly alleviated by the Dotials who, though only engaged as far as Joshimath, were now eager to remain with us. This enthusiasm was the more surprising as most of them had only just arrived after a twelve hour day, and although we painted a gloomy picture of the perils and hardships awaiting them in the Rishi (not inaccurately as it happened) nothing would shake them.

Next day was a Sunday, but there was no rest for us. We began work at 6 a.m.; nor did Tilman need to have his first job, the killing of a scorpion, pointed out to him. It was curled up in his bedding and very gratifying it was to see the 'early bird' and the sluggard for once receiving their respective dues – it might so easily have been the other way round. Curiously enough later in the day we killed a snake close by, but these two specimens must not be taken as typical Joshimath fauna, which consists almost entirely of the more homely but equally venomous fly.

Before getting down to sorting and weighing loads we sent off one of the Sherpas to scour the surrounding country for eggs. We reasoned that as Joshimath was a considerable village on the very populous Pilgrim Route such things ought not to be beyond the bounds of possibility. It is a place of some antiquity and lies 1,500 feet above the deep gorge where the Dhauli and Alaknanda rivers unite. The junction is called Vishnuprayag and has many sacred associations but there is nothing there save a shrine and a few huts. Joshimath itself is a long straggling village built on a projecting spur, and besides two bazaars, nearly half a mile apart , there is a hospital, a school, a post office, and one or two large houses. One of these belongs to the rawal of the Badrinath temple who passes the winter here. The villagers' houses are solidly built of stone, with two stories and a stone roof. The living room is on the first floor which opens out in front on to a wooden balcony, the ground floor being used as a stable, store, or shop. The timber for the houses is all cut by hand and is very massive, and on the lintels and balcony there is sometimes elaborate carving.

For all its two bazaars no one living in Joshimath could have made much of a hole in his pocket or wasted his substance on riotous living. Once or twice we succumbed to the temptations of the sweetmeat sellers, but we always found sickness intervened before a whole rupee had been spent. Nevertheless, the cost of the few things we wanted and which were obtainable was quite high enough, and the bazaar fraternity had the fine independent air assumed by the owners of seaside lodgings at the height of a good summer season.

Towards evening the scattered debris of the loads had at least begun to resolve itself into two piles, one to go with us and one to remain, and the first was even shaping itself into approximate loads. But the strain was telling, the spring balance was now, through overwork, registering several pounds with nothing on it, and we were not sorry when an interruption came.

It was the Sherpa, faint but triumphant, accompanied by the owner of three eggs. We were too pleased to argue about the very stiff price, but put them straight into a bucket of water where, to our dismay, they bobbed about merrily on the surface, obviously, by all the laws, in a fairly advanced state. Wiser men would have called the deal off but second thoughts suggested that after all eggs were eggs, and the water test, infallible as we knew in Africa, might not apply to Indian eggs. Further than that Joshimath was 6,000 feet above the sea, and though neither of us was a physicist, we knew that altitude had queer effects on boiling water and why not on the buoyancy factor? Anyway, for better or for worse, we decided to take them, but unfortunately three into two won't go so, in a spirit worthy of Mrs Beeton, we recklessly sank all three in an omelette, telling Angtharkay not to spare the ghee in the frying, for it has a powerful taste of its own. The result was as excellent as it was surprising and worthy of more than our somewhat sententious remarks, I observing that 'the highest wisdom is not to be too wise,' while all Tilman could find to say was: *'De l'audace, toujours de l'audace.'* Had our heads not been in a whirl of figures relating to rations, days, and rupees (we had just counted the contents of our bag of rupees for the tenth time, to make sure we really had lost some) we might have worked out a learned thesis on 'Altitude and the Specific Gravity of the Egg'; as it was we had one more unsuccessful count and turned in.

I am afraid that night we were unfeignedly glad that this delightful ten-day prelude was over and that the morrow would see the beginning of more serious work, and our impatience was no doubt the reason why we did not enjoy the preliminary march to the full. At the back of our minds was regret at the apparent waste of time, regret which became more poignant as fine day succeeded fine day, for we well knew that this pre-monsoon weather was the best we should ever have. But for that we might have been content to put no limit to our wanderings in a country of such loveliness, where the air and the rivers, the flowers and the trees filled one with the joy of living.

Now, however, impatience was to be satisfied and though we should find nature in a sterner mood, there would be no carking care to prevent us echoing Petulengro's 'Life is very sweet ...'

7   Chapter 7

Light rain had fallen during the morning and the air was fresh and invigorating as we marched out of Joshimath along the well-made path that runs high up along the south side of the Dhaoli Valley. To the north dark precipices rose from the water's edge in a continuous sweep, to lose themselves in the clouds some thousands of feet above us. At irregular intervals these walls were cleft by narrow, ravine-like valleys, cut in the rock by streams descending from the glaciers of the great peaks above. I can never see such configuration without experiencing an almost irrepressible desire to select a valley at random and wander up into its mysterious recesses, and on such a day as this, when the clouds, darkening the upper reaches of the gorge, accentuated its apparent depth, it was hard to resist the temptation to make a drastic change of plan.

Our path, which started at Joshimath some 1,500 feet above the river, remained fairly level throughout the short day's march, and at the village of Tapoban ran only a few feet above the floor of the valley. Here we caught up the Dotials, who had left some hours ahead of us, and a mile beyond the village, in a pleasantly wooded side-valley, we camped.

The evening was a fine one. Four miles upstream we could see the junction-point between the Rishi Nala and the main Dhaoli Valley. In the corner formed by these two valleys is a prominent forest-clad knoll called Lata after the village at its foot. It really forms the butt end of the great western ridge of Dunagiri, and we could see at a glance that the summit of this hill must command a fine view up the Rishi Nala, a view which might well prove invaluable to us later on. It was decided, therefore, that Kusang and Angtharkay should go with the Dotials on the following day, and that Pasang, Tilman and I should climb Lata and join the others in the evening at Surai Tota, where we had made arrangements with the Bania to pick up our supplies of satu and ata.

Five a.m. saw the three of us again striding along the path by the side of the river. We moved at a good speed as we had a long day's work before us: five miles along the path, 6,500 feet of ascent and descent over the rough wooded hillside, and then some more miles of path to be accomplished before nightfall.

The morning was one of exquisite beauty. The air, cleansed and purified by the rain of the previous day, was filled with the delicate scents of the pine-woods. From behind the great ice-peaks came the beams of the newly-risen sun, in magnificent contrast to the sombre, heavily forested country about us. The trees with their drowsy limbs still wet with the dew, the song of the birds sharing with us the exaltation of the new-born day, the streams splashing down in silver waterfalls or lying dormant in deep-blue pools, all played their part in this – the second act of Nature's pageantry of dawn. A fine morning, when all consideration of time and distance was eclipsed by the pure delight in one's surroundings.

We had been going for an hour and a half when we came to a northward bend in the Dhaoli River, which marked the point where the Rishi Ganga joins it. There we paused for a moment to look into that section of the gorge up which Graham had made an attempt to force a route as far back as 1883: a gorge which has never yet been penetrated by anyone. As our object was to get into the Nanda Devi Basin, we could not afford to spend any time trying to explore this section of the Rishi Ganga. We knew of a practicable route into the middle section, and a failure to get up this lower section would cost us valuable time.

But it was interesting to have a close view of the river which, in its higher reaches, was going to play such an important part in our adventures of the next few weeks. There was less water in it than I had expected, and we became hopeful of being able to wade up it in parts where there was no other route – poor innocents that we were. I had an idea too that once the winter snows had gone from the lower mountain sides, the volume of water in the rivers would decrease considerably, and never regain its present proportions for the rest of the year. In this I was entirely wrong. In actual fact, as soon as the melting of the glacier ice sets in, after the departure of the winter snow, the rivers increase enormously in size. This I think is an impressive indication of the immense area of the glaciers in the district.

A mile beyond the mouth of the Rishi, we turned to the right and started mounting the steep slope of Lata, finding the going more complicated and strenuous than we had expected. The hillside was covered with dense undergrowth, through which it was hard work to make our way. The ground was steep, and every now and then we were faced by a little cliff which had been masked by the undergrowth. Moreover we had had no chance to make a selection of a suitable route from afar, and now we could not see far enough ahead to choose out the best line. Our pace was slow, the day waxed hot, and our throats became unpleasantly dry. Sometimes we were forced to descend a considerable way in order to avoid some overhanging cliff, which tried our tempers sorely. At eleven o'clock we arrived at the foot of a cliff of larger proportions than usual. This we saw would demand a long descent before we would be able to outflank it. Like the rawest novices we elected to try and climb the crag direct, though the upper section was screened from view. After an hour of stiff rock-climbing, we succeeded in getting down again to the spot from which we had started. More heated than ever, we started on the outflanking movement. This accomplished, we toiled upwards once more, feeling not a little humbled by the heavy weather we were making of this little knoll. Clinging on to mossy roots, which not infrequently came away from the hillside, showering earth into our mouths and down our backs, we reached at 2.30 p.m. a little bald rocky patch, which formed the summit of Lata.

A glance at the view changed our gloomy outlook on life to one of thrilling exultation. The afternoon was clear and still. All round us were scenes of grandeur, the scale of which was too vast for human conception. To the north, across the Dhaoli Valley, rose the grim turrets and delicate spires of the Hathi Parbat group, so complex in structure that we could not begin to understand its tangled topography. Eastwards was the lovely cone of Dunagiri, displaying to full advantage its beautifully proportioned curves. West of us was the Trisul range, its vast ice plateau dazzlingly white in the torrid rays of the afternoon sun. And to the south Nanda Devi, queen of them all, held aloft her proud shapely head, her slender shoulders draped with snow-white braid.

Coming down to earth, we erected the plane-table, and worked with it for an hour. The views we had obtained of the Rishi Nala provided food for much thought.

Soon after four o'clock we started to descend. We got into a steep leaf-filled gully in the forest, and down this we plunged at a fine speed. I was still wearing my tennis shoes, and gave my bad toe several cracks which nearly sent me head first down the steep slope.

Since leaving the valley in the early morning, we had not come across a drop of water, nor did we find any now. The day was hot, we had been working hard, and by now were unpleasantly parched in tongue and throat. For my part this was accountable for the turn of speed which landed us on the shore of the Dhaoli River at six o'clock – a descent of six thousand odd feet in under two hours. To the infinite astonishment of a company of Bhotias who were camping on the shore close by, Tilman stripped and plunged into the turbulent waters of the river. I was more circumspect and performed my ablutions from a convenient boulder. Pasang, a true Tibetan, merely drank.

In the cool of the evening we marched silently up the valley. A fresh breeze blowing down from the peaks, and limbs just pleasantly tired, put me in sympathy with the subdued colouring of dusk, while I mused over the glimpse we had had into the mysterious country beyond the Rishi Ganga.

It was quite dark before we reached Surai Tota. Our camp was pitched on a flat stretch of grassland above the river, and a fine fire was blazing outside the tents. A large dish of lentils, followed by inexhaustible supplies of tea put us at peace with the world, and quite incapable of coping with a voluble flow of Hindustani from Kesar Singh, who had awaited our arrival in the village. [1] The

---

1 Kesar Singh had accompanied us on the Kamet expedition and lived hereabouts.

night was warm, and we fell into luxurious slumber by the fireside, knowing nothing more until roused by the first beams of the morning sun.

Kesar Singh had arranged for eight Surai Tota men to come with us up the Rishi. They were to be paid at the same rate as the Dotials and receive the same rations, i.e., tea, salt, cigarettes and ata. Kesar Singh said he knew the men well, and according to him they were sure-footed, brave, strong, and absolutely reliable: in fact, it appeared that they were very paragons of virtue. The ata, it appeared, was bagged and ready; but the satu would not be ready until later in the morning. However, it was arranged that we should start on with three of the 'locals' who knew the route, and the other five would follow on with the satu when it was ready. Our destination that day was a little alp known as Hyetui Kharak, situated near the upper limit of the forest at an altitude of about 11,700 feet. The men who were coming with us assured us that they all knew the way well and, completing a touching farewell ceremony with Kesar Singh, we made our departure with his assurances that we would have no trouble from *his* men at least.

A rough track led steeply up through the forest which covered the southern side of the Dhaoli Valley, the floor of which at this point is about 7,500 feet. An hour's steady going along this track took us to the tiny village of Tolma, a charming spot built high on the steep mountain side under the shade of some gigantic conifers.

Life in these little mountain villages is delightfully simple, and the inhabitants are almost entirely self-supporting. A few stony fields, terraced out of the steep hillside by their ancestors, supply all the food they require. A flock of sheep and goats, tended in summer by the youth of the community on the high mountain pastures, provides them with wool for their clothing. This wool is spun into yarn by the men, who carry their simple apparatus about with them wherever they go, so that they can be constantly spinning, while carrying loads, tending sheep, or performing any job that does not involve the use of their hands. The yarn is then woven into cloth by the women, who sit outside their houses, manipulating complicated machines with astonishing skill. Thus all are busily employed, all are well-fed and clothed, and all are happy. Any surplus farm produce is exchanged with itinerant traders for such luxuries as salt, tobacco, etcetera.

We paused awhile to converse with some of the weavers, and to try and puzzle out how their machines worked, then continued on our ascent. Our newly enrolled Surai Tota men already seemed a bit doubtful of the way and we inquired of some ploughmen, whether or not the path to Hyetue Kharak was well defined. We gathered from them that we could not possibly miss it if we kept our eyes open. Nevertheless we were no sooner clear of the fields than we were floundering in dense forest, trying in vain to find the least vestige of a track. The 'locals' assured us that we had just got to keep on up and we would be all right. But only when, after wading for some hours through the forest, we reached the brink of a 1,500-foot precipice, did they admit that the only two of the eight who knew the way were among those who had waited at Surai Tota for the satu! They thought that we had come too high and that the alp was somewhere below us.

It was obvious to us from Dr Longstaff's descriptions of the country that it was still *above* us, and taking the matter of route finding into our own hands we reached the 'kharak' in the middle of the afternoon. (Kharak, by the way, is a word used in these parts to mean a summer grazing ground. As the winter snows depart from the lowest of their pastures, so the shepherds and their flocks come up into occupation; later in the year they move to a still higher alp.)

The highest of these kharaks are about 14,000 feet in altitude, and are occupied for a bare two months each year. Hyetui Kharak was not yet occupied, as a quantity of snow still lingered on its higher slopes. It was a pleasant spot – a wide stretch of meadowland bordered on three sides by the forest, and we spent the remainder of the afternoon lying stretched out on the grass, dozing in the warm sunshine.

Towards dusk we began to get anxious about the non-arrival of the five satu men. Now that we had left the Dhaoli Valley, we could not afford to waste a day; for with such a large company of porters, each day spent in getting to our base in the Rishi Nala meant a large amount less food with which to carry out our work beyond. When night fell and there was still no sign of the missing five, we began to curse our folly in starting without them. We fully expected that they, like their fellows, had not the least idea of the way. However, at eight o'clock our anxiety was relieved by their arrival.

We slept out in the open again, and were up as soon as it was light, for we knew that we were in for a hard day's work. Not far above us, at an altitude of about 12,500 feet, the forest zone ended abruptly. Above this line the snow was lying deep on the ground. This winter snow in the process of melting is vile stuff to get through. Soft and sodden, it allows one to sink in to the extent of its depth, but is sufficiently heavy to put up a formidable resistance against any forward progress.

The porters knew this as well as we did, and, as we were getting ready for an early start, the Surai Tota men came to us to say that they must have a ration of ghee before they could consent to go any further. Except for a small quantity of ghee intended for the use of the Sherpas high up, we had none to give them. But it was obvious that they had little intention of going any further, and I told them that they could do as they liked; to which they replied that they would go down and leave us! Indeed, I suspect that that had been their idea all along: to come with us as far as Hyetui Kharak, a very easy day's march from Surai Tota, to collect their pay, and clear off before they were involved in any hard work. In this they were disappointed, as of course we refused to pay them unless they fulfilled their agreement to come with us into the Rishi Nala. I would like to say here, however, that this was the only time in all our dealings with the people of this district that we were let down in any way.

The desertion of the Surai Tota men put us in a serious predicament, and threatened to wreck at the very outset our plans for the exploration of the Nanda Devi Basin. We summoned the Dotials, who were camped a hundred yards away, and explained the situation to them. Without a moment's hesitation they volunteered to carry as much as they could manage of the abandoned loads. We warned them that the going would be extremely bad, but they held to their offer, and added so much of the satu and ata to the loads which they had been carrying on the previous day, that only two loads of ata remained. These were dragged off to the forest and hidden, to be picked up on their return. Staggering under loads weighing more than eighty pounds each they cheerfully faced the steep slopes above the alp. Thus did these low-caste Dotials by their loyalty make it possible for us to go through with our plans.

These negotiations delayed our start, and it was 7.40 a.m. before we were on the move. We were making for the crest of that same ridge running down from the Dunagiri massif, whose westerly end culminated in the little peak of Lata, which we had climbed two days before. We knew that our route lay across a gap in this ridge, some 14,700 feet in height, to a grazing ground used in summer by the shepherds of Tolma and Lata, and known to them as Durashi. This kharak was not generally visited until the beginning of July, owing to the winter snow which makes the pass impossible for the transit of sheep. It was now 24 May and the track was still buried under deep snow.

From the summit of a spur above Hyetui we got a good view of the ridge above us, and saw that there were no less than three gaps to choose from, each just as promising as the other. Moreover the ridge was serrated, and the condition of the snow made it impossible to get from one gap to another by following the crest. The only thing to do was to make a guess at which was the right one, and trust to luck.

Soon after leaving the forest we plunged into a morass of soft snow, through which we had to flog a track. At first it was not particularly deep and, keeping to the crest of a spur, the first gap was reached in a couple of hours. From here we looked down a sheer precipice of several thousand feet. We were obviously in the wrong gap, and a traverse had to be made round to the next one. Once off the spur our difficulties began. We sank first up to our knees, then up to our waists; sometimes we were floundering up to our armpits in the sodden snow. The day was fine, without a breath of wind. The blazing sun and the torrid glare from the snow produced a feeling of lassitude such as I have never experienced elsewhere except on enclosed glaciers at great altitudes.

Tilman and I took turns of twenty minutes each at the task of track making, while the others remained behind to assist the porters, whose cruel loads frequently caused them to overbalance. It was terribly hard work for them; but they stuck to it wonderfully, cheerfully chiding one another as they fell into some deep drift, from which they had to be extricated. The ground too was steep and very rough, and they avoided an accident only by their surprising skill.

It was a weary struggle and our progress seemed painfully slow. Beating with our ice axes, kicking and stamping, we continued without pause until 2.30 p.m., when we reached the second gap, only to find that the third was the true pass. We made an attempt to get along the ridge towards it, but after some hard work we had to give this up on account of the difficulty of the climbing which made even the Dotials lose their cheerfulness. Descending a few hundred feet we reached a small rocky ledge sticking out of the snow. It was now five o'clock, and we decided to bivouac here for the night. We melted some snow and brewed tea; never was a drink more welcome.

The outcrop we were on was sloping steeply downwards, so we built up platforms on which to sleep. It was a commanding position, 6,000 feet above the Dhaoli River, and one from which the surrounding peaks could be seen to their best advantage.

It was a perfect evening. As I lay on my little platform, the multi-coloured afterglow of sunset spreading over the vast mountain world about me, I was filled with a deep content, untroubled either by the memory of the failures of that day, or by the prospect of further trials on the morrow. A vision of such beauty was worth a world of striving.

The last tint of sunset died, and a young moon, hanging over the ice buttresses of the giant peak of Dunagiri, held undisputed right to shed her pale light over an enchanted world. The snowy crests stood now in superb contrast to the abysmal gloom of the valleys. Interwoven with my dreams, I was vaguely conscious of these sublime impressions throughout the night, until a new day was heralded by the first faint flush of dawn.

We made full use of the cold of the early morning in resuming our toil through the snow and with this ally we made more rapid progress. Now at last we were on the right route, and at 10.30 a.m. we reached the true pass. There we found a well-defined track running along the face of a steep precipice. The rocks still held a good deal of ice and snow, especially in the gullies, and much step cutting was required in order to get along the track. It was a remarkable place. The cliffs were exceedingly steep and dropped in an almost unbroken plunge for some 8,000 feet, and yet there was this narrow ledge, along which it was possible for the shepherds to take their sheep in the summer time. The length of the cliff was about half a mile.

My heart was in my mouth as I watched the Dotials coming along the track, for the ice made the passage of certain sections exceedingly delicate work. But we soon discovered that they were as sure-footed as cats, and needed very little assistance, in spite of their formidable loads. Cutting steps for prolonged periods is tiring work, but it was infinitely preferable to the heart-breaking toil of the previous day. At the further end of the terrace was a deep gully into which we had to descend for several hundred feet; when a climb up a boulder-strewn slope took us to a small gap, from which we looked down gentle grassy slopes to Durashi. The contrast could not have been more sudden and unexpected. There at our feet lay a little stretch of country, enclosed by gently rolling hills, for all the world like some quiet corner of the English Lake District. There was about it not the least suggestion of the vast ruggedness of the land from which we had just come.

The little vale of Durashi is really a hanging valley, lying high up on the northern side of the Rishi Nala. On three sides it is enclosed by these grassy hills, and on the fourth it opens out above the precipice which forms the side of the main valley. It seems to be entirely cut off from the outside world. Indeed if it were not for the cliff track, its luxuriant pastures would be inaccessible to the shepherds and their flocks. We found several stone shelters there, which were gladly occupied by the Dotials. Water and firewood were scarce and difficult of access.

In the evening we wandered down to the lower end of the valley, and looked straight down a 5,000-foot precipice into what must be one of the most fantastic gorges in the world. It has never yet been penetrated by any human being, and is believed by the locals to be the abode of demons – a superstition we were quite ready to share. The precipice was far too steep for us to be able to examine the near side of the valley, but the other side was almost grotesque in its structure. It was built up of tier upon tier of gigantic steeply inclined slabs, which culminated 10,000 feet above the river in a multitude of sharp rocky peaks set at a rakish angle. The river itself, only just visible in the depths below us, sent up a roar like that of Niagara. What a subject for an artist illustrating an old-fashioned travel book! No conception, even of Gustave Doré, could appear exaggerated beside the cliffs and turrets towering above that amazing canyon. To us the view was anything but encouraging.

The evening was overcast and we began to fear that our spell of fine weather was coming to an end. A little rain fell in the night, but we awoke to another cloudless morning. We started at seven o'clock and climbed up to a saddle in the ridge which enclosed the head of the little Durashi glen. This ridge has been aptly named 'the curtain' by Dr Longstaff, for it is an offshoot of the main Dunagiri-Lata ridge which we had crossed the day before, and runs down at right angles into the Rishi Ganga, completely screening the upper part of that valley from Durashi. Before starting on its final plunge into the Rishi Ganga, the ridge rises to a little peak, which we called for want of a better name Durashi Peak. This was only about 600 feet above our saddle and, leaving the porters to rest awhile, Tilman and I ascended the peak with the plane-table, and spent two hours on top, studying the geography of the upper gorge and its surroundings, of which we commanded a fairly comprehensive view.

We could identify the furthest points reached by the Graham and Longstaff parties, just beyond the junction of the Rhamani Valley with the Rishi Nala, and it was about there that we proposed to put our base camp. Beyond was the untrodden section of the gorge, the key to the sanctuary of the Nanda Devi Basin. The view we got of it from here proved of the greatest value to us later.

Clouds soon began to form on the peaks around, but Nanda Devi remained clear. Indeed, this was a peculiarity of the mountain, which we came to recognise. Often when all the other peaks were obscured from view, wrapped in a dense mantle of cloud, the summit of Nanda Devi would remain clear. (This is directly contrary to general rule, for it is nearly always the big isolated rock mountains which first attract cloud, especially when they happen to be the highest in their particular district.) Now we obtained an uninterrupted view of the great southern ridge of the mountain. It was by this ridge that we entertained some slight hope of finding a practicable route to the summit, although we were not sufficiently equipped to make the attempt that year. But as we looked at the mighty upward sweep of the ridge all hope died, for the thing appeared utterly unclimbable, as indeed I still think it is.

At 10.30 a.m. we rejoined the porters on the saddle. From here we looked down some three thousand feet into a thickly-wooded nala, descending from a glacier-covered south-westerly spur of Dunagiri. The nala was cut into two parts by streams which united further down. Between them, completely surrounded by a forest of tall pines, lay a beautiful strip of pasture land, known to the locals as Dibrughita. This too was used as a summer grazing ground. We were told later that nowadays it is very seldom visited by shepherds, presumably because of the difficulty of access, for the grazing must be very valuable.

The descent was steep and, owing to the loads, took a long time, but it was devoid of difficulties. Unluckily we crossed the stream in a bad place, and had considerable difficulty in getting up the other side. Later, however, we found an easy crossing, which was obviously the one used by the shepherds. It will have been noted by now that many of our difficulties at this early stage were due to our lack of local knowledge. This we had thought to provide against, by engaging Kesar Singh's friends at Surai Tota, some of whom I have no doubt knew the route well. Their desertion put us at a bad disadvantage. We had expected to have no difficulties in the matter of route-finding, at least until one march beyond Dibrughita. We were too pressed for time and food to employ any time in reconnaissance, and a false move meant hours of extra toil for ourselves and the unfortunate Dotials.

We had intended to camp on the alp, but we could not find any water there, and we were forced to go on beyond. This was disappointing, as it was undoubtedly one of the most lovely spots it had ever been my good fortune to behold. Dr Longstaff had described it to me when I was staying with him in England, but even his well-known enthusiasm could not provide me with a picture to compare with the reality. Lying on the soft grass, surrounded by a luxuriant growth of wild flowers, the forest of tall stately pines bordering the alp on every side, and with only a glimpse here and there of some icy peak, it was impossible to imagine the grimly terrifying aspect of the main valley so close at hand. Tilman's remark that it was like 'a horizontal oasis in a vertical desert' was one whose aptness we were afterwards to appreciate more fully.

Our camp that night was in the nala beyond Dibrughita. Close beside, a clear stream splashed its joyous way through the forest. Here the vegetation was neither dense nor oppressive, and the trees, great gnarled veterans, each possessed a striking individuality, as in a wood at home.

We had a long climb through the forest next morning to get out of the nala, and when we did so we found ourselves for the first time in the main valley of the Rishi Ganga. Looking back across the Dibrughita Nala we saw to full advantage the huge mass of 'the curtain'. We saw that it too was composed of gigantic steeply sloping slabs such as we had seen from Durashi on the other side of the valley. And very different it looked now from those gentle grassy slopes on which we had camped two nights before.

We now had our first taste of what moving about in the Rishi Nala was like. Having no local knowledge to guide us, we did not know whether to keep high up on the mountain side or low down, or which was the best route to take. We were then about 2,000 feet above the river, and decided to take a line at about that level. The valley-side was steep, and cut by innumerable deep gullies and cliffs. We could rarely get a clear view of the ground for more than a hundred yards ahead, and we were constantly toiling up some steep slope only to find that we had arrived at some impassable cut-off, which could only be avoided by making a long detour above or below. Tilman and I would go ahead taking different routes, and signal to the others behind to follow the better line. But even so we were continually making big mistakes, which cost us hours of needless toil. Some months later, when we came this way again with a party of porters, we had no difficulty whatever in picking out a good line, simply because we had already been over the country twice and knew it well. But on our first journey it was a worrying job, more particularly as we were in a hurry, and were relying entirely upon the good nature and steadiness of the Dotials.

At about one o'clock we reached a point from which we could proceed no further at our present level, and we decided to descend to the river. This was easier said than done, however, and we searched for a long while before we discovered a steep gully down which we could climb. In two places the loads had to be lowered by means of a rope. At one of these I had climbed down first, and was standing on a ledge ready to guide the loads down, when someone dislodged a rock from above, which hit me on the back of the head. It did not quite knock me out, but I was dizzy and sick for some little while afterwards. The accident was more spectacular than serious, however, as the resulting scalp wound bled with a freedom out of all proportion to the size of the cut. This elicited much tender sympathy from the Dotials, particularly from their old 'Captain', and for the remainder of the day they worked with redoubled energy.

A few hundred feet above the river we got into bad bramble, through which a way had to be cut, and at 4.30 p.m. we reached the water's edge at a point about half a mile below the Trisuli Nala. We recognised it as the place at which Longstaff had crossed the river on his way to make his famous ascent of Trisul, twenty-seven years before. We decided to camp here for the night.

When we had distributed the rations and had drunk a cup of tea, Tilman and I went off to make a reconnaissance, and to try to decide on tomorrow's route before nightfall.

I had hoped to reach the junction of the Rhamani and Rishi rivers on the following day but we had made very poor progress that day and the difficulties ahead appeared considerable. A number of large boulders in the river bed offered us an easy place for bridging the river. Dr Longstaff's party had reached the Rhamani junction by crossing the river at this point; but they had been a lightly-equipped party, and even so had found considerable difficulties beyond the Trisuli Nala. We had no idea whether a route along the northern bank was practicable. However, after a careful consideration of the matter, it was decided upon as being at least the more direct one. I was in a hurry, because each day that we spent in getting to our proposed base camp meant at least three days' less time for the job above as, so long as the Dotials were with us, we were consuming our food supply at the rate of thirty-two pounds per day.

By now the loads were appreciably lighter for, besides the food which was being consumed, we had left a dump of flour at Durashi for the use of the Dotials on their return, and here another dump was left.

We got away at about 6.30 on the morning of 28 May. After a few hundred yards we struck very bad going, but later in the morning we began to make quite satisfactory progress, though held up from time to time by small land-slips, or by fearful tangles of thorn-scrub and bramble. At midday we reached a big scar in the hillside, beyond which we could make no further progress along the river bank. We climbed up for a thousand feet or so and got on to a terrace which took us to a bend in the valley half a mile further on.

The mountain side we were on now steepened up enormously, and it looked very much as if we had reached a dead end. The porters were some way behind so, leaving his load, Tilman went off to prospect round the corner while I waited to rally the men. Now for the first time the Dotials showed signs of despondency. They said they had had enough and they wanted to leave their loads here and go back, and anyhow, they added, they would not face any more difficult or dangerous bits.

It was nearly an hour before Tilman reappeared. He reported that he had got right into a side valley which must have been the Rhamani, and that from the point he had reached it would have been a comparatively simple matter to descend to the stream but that, in getting there, he had had to traverse a tiny sloping ledge without any hand holds to keep him in balance above a sheer precipice of several hundred feet. He did not think it fair to ask heavily-laden men to go across.

We went on for a bit until we arrived at the edge of a deep gully which descended steeply to the Rishi. While Tilman and I examined the possibility of getting on to a higher line of traverse, Kusang and Angtharkay went down the gully to see if the shore of the river would help us. By now the sky had become very dark and a fierce gusty wind was blowing up the valley. It was evident that we were in for a fairly considerable storm. The Dotials huddled together, their teeth chattering.

When the two Sherpas returned with the news that they had only been able to get a hundred yards or so along the shore, we nevertheless gave the word for a general descent to the river, for it was obvious that, apart from everything else, the storm would prevent any intricate climbing on the precipitous ground in front of us. On reaching the river we set to work cutting down trees for the construction of a bridge, while the Dotials made fires on the shore and squatted round them. The actual bridging was not a difficult task with so many hands to assist, as the river was now quite low. By 5.30 p.m. the whole party was safely across.

With a good deal of persuasion we induced the Dotials to come on a little further, telling them that if they did reach the Rhamani junction that night, we would discharge them on the following morning. We told them too that it would take another two hours (though we had not ourselves the haziest notion of how long we should need). A strip of pine forest lay along the southern shore at this point, and as this was free from undergrowth and offered such excellent going, we had actually reached our goal by 6.15. A few minutes later the storm broke, and in a whirl of falling snow we pitched the tents and struggled with a reluctant fire, while the Dotials made themselves snug in a little cave beyond. We did not bother much about food that evening, as darkness had fallen before we had stowed our kit away, and the whirling snow made a mockery of all our efforts to get a fire going.

8 Chapter 8

When preparations for the night were complete, Pasang and I retired to the shelter of a small overhanging rock, while the others took to the tents. Until late into the night the two of us sat huddled over a fire which, after many unsuccessful attempts, we had managed to light in our shelter. Pasang had been suffering from 'tummy trouble' for some time, and the heavy work of the last few days had made him feel very weak. It continued to snow heavily throughout the night, and about one o'clock I was woken up by Tilman, who had come up to join us, his tent having collapsed under the weight of the snow. He managed to fit some of himself under the shelter of our overhang.

The snow stopped falling in the early hours of the morning and the dawn broke on a cloudless sky. The Dotials paid us an early visit, and we gave them their well-earned pay. They said they did not like leaving us up here alone, but after a touching farewell ceremony, they took their departure. And sorry I was to see them go. They had served us well and faithfully, carrying huge loads over country where a slip would have had serious consequences. Nor should I easily forget their pleasant humour and their courtesy.

The morning was spent in moving our stuff over to the overhang which had been occupied by the Dotials, sorting things out, taking stock of food, and many other little jobs. We found that we had thirty-five days food left.

This section of the Rishi Nala is a fine example of a box-canyon, that is to say, a canyon whose sides rise perpendicularly from the water's edge. The walls of this gorge maintained a tremendous steepness and culminated in peaks of 20,000 feet. Our present altitude was 11,800 feet, and our camp was situated on a small strip of shore on the southern side of the river. The cliffs overhung the shore for about eighty feet above our heads, and afforded fine protection from the rain. In addition, the valley was running nearly east–west, and so our camp enjoyed more sun than would be supposed from the depth of the valley. One drawback to an otherwise ideal site was the lack of clean water. The Rishi was thick with a whitish glacier mud and, though there were several side-streams near by, we could not reach any of them. As we were having our evening meal one night, Angtharkay remarked that now at any rate we had milk with our tea – the milk of the great Nanda Devi!

Our camp was about 200 yards above the point where Rhamani stream comes into the Rishi Ganga from the north. At the junction itself a huge rock had fallen across the Rishi stream, forming a natural bridge. The crossing was not easy though, and involved some delicate work, especially when crossing with loads. However, it gave us access to the northern side in our search for a route up the gorge, and later was more than useful in our retreat down the valley.

On the afternoon following our arrival, Tilman and I crossed the river to make a reconnaissance on the northern side of the gorge. A hundred feet or so above the rock-bridge we came upon Dr Longstaff's old campsite – a level grassy platform by an overhanging rock. We climbed up the steep slopes behind it until we could command a good view of the cliffs above our base camp. It was soon evident that it would be impossible to make our way up the gorge at a low level, and that we would have to climb at least 1,200 feet before we could start traversing. We could not see how far this line would get us, but it seemed to be our only chance to get along the southern side of the valley, and it was on that side that Dr Longstaff had told us to concentrate all our energies.

I found myself to be very nervous and shaky on the steep grass slopes and slabs on which we had to climb. This was due to the fact that I was not yet used to the immense scale of the gorge and its surroundings. Tilman suffered from the same complaint. We also had great difficulty in judging the size and angle of minor features. This made route-finding from a distance very difficult indeed, and we were continually finding ourselves in error. However, the eye gradually adjusted itself, and soon we began to move with more confidence.

That night I could hardly control my impatience to get up on to the cliffs above and start our search for a route through the upper gorge. For a long time I lay awake weighing up in my mind our chances of success. The morrow would show us much, for our reconnaissance that evening had proved to us that there, at the beginning, was but one line of possibility. Should this fail, we should be check-mated at the very outset.

Whatever may have been my enthusiasm or impatience to be up and doing on the night before, the hour for getting up always finds me with no other ambition in the world than to be permitted to lie where I am and sleep, sleep, sleep. Not so Tilman. I have never met anyone with such a complete disregard for the sublime comforts of the early morning bed. However monstrously early we might decide, the night before, to get up, he was about at least half an hour before the time. He was generally very good about it, and used to sit placidly smoking his pipe over the fire, with no more than a few mild suggestions that it might be a good idea to think about starting. Nevertheless, I always boiled (so far as my sleepy state allowed) with indignation, and thought of many crushing arguments (never uttered) why I should be allowed to sleep. Unfortunately it was easier to be a passive obstacle than an active force, and I generally got the better of the silent dispute. But on the morning of 30 May,

Tilman's efforts resulted in our leaving camp at 5.20 a.m., that is to say, only twenty minutes late.

Mounting in a series of wide zigzags, we followed the route we had worked out on the previous afternoon from the opposite side of the valley. After two hours' climbing we reached the crest of a little spur which we had taken to be the start of a possible line of traverse, and beyond which we had not been able to see. The spur commanded a fine view of the upper gorge. The immediate prospect looked anything but hopeful, while some two miles further up we saw a huge dark buttress, which appeared to descend in an unbroken sweep from great heights above to the water's edge, and looked to be utterly impassable. This buttress came to be called 'Pisgah', for we felt that if we could climb it we would have access to the 'Promised Land' beyond.

Directly in front of us was a gully, and beyond the gully was a little terrace running steeply downwards across the face of the precipice we were on. This looked so unpromising that we decided to try it only as a last resort. We climbed the gully for a couple of hundred feet, but were soon brought up short by a line of overhanging rock, and were forced to retreat to the terrace. This led us further than we had expected and we had progressed along the face for some 200 yards before it petered out below a great scar in the side of the valley caused by a recent landslip. There was no alternative but to climb up to the top of the scar and hope for the best. The rock was 'slabby' and very rotten, and we had some unpleasant moments before we surmounted the difficulty. When we reached the top of the crag it seemed as if it would be impossible to get any further, but a search revealed a tiny flaw which enabled us to get round the next corner on to a further sloping terrace.

Our luck held throughout the morning. Above and below us the cliffs were impregnable, and had our present line of traverse failed, I think we should have had to admit defeat; but by a remarkable freak of chance the slender chain of ledges continued unbroken. The complete lack of any alternative, too, enabled us to make good progress, and our eagerness grew as we rapidly approached the gaunt cliffs of 'Pisgah'. Over and over again the terrace we were on would peter out in some deep cleft, and further advance would seem impossible, but on each occasion there would be a kindly fault in the rock which would enable us to climb over to the continuation of the terrace beyond. Some of the sections were very 'thin', and we began to wonder if the route would be possible with loads.

All the terraces were dipping towards the east, and when we reached a point about a quarter of a mile from 'Pisgah', we were only 300 feet above the river. Then came the most sensational, though not the most difficult, section of the route. In rounding a spur the terrace or ledge narrowed to a foot in width and actually overhung the river. The passage along it was exhilarating, and it was difficult to believe that a kindly providence had not placed it there to wind up that long chain of improbabilities.

On the opposite side of the river was a strip of shore which ran along the water's edge, until a bend in the river screened it from view. It was possible that if we could get across to it, it might take us past the buttress. We decided to attempt to ford the river and see. It was now one o'clock. We should have turned back, but I was desperately keen to 'prove' the route we were on, as, if we could do that, further time need not be wasted in prospecting. We took off our lower garments and waded out into the swiftly flowing stream. The water did not reach much above our thighs, but the current was so strong that it was only with the greatest difficulty that we could retain our balance. Also the water was icy cold, and our legs soon lost all sensation. We got across; the passage was painful and unpleasant, but we considered that with due precautions it was safe enough.

The strip of shore did not lead us far and we had to make five more crossings before we were clear of the buttress, and could make our way along the southern side of the valley once more. But it was now getting late, and we had to hurry back. The river of course had to be crossed six times on the way back, making twelve crossings in all, and by the time we reached the gully at the end of the traverse, we had had enough of aquatic sports to last us for some time.

The route we had discovered was far from satisfactory. Many sections of the traverse would be extremely difficult to negotiate with loads; and a route which relied for its practicability on the state of the river was obviously bad. But in the absence of an alternative it would have to serve. Any alternative to the traverse on this side of the river was out of the question, as from what we had seen of the vast precipices of the northern side our chances over there would be remote indeed. Only freak rock formations had made the traverse possible. As for the river, I have already mentioned my reasons for believing that we need not expect a great increase in the volume of water. Also we fancied that, by exercising our ingenuity, some of the crossings could be bridged.

Therefore, after the matter had been discussed at some length, it was decided that we should start at once, relaying the loads along the route discovered that day.

Food was the factor on which all our plans depended. We now had a supply sufficient to last us for thirty-four days. The minimum we could afford to leave at our base for the retreat down the Rishi Nala was enough for three days. That left us thirty-one days for the work ahead of us. A total of 550 pounds of food and kit had to be shifted.

There were still a good many odd jobs to be done on the morning of 31 May, and we did not get started on our first relay until 11.30. We left Pasang behind for another day's rest, as he had not yet recovered from his 'tummy trouble', and we took with us a considerable quantity of light rope and iron pegs with which to construct handrails across the more difficult sections of the traverse, one of which lay just above our base. Here and there we managed to improve upon our previous route, but in the main we were obliged to stick closely to it. At first the work of carrying heavy loads over such difficult ground was exhausting, but gradually we acquired a new rhythm of movement, and the body adjusted itself to the strain imposed upon it. On these occasions my shoulders always gave me most trouble and it generally takes some time for the muscles to get set. The Sherpas support the weight of their loads by means of head bands instead of shoulder straps. This method is much the less tiring of the two, but needs considerable practice. I have tried to use a head band, but cannot manage it over difficult ground.

We decided to make our first camp above the base on the little spur from which we had got our first view of the upper part of the Rishi. It was agreed too to move all our stuff up to the first stage, before going on to the second, and so on. Thus everything was staked on our being able to get through by this route.

The next day, with Pasang to help, we started early, and by making two journeys we got everything on to the spur, where we built up a platform and pitched camp. There was a good supply of juniper fuel with which to make a fire, and we set about the preparation of that ever important item, the cup of tea. It was then discovered that the tea had somehow been left behind with the food dump at the base! I was in favour of leaving it there, but the others would not hear of that, so we drew lots to decide who should make the third journey of the day. Tilman lost and started down at once. However, I think he had the best of the bargain for, as there was still plenty of daylight left, Angtharkay, Kusang and I went off to fix ropes over the big scar at the end of the first traverse. This proved to be an exceedingly tricky job, and was complicated by the advent of a short sharp snow storm. We returned to camp as night was falling, to find Tilman already returned, and a welcome brew of tea awaiting us.

Seven o'clock the next morning saw us descending into the gully beyond the spur, carrying between us 230 pounds of gear. All our concentration was needed for the job, for a slip was not to be thought of. (I have often found that so long as the work does not involve complicated movements, carrying a load improves one's climbing technique. Far greater precision is needed, and one naturally abandons all superfluous movements of the body, which often more than counterbalances the weight of the load. This is one reason why a man who is used to carrying loads uphill, when deprived of his load, very often cannot climb as fast or as far as a man who is not used to carrying loads; his movements become jerky, and he finds it very difficult to adjust his rhythm to the altered conditions. Indeed, it is easier to learn to carry a load than to learn how not to carry one. The fact is very evident with the Sherpas, potentially some of the finest mountaineers in the world, but suffering from a tremendous handicap of not being able to adjust the rhythm of their movements as the weight of their loads, or altered conditions of snow, require.)

The scar caused us a lot of trouble. We could not climb the steep crumbling rocks carrying our loads. Three of us had to climb to a stance halfway up, throw a rope down and haul up each load in turn, while those below did their best to prevent it sticking half way, by means of another rope from below. This performance was then repeated on the upper section of the crag. Beyond this was a gully, to cross which the Sherpas removed their boots, so as to be more sure of their footing on the treacherous grass-covered rock.

Climbing out of the gully on the further side, we halted for a moment's rest on a small ridge beyond. While we were there, one of the loads overbalanced and crashed down into the gully some 200 feet below us. It split open, but most fortunately got hung up on a ledge, which saved it from total destruction at the bottom of the gorge, 1,500 feet below. When we reached the battered sack, we found that some twenty pounds of lentils and rice had been lost, together with some candles. The loss of the food was most annoying, as it represented some two days of our valuable time. But the mishap might easily have been very much more serious, and it taught us to exercise greater care when handling our loads in such unusually steep country.

It was useless trying to hurry along the traverse. Each section had to be tackled with the utmost caution. It was slow work, but very far from tedious, as the job required all our attention. As we gradually became used to the gigantic depth of the ravine above which we were making our way, the early feeling of nervousness changed to one of exhilaration, a glorious feeling almost of being part of this giant creation of nature. Towards the end of the traverse, the links became very fragile. One spot in particular caused us such trouble that it produced a fairly forceful protest from Angtharkay, and caused Kusang to pause momentarily in his monotonous flow of song. But above and below us the cliffs were smooth and sheer, and the passage could not be avoided. This section came to be known as the 'Mauvais Pas', and was certainly the most hair-raising bit of the traverse. The last bit went comparatively easily, and by the middle of the afternoon we reached the river at the point where we had made our first crossing three days before. After stowing the loads under a rock, we hurriedly retreated along the traverse, and reached our camp before dark.

The dawn of 3 June gave warning of bad weather, and it was in some anxiety that we packed up the remainder of our baggage and hastily got under way. The route was now becoming familiar, and difficulties which had cost us much time and labour before were now being tackled with the confidence and ease of familiarity. We made good time on the slabs of the scar, and the gullies which followed had lost much of their sting. But fast as we went we were still too slow for the weather. By ten o'clock the lower valley was filled with cloud and by eleven o'clock snow was falling gently in large woolly flakes. This spurred us on to yet greater energy, as the thought of the Mauvais Pas under a covering of snow was not a pleasant one and, if we failed to get across it today, there was no knowing how long we should be held up; for it looked as if the snow had come to stay for some time.

The weight of our loads was forgotten as we raced along the little ledges of the traverse at a frantic speed. By twelve o'clock snow was falling heavily and, when we reached the Mauvais Pas, all the ledges and crannies were hidden under a thick white canopy. We removed our boots in order to be sure of our footholds, and proceeded with the utmost deliberation, clearing the snow from the ledges as we went. It was not easy to find places on which to anchor the rope and, though we moved one at a time, a slip would have had very serious consequences. About half way across a narrow slanting cleft had to be negotiated in order to get on to a lower ledge. This was the worst section, as one's load was apt to catch and throw one off one's balance, and my heart was in my mouth as I watched each member of the party negotiate it. The Sherpas worked with a wonderful steadiness and composure, only giving vent to their pent-up feelings when they reached the comparative security of the terrace beyond. Here we halted a moment to rub our feet and put on our boots. A wind started to blow down the valley, driving the snow into our faces as we made our way slowly across the face of the precipice, and Angtharkay suggested that we should stop where we were until the storm had blown over. A more unpleasant idea would have been difficult to conceive, though I must admit conditions had made progress not a little dangerous. By going slowly, however, and taking every precaution, we eventually reached the end of the traverse without a mishap.

Cold and wet, we huddled under the lee of the cliff rising from the little strip of shore by the water's edge. A few sodden pieces of wood lay about the beach, having been deposited there when the river was in flood. With the aid of a couple of candles and a good deal of patience we got some sort of a fire started, and 'smoked ourselves' until, towards evening, the snow slackened.

On the opposite side of the river there was a wider strip of shore, on which grew a small clump of stunted birches. There was also a fair-sized cave. It was obviously the ideal base from which to tackle the final section of the upper gorge, and the sooner we got there and made ourselves snug, the better, so as soon as the snowstorm had abated we collected all the loads at the water's edge, and prepared for the crossing.

There were ten loads to be carried across. The river appeared to be slightly swollen but, as the snow had been melting as it fell, this was only to be expected. We did not anticipate that the difficulties would be much greater than they had been before.

Fastening an end of the rope to my waist and shouldering a load, I paddled up the edge of the stream, probing with my ice axe and searching for the best place to begin the crossing. Then I started to wade slowly out into the raging waters. I soon realised that, although the river appeared only slightly higher than it had been before, it confronted us with an obstacle twice as formidable. The force of the current was terrific. As I moved a foot forward, it would be whirled sideways, and it was only by shuffling along that I could make any headway. My legs were slashed by stones swept down by the force of the river, but soon the numbing cold robbed my lower limbs of all sensation. The whirling motion of the water made me giddy, and I was hard put to it to keep my balance. In mid-stream the water was nearly up to my waist; had it been an inch higher it must have carried me away, but by a desperate effort I kept my feet. I tried to turn round, but found that the current was impossible to face, so I had to go on, and at length emerged with bleeding legs upon the opposite beach.

Tilman was a short way behind me. Being shorter, he was having an even tougher struggle. Pasang and Angtharkay were already well in the water, holding on to each other, and on to the rope which was now stretched across the river. My wits must have been numbed by the cold, for I missed the brief opportunity I had of preventing them from coming any further. Too late I realised what they were in for. Pasang was carrying a load of satu, Angtharkay had a load of clothes and bedding, which came down to his buttocks. He was very slight of build and easily the shortest of the five. When he got out towards the middle of the stream, the water was well above his waist, and it was obvious that he was prevented from being swept away only by hanging on to the rope and Pasang's firm hand, which clutched him by the arm. Soon, however, his load became water-logged, and started to drag him down. How he managed to keep his feet will always remain a mystery to me for, in spite of the help afforded him by the rope, his difficulties must have been vastly greater than my own, and I knew that I had had just as much as I could cope with. But then these Sherpas have standards of their own. As they were approaching the northern bank, however, Angtharkay actually did lose his balance and, as he went in up to his neck, I thought he was lost. But he retained his hold on the rope, and Pasang, clutching frantically at his arm, dragged him ashore. They were both rather badly shaken, but immediately set about the task of pitching camp and lighting a fire.

Tilman and I each made two more journeys across with the remaining loads (we left one bag of satu on the southern shore), and on his third trip Tilman came over with Kusang, who had been patiently holding the other end of the rope for us. This time he missed his footing and was submerged, fortunately in the shallow water near the shore. Dusk was falling as, painfully, we lugged the loads across the beach.

It was a cheerless party which sat huddled round the weakly smouldering logs under the shelter of the cave, silent save for the continuous chatter of teeth. I felt very humble indeed for having been fool enough to tackle the river in such haste. It was obvious now that a route which involved several such crossings was out of the question, and except for the fact that we had a decent campsite, we would have been much better off on the southern shore of the stream. However, one must pay for experience, and we were later to find that much was needed in dealing with these fierce glacier streams.

Tilman's pipe had been washed away out of his pocket down the river. He is a confirmed pipe-smoker, and I think that the prospect of a month without one was gloomy, to say the least. Fortunately for him, I had been travelling in southern Tibet the previous year with Laurence Wager, who had insisted on my smoking a pipe in the evening to keep me from talking. Since then I had continued the habit, and now Tilman was able to get a smoke at the expense of an increased flow of argumentative conversation!

No rain or snow was falling next morning, but it was a dull and cheerless dawn. After an early breakfast, we walked along the little strip of shore to examine the possibility of bridging the river. A little downstream, at the point where the river entered the box-canyon, which stretched almost unbroken for the two miles separating us from our base camp, we found a place where huge boulders in the bed of the stream formed a natural foundation for a bridge. A clump of twisted birches, however, offered us poor material, and it was midday before we had spanned the river with a fragile and rickety structure. Considerable dexterity was necessary to cross the bridge, but it served our purpose so long as it was not washed away.

We now commanded both sides of the river, and it was decided that Tilman and Angtharkay should explore the possibilities of the southern side, while Pasang and I tried to get through on the northern side. I confess that when we started out on our respective jobs, I thought that if anyone got through, it would be Pasang and me; for to get past 'Pisgah' on the southern side appeared to be a hopeless task.

Edging along the base of the cliffs at the water's edge, we reached another strip of sandy shore a hundred yards further upstream. From here a steeply sloping corridor led back across the face of the precipice. All the strata we had encountered in the Rishi Nala sloped from west to east in this manner, and we hoped that by following this corridor we might be able to climb on to a terrace which would at least carry us past that formidable buttress on the southern side. But the corridor became more and more difficult to follow, and finally ended in a little platform 500 feet above the river, completely isolated save for the way by which we had come. Further advance in any direction was impossible. We sat down disconsolately, and scanned the cliffs of the southern side of the gorge. High above us, like ants on a gigantic wall, we saw the other two climbing slowly upwards. Presently they started traversing horizontally, and we saw that they were making for the one point in the great buttress where, we had agreed before, lay the only slender chance of success. They reached it and disappeared from view. When after a short while they reappeared, and started up a vile-looking gully, my heart sank. It appeared that the last chance on the southern side had failed, and now it was up to Pasang and me to find a way by hook or by crook.

We descended to the river again and with great difficulty managed to make another 200 yards upstream, before an overhanging cliff brought us to a dead stop. We tried wading, but the river was even higher than it had been on the previous evening, and we could make no headway. Then we began to search every inch of the 300 yards we had come from our camp, in the hope of at least being able to climb out of the gloomy canyon we were in. We tried places which were obviously quite ridiculous; just as one searches under the teapot or in the coal-scuttle for a lost fountain pen when one has exhausted every likely place, and I had a similar feeling of hopelessness. But after some desperate rock-climbing, we were forced to admit defeat, and returned to camp, satisfied that at least there was no route along the northern side of the gorge.

It was a cold grey afternoon, and towards evening rain began to fall gently. The gorge wore a grim and desolate aspect, which increased my dejection as I sat in the cave, waiting for the others to return and wondering what our next move would be. If we were forced to retreat from here, we would have to abandon our attempt to penetrate into the Nanda Devi Basin, as there was no other line of possibility. As the evening wore on, we began to scan the crags of the opposite side anxiously for any sign of the others. Their delay in returning gave me some hope that they might after all have found a way; but towards dark I began to fear that an accident had occurred, for they must have realised our failure, and desperation is apt to make people run unjustifiable risks. Then all at once we spotted them, descending through the mist at a seemingly reckless speed. As they approached the river I went over to the bridge to await them. Angtharkay was in front and, as he came nearer, I could see that he was in a state of great excitement; as he balanced his way precariously over the water, above the roar of the torrent I caught the words: 'Bahut achcha, sahib, bahut achcha.'

When Tilman arrived, I heard from him the glad news that they had found, 1,500 feet above the river, a break in that last formidable buttress, guarding the mystic shrine of the 'Blessed Goddess'. From where they had stood they could see that the way was clear into the Nanda Devi Basin. The last frail link in that extraordinary chain of rock-faults, which had made it possible to make our way along the grim precipices of the gorge, had been discovered; and this meant at least a certain measure of success to our undertaking.

As I lay in the mouth of the cave after our evening meal, watching the spectral shadows hover in the ghostly clefts of the opposite wall of the gorge, and listening to the mighty boom of the torrent echoing to a great height above our heads, my feeling of despondency was changed to one of deep content.

9   Chapter 9

The task next morning of getting the loads back across the river over the bridge was one which required delicate handling. It was easy enough to balance across unencumbered by any weight, but to do so with a heavy load strapped to one's back was a very different proposition. The bridge sagged unpleasantly in the middle, and, as it took the weight of the body, water swept over it. A rope stretched across the river served as an unreliable handrail. Curiously enough Kusang, normally very sure of foot and steady of head, could not face it. It was as much as he could do to get across without a load, so the rest of us each had to make several of these perilous trips. It was a painfully cold job too in the bitter morning air. But all went well, and by nine o'clock we were across, bag and baggage, fervently hoping that this was to be our last encounter with the river.

Shouldering five of the loads, we climbed slowly up the mountain side. We encountered several difficult sections, but managed to negotiate each successfully. Twelve hundred feet above the river, we climbed on to a sloping ledge, which led us across the face of 'Pisgah' buttress to the foot of the gully up which Pasang and I had watched the other two making their way the previous day. Though there were one or two awkward bits, the gully was easier than it had appeared from below, and after climbing some 800 feet up it, we were able to escape by way of a narrow chimney, which landed us on the crest of the great ridge which had come so near to destroying our hopes. From here we could see right into the Nanda Devi Basin, though heavy rain clouds obscured all but the mighty ramparts at the base of the great peak.

A short way beyond we came upon two small caves. There was also a plentiful supply of juniper and a small spring; altogether an ideal site for a camp. So we stowed our loads away out of reach of the rain, which was now starting to fall, and romped down the 2,000 feet to the river at a breakneck speed. The second journey up the slopes carrying the remainder of the loads was a slow and tedious business; but when at length we reached the ridge once more, we were rewarded by the pleasant knowledge that for the time being we had finished with the grim austerity of that fearful gorge, and that ahead of us was a new and wonderful world to explore.

Growing in the vicinity of our new camp was a great quantity of wild rhubarb. We had found it lower down the valley, but there it had been scarce. That night we consumed a quantity which now makes me sick to remember!

Towards sunset the rain cleared off and, as we sat round our juniper fire, we witnessed a heavenly unveiling of the great peaks of the basin. First appeared the majestic head of Nanda Devi herself, frowning down upon us from an incredible height, utterly detached from the earth. One by one the white giants of the un-named ranges to the north followed suit; until at last it seemed as if the entire mountain realm stood before us bathed in the splendour of the dying sun, paying homage to the majesty of their peerless queen.

It was after eight o'clock when we got away next morning. We cached twenty pounds of food in the cave, together with the remainder of the rope and iron stakes we had brought for the roping up of the difficult sections of the gorge. This left us with 380 pounds of baggage to be transported through into the basin. It was obvious from what we had seen that we could not hope to make even a rough exploration of the whole thing in the time available before our food ran out. We therefore decided to concentrate on the northern half of the basin, and to return in August, when we hoped that the main force of the monsoon would have spent itself, to explore the southern section. The distance we would be able to cover depended on the difficulty of the ground, and my previous experience of Himalayan glaciers had made me not over optimistic.

The going now became distinctly easier, and by noon we got on to the gentle grassy slopes above the junction of the two streams which came down from the main glaciers of the northern and southern sections of the basin to form the Rishi Ganga river. Half a mile below the junction, we could see a stretch of sand flats where the river broadened out, and, becoming comparatively slug- gish, appeared to offer a good fording place. To cross here would save us several hours of toil, which would be necessary if we were to cross the two streams above the junction. But we sadly underestimated the difficulties, for although we succeeded in getting across, the struggle was almost as severe as it had been in the gorge a few days before and, as there was no possibility of bridging the river at this point, a better way had to be found.

We pitched camp in a little nala formed by a stream coming down from the glaciers of the westerly rim of the basin; then, leaving Kusang to prepare our evening meal, we started out to visit the junction, and to find a better way of getting across into the northern section.

We were now actually in the inner sanctuary of the Nanda Devi Basin, and at each step I experienced that subtle thrill which anyone of imagination must feel when treading hitherto unexplored country. Each corner held some thrill- ing secret to be revealed for the trouble of looking. My most blissful dream as a child was to be in some such valley, free to wander where I liked, and dis- cover for myself some hitherto unrevealed glory of Nature. Now the reality was no less wonderful than that half-forgotten dream; and of how many child- ish fancies can that be said, in this age of disillusionment?

Immediately above the junction of the two streams was a curious little plateau, rather resembling a giant tennis-court, which commanded a fine view up each of the rivers. About a mile and a half up the left-hand valley (facing up), we could see the snout of a great glacier. This later came to be known by us as the Main Glacier, and was formed by the ice of all the larger glaciers of the northern section. But although we had a clear view for nearly three miles up the southern stream, we could see no sign of a glacier, though the character of the stream told us that one must exist. This southern stream too contained only half as much water as the other; a clear indication that we must expect a vaster and more complicated glacier system in the section we were about to visit.

It had been decided that on the following day, while Tilman and I were at work with the plane-table, the others would go back to the previous camp for the rest of the stuff. After some discussion the Sherpas assured us that they would be able to find a way back above the junction and, as it was getting late, we decided that it was not necessary to go further that evening. On the plateau we found a quantity of wild onions, which greatly pleased the Sherpas. Beyond the junction, peacefully grazing on the gentle grassy slopes, was a small herd of bharal. We estimated the height of the junction to be about 13,100 feet.

The Sherpas were away shortly after dawn on the following morning, while Tilman and I left camp a little later on our first reconnaissance into the unknown basin. Following a ridge which came down from some of the westerly peaks, we reached at an altitude of about 15,500 feet the crest of a little shoulder, from which we obtained a good view over the lower part of the Main Glacier. I was very surprised at the type of country which lay before us. On the true left bank of the glacier the giant cliffs of Nanda Devi rose sheer and forbidding in true Himalayan style; but, bounding the glacier on the right-hand side, beyond a well-defined lateral moraine, an expanse of undulating grassland stretched for miles, in lovely contrast with the desolation of the moraine-covered glacier. If the shepherds of the Dhaoli and Niti valleys could only get their flocks through the grim gorges of the Rishi Ganga, they would find here almost unlimited grazing. Now this pasturage is a sanctuary where thousands of wild animals live unmolested. Long may it remain so!

It was a great relief to see that when making our way up the valley we would not be confined to travel on the glacier itself; for conveying loads about on the lower reaches of a Himalayan glacier is a task which demands much time and infinite patience. The ice is generally completely covered with a thick deposit of gravel and boulders. The whole surface is rent and broken into a sea of cliffs and fissures, ridges and hollows. It is almost impossible to work out a good line beforehand, and the traveller has to worry his way through a perfect maze of obstacles. From the point we had reached we could see that by the side of the glacier there stretched gently undulating grassland, which would provide us with excellent going for the first few miles at least.

Though the views we got were of great interest, we did not have much success with the plane-table, as there was a lot of cloud about, and we could not fix our position with any degree of certainty. Eventually, we were driven down by a shower of sleet and rain. We got back to camp at seven o'clock, and were surprised to find that the Sherpas had not returned. When darkness fell, and there was still no sign of them, we became seriously alarmed. We were contemplating going out to search for them when from a distance we caught the sound of their voices, and presently they appeared, without loads and obviously tired. We learnt from them that they had had great difficulty in finding an alternative route above the junction of the stream, and that, being overtaken by night, had dumped their loads on the far side of the northern stream.

The next morning (8 June), there was a great feeling of slackness, and though we got away by 7.20 a.m., we walked without much energy, stopping frequently. The ground, however, was easy and in a few hours we reached the snout of the Main Glacier.

In the afternoon, while the Sherpas went off to fetch the loads they had left on the previous day, Tilman and I climbed over the snout of the glacier, and mounted up the lower buttresses of the main peak of Nanda Devi. We climbed for some hours over rough broken rocks, and emerged at length on the crest of a sharp spur, which commanded a grand view down the Rishi Nala. We saw to its best advantage the majestic sweep of the northern cliffs of the gorge, which culminated in a formidable barrier of mountains forming the western rim of the basin. We worked for an hour with the plane-table, before a mass of evil-looking clouds blowing up from the black depths of the gorge blotted out the view, and we were driven down again, this time by a storm of hail.

Sitting round a blazing fire of juniper that night, Tilman reminded me that in the course of that afternoon we had been the first human beings to have set foot on the main peak of Nanda Devi, a point we had both neglected to observe before!

We cached a further small dump of food at the snout of the Main Glacier, when we left early next morning. We then mounted to a little moraine ledge at the side of the glacier, and soon reached the gentle grassy slopes we had seen two days before. The going could not have been pleasanter: soft springing turf with the grass still short, having only lately got rid of its burden of winter snow. And, owing to our ease of movement, we were able to give our whole attention to the enjoyment of this wonderful new world we were in. Every few hundred yards, some new feature would reveal itself – here a side valley to look up, and to speculate as to where it would lead, there some graceful ice-clad summit appearing from behind a buttress, and looking, in the newness of its form, lovelier than any of its neighbours; there again, a herd of wild mountain sheep gazing indignantly at these intruders who had violated the sanctity of their seclusion. In spite of the heavy load I was carrying, I frequently had difficulty in refraining from running in my eagerness to see round the next corner, or to get a better view of some fresh and slender spire which had just made its appearance.

Towards midday we reached the edge of a big glacier, coming in from the west. After crossing this, we came upon a beautiful lake, shut in on three sides by great mounds of moraine deposit, and on the fourth by dark, frowning cliffs. On the placid waters were reflected the icy crests of the great peaks. We had intended going further that day, but we could not resist the prospect of a camp in such surroundings.

We had previously agreed that not a moment of our time in the basin should be wasted if we could possibly help it. It was all too short as it was, and we were determined to get through as much as we could while our food lasted. Accordingly, as soon as camp had been pitched, we set off to reconnoitre the lateral glacier we had just crossed. The sky was dull and overcast, and presently snow started falling heavily. We climbed on to a ridge which bounded the glacier on the right, and followed it until we were some 2,000 feet above the lake. At four o'clock the snow stopped falling, and we erected the plane-table, and waited in a bitterly cold wind for the evening clearing of the mists. At half-past five our patience was rewarded. A rift appeared to the west, and framed in it was a dome of rock and ice, which could belong to only one mountain – Changabang. There was no mistaking it. Often had I gazed at that wonderful photograph taken by Dr Longstaff from the Bagini Pass on the opposite side: and here before us was an almost exact replica of that splendid face which Dr Longstaff describes as 'the most superbly beautiful mountain I have ever seen: its north-west face, a sheer precipice of over 5,000 feet, being composed of such pale granite that it is at first taken for snow lying on the cliffs at an impossibly steep angle.' As is generally the case with such views, the mountain summit appeared as something detached from the earth, floating in the upper air at a fantastic height above our heads; and moving along swiftly in a direction opposite to that of the drifting mist.

Presently Changabang's sister-peak, Kalanka, made her appearance, and we saw that the glacier at our feet originated in a vast coombe formed by the ridge of the two peaks. Tilman suggested the name 'Changalanka' for the glacier, and appeared disappointed when I expressed doubt as to whether that name would be accepted by the authorities!

Soon other summits appeared, each tinted with the fires of the dying sun, and vying with one another to tax the credibility of their puny audience. But nature is a perfect stage-manager, and when the majesty of the vision was at its height, the curtain of cloud fell about us once more, so, with numbed fingers we packed up the plane-table, and scrambled down to camp in the gathering dusk.

From above the lake we had a view right up the main valley, along the north-ern base of Nanda Devi. A series of subsidiary valleys coming in from the north-eastern rim offered us a means of exploring that section, and we decided to devote the next week to that task.

The red sunset of that evening was a sure indication of better weather, and we awoke at dawn the next morning (10 June) to a chorus of birds heralding a gloriously fine day. We ate a hasty breakfast in the frosty air and were away before the sun had reached us, carrying light loads, and having enough food with us to keep Tilman and myself in the necessities of life for three or four days. It was our intention to push as far as we could up one of the eastern val-leys, and camp there while the Sherpas came down to relay the rest of the stuff up to a more suitable base. Making our way round the eastern shore of the lake we climbed over the wall of moraine deposit, and were soon worrying our way through the intricacies of a big ice stream coming in from the north. This came to be known later as the Great North Glacier. At its junction with the Main North Glacier we found an easy route across, and within two hours of leaving camp we found ourselves in a pleasant meadow on the far side of the Great Glacier.

From here the travelling was extremely easy. A wide corridor of flat grass-land ran outside a very well-defined lateral moraine on the right bank of the Main Glacier, and we were able to stride along at a quick walk, until we were abreast of the entrance to the valley we were making for. Then we turned left and plodded up nearly 2,000 feet of slaty shingle, which had been left when the side glaciers shrank to their present dimensions.

By two o'clock we had got fairly into the valley and decided to camp at an altitude of about 17,500 feet. The Sherpas built a small stone wall to protect us from the wind, and left us with a promise to return in three days' time.

Later that afternoon Tilyian and I went off in opposite directions to make a preliminary reconnaissance of the valley we were in, in order to be able to come to a decision as to our course of action. I took the plane-table with me. Climbing up the scree and snow-covered slope above the camp, I came, at an altitude of about 18,000 feet, to the crest of a ridge. As I did so, I saw a solitary bharal, some twenty-five yards away. He was a noble specimen, and stood so still that he might have been a stuffed beast in the Natural History Museum. We stood regarding one another for some minutes before his curiosity was satisfied, and then he stalked leisurely away and disappeared round the corner of a cliff. Most unfortunately I had left my camera in camp (as was usually the case when I happened upon something which would make a good photo-graph!) It was difficult to understand what brings these animals to such altitudes. Three thousand feet below was perfect grazing, and neither man nor beast to molest them. Their lives must be wonderfully care-free and one would expect them to be content to grow fat and lazy down below; instead of which they seemed to spend most of their time climbing about precipices of astonishing steepness, risking their necks on crevasse-covered glaciers, and going as far away as possible from food and comfort. Surely then they too have the capacity to appreciate the savage beauty of high mountain places, and to revel in the rhythm of practised movement over difficult ground.

I returned to camp at 5.30 to find Tilman was just back. We compared notes, and formulated a plan for the employment of our time in the valley. We decided first to attempt to reach a col at its head, which we concluded must lie on the eastern rim of the basin. From it we hoped to get a view out of the basin towards the peaks of the Nepal-Tibet border. After that we proposed to attempt to find a high level route into the next valley-system.

We consumed a dish of pemmican soup and, as the sun disappeared behind the distant ranges, we crept into our sleeping bags, to watch the world give itself over to frozen night. We had with us our tiny bivouac tent, but we had by now got firmly into the habit of sleeping out, using the tent canvas as a blanket. This was due mainly to the discomfort of squashing ourselves into the minute space it afforded, though personally I dislike all tents and use them as little as necessity permits.

The ledge on which we were lying being high above the floor of the main valley on the north side, it commanded a superb view of the colossal northern face of the twin peaks of Nanda Devi. The two peaks were joined by a horizontal rock ridge, some two miles in length. From this ridge, the precipice fell in one unbroken sweep to the glacier which lay at its foot, 9,000 feet below the summit. The rock wall thus formed is perhaps without an equal anywhere in the world. We had recovered by now from the shock which we had experienced on coming for the first time face to face with this sight, but, as I lay there and watched the rays of the setting sun bespangle the mountain with a score of rapidly changing shades, the whole scale of height and depth appeared enhanced beyond belief.

We passed a restless night due, I suppose, to the fact that it was our first visit to that particular altitude that season. We were both wide awake at 2 a.m., though we did not want to be off much before daylight. The little streamlets about us were hard-frozen, and we spent some time melting sufficient ice for what we knew would be our last drink for many thirsty hours of toil to come. We left our bivouac just after 3.30 a.m., about a quarter of an hour before the first glimmer of dawn, and in sleepy moroseness climbed over the boulder-strewn slope to the edge of the dry ice of the glacier. Mounting on to this, we soon settled down to that gentle rhythm which alone makes early morning climbing at high altitudes bearable. For an hour and a half we plodded along in a dreamy silence, only roused every now and then when some large crevasse necessitated an altering of the course. The dry ice gave place to frozen snow, and presently one of us suggested that perhaps it was about time we put on the rope. It was then quite light and, looking back, we saw that Nanda Devi was already bathed in the warmth and splendour of the morning sun, and with this sight a modicum of enthusiasm stirred our lethargy.

The work now became intricate, and several crevasses gave us food for serious thought before we were able to cross them. At about 6.40 we were standing at the foot of a steep slope some 400 feet below the col. Working on a short rope we started up it, and found it to be composed of a vixenish layer of hard frozen snow, covering pure ice. While the snow remained frozen it was safe enough to kick shallow steps up the incline, but directly the sun came over the col the snow would melt and form an exceedingly dangerous avalanche trap. By first cutting through the snow, and then making large steps in the ice, the slope could probably be negotiated later in the day, but it would be a prolonged and hazardous business, as the gradient was continuously steep and afforded no safeguards whatever. Moreover, the task of cutting such a staircase under the present conditions would take nearly all day. However, from the point he had reached in the course of his reconnaissance on the previous day, Tilman had seen that by climbing one of the peaks adjacent to the col, we would find an alternative route down to the lower part of the glacier we were on; and we decided, after some discussion, that we were justified in continuing the climb by relying on the snow crust alone.

This crust became thinner and thinner as we mounted, and at last we were forced into a longish bout of step-cutting in order to reach some ice-covered rocks just below the col. These too required some careful handling, before we drew ourselves up on to the knife-like crest of the ridge which formed at this point part of the eastern rim of the basin. We sat on a ledge protected from the cold wind and beat our numbed extremities back to a painful life. It was nine o'clock. With the aid of our barometer we estimated our height at 20,300 feet.

The day was gloriously fine. The view to the east was bewildering. I had never expected to see such an extraordinary array of peaks, and we could make but a poor effort at sorting out the tangled topography. Except for Nanda Kot to the south, there was no particularly dominating feature, but as far as the eye could see there stretched a sea of glistening spires and domes, ridges and icy plateaux, in dazzling profusion and complexity, while in the distance we could discern some mighty giants, evidently belonging to the ranges of western Nepal.

At our feet, far below, we looked down into a wide valley whose glacier flowed away from us into another and much larger one, which we identified as the Milam Glacier.

We were anxious to find a way of escape from the basin in this direction, but even had there been a practicable route down to the Milam Glacier from this point, it would have been an impossible task to get our loads up the ice slopes we had just climbed.

Tilman was feeling the effects of altitude a good deal, and was suffering from the usual sickness and weakness. However, by now our retreat was cut off, and we had to go through with the traverse of a 21,000-foot peak to our north. We sat on the ledge near the col for half an hour, during which time we occupied ourselves by studying the view, forcing bits of biscuit down somewhat unwilling throats, and thawing our chilled limbs. Then we rose to tackle the eight or nine hundred feet of rock and ice which separated us from the summit of the peak. The climbing was not difficult until we got on to a sharp ice ridge which led to the summit. A cold wind was blowing, and it was a tricky job to retain one's balance in the small steps which it was necessary to cut in the crest of the ridge. This was a type of climbing which I disliked, as one had to trust to one's feet alone, and the slightest slip would be impossible to check. But it was exhilarating to see the Milam Glacier system beneath one heel and the Nanda Devi Basin beneath the other; and it is not often that these Himalayan ice ridges are even possible to climb along.

The wind was too cold and the ridge too narrow for us to stop even for a minute on the summit, and we passed straight over and continued climbing down along the ridge on the other side. Soon we were brought up by a vertical cleft in it, and we were forced to cut steps for some distance down the Milam side before we could get round this.

There now followed a very long bout of downhill step-cutting along a ridge which never allowed any relaxation while we were on it. I felt a mighty relief when after some hours we reached a steep snow gully leading down to the tracks of the morning, and found the snow to be in a safe condition. The snow on the glacier itself was soft and we broke through several times into small crevasses. Nevertheless, we made a very rapid descent and were back in camp by the middle of the afternoon.

As I have said, Tilman had suffered severely from mountain sickness throughout the day, but I was feeling remarkably fit, considering it was the first bit of serious mountaineering that we had been engaged upon at any altitude that year. Presently I felt a considerable pain in the groin, at the top of the right leg. I thought I must have strained the leg slightly in one of the crevasses we had encountered on our descent, but I have since connected it with a mysterious fever which attacked me a few minutes later. It began with a violent attack of shivering, which caused me to pile on all my spare clothing and roll myself up in my double sleeping bag, despite the scorching afternoon sun. My memory of the next twenty-four hours was distorted by delirium. I had a curious impression that I was lying there in the open for several days, during the whole of which time I was either trying to escape from a fierce tropical sun or from a dead Arctic cold, while the ever-changing face of Nanda Devi writhed itself into hideous grimaces. The fever lasted for about thirty-six hours and then left me as suddenly as it had come. When the Sherpas came on the morning of the

13th, I was able to hobble slowly down with them to a base which they had by now established above the junction of the Great North Glacier with the main ice stream, and well stocked with juniper fuel collected from the area below the lake.

Having regained my senses, I was extremely annoyed at having lost two days of our valuable time in the basin. Tilman, however, had put in some good work in the meantime, and rejoined us at what came to be known as 'Glacier Junction Camp', on the evening of the 13th.

The next morning we started out again, this time with provisions for only one night, for a bivouac in another of the valleys coming down from the peaks of the eastern rim. I still felt very weak, but as I was carrying no load, I managed to follow the others without delaying them too much. This new valley we found to be divided into two sections, and we decided to devote a day to the exploration of the right-hand one, if possible climbing once more on to the eastern rim, where we hoped to be in a position to make a close examination of a complicated knot of peaks to the north which had aroused our curiosity a few days before. We were still hoping too to discover a means of escape which we could use when the time came as an alternative to a retreat down the Rishi Gorge. In this we had small hope of success, however, as a strong party consisting of Mr Ruttledge, Dr Somervell and General Wilson, had made an abortive attempt some years previously to find a route into the basin from the Milam Glacier.

As we brewed our evening pemmican, we observed signs which promised an early change in the weather. The evening was warm and still, and our barometer was behaving in an extraordinary manner. However, we 'dossed down' in the usual way, using our ridiculous little tent merely as a covering. [1]

I had slept for about an hour when I was awakened by soft wet snow falling on my face. The tent, an intricate tangle of sodden guy ropes, flaps and ridges, offered very poor covering, as the snow melted and lay in pools of water in the folds of the canvas, and from time to time these would empty themselves

---

1 Since then I have come to the conclusion that for the purpose of these lightweight bivouac camps a thin waterproof sheet would be lighter and more satisfactory than one of the small tents people have been at such pains to design of recent years. Tents with accommodation for two people and weighting fifteen pounds or more can be made to stand up against almost any conditions of weather, but I do not think a cloth has yet been discovered which, if made into a tent of less than eight pounds, will stand up against weather such as one must be prepared for when doing a series of bivouacs at great altitudes. Such a tent will generally collapse under a heavy weight of snow; it will be torn to shreds if exposed to a really bad blizzard, and will leak even in light rain. Under a single waterproof sheet one is at least as comfortable; it is no trouble to either pitch or pack up, while in fine weather one need not suffer from the unbearable stuffiness of the midget tent.

playfully down our necks. This prevented us both from sleeping until about one o'clock, when it started to freeze, and though the snow continued to fall our rest was no longer disturbed.

We awoke at six o'clock to a dreary morning. The snow had stopped falling, however, and we started up the glacier. Here we encountered the vile snow conditions which were to prevail throughout the summer, and this was to prove to be one of the most serious obstacles with which we had to contend. But the climbing was not difficult, and at 12.30 p.m. we reached another point on the eastern 'rim', at an altitude of just about 20,000 feet. A cold wind was blowing sleet into our faces as we peered down from the crest of the narrow ridge. We caught a further glimpse of the valley which contained the Milam Glacier, but beyond that all was obscured in mist. Two thousand feet of steep snow-covered rocks lay at our feet. It might have been possible to climb down, though with loads the risk of snow avalanches would have been too great. From where we stood we were able to get some slight idea of the topography of that part of the watershed, though ten minutes after we had arrived all our surroundings were blotted out and visibility was restricted to a few yards.

The descent to our bivouac took only two hours. The Sherpas were waiting for us, and, packing up the loads, we ran on down to the junction camp as fast as we could.

The present weather was obviously better suited to travel than to the mapping of intricate side valleys, and we decided that on the following day we should push as far as possible up the Great North Valley, so as to be in a position, when the weather cleared, to explore its head. Accordingly, soon after dawn we started in a northerly direction, carrying with us enough food and fuel for six days.

The morning was reasonably fine and it was not until about ten o'clock that the more distant views became obscured. Travel in the Great North Valley we found to be very different from the easy progress we had made over the gently undulating slopes which bounded the Main Glacier, steep precipices continually forcing us on to the shattered moraine-covered surface of the ice.

We had been going for an hour or so, when Tilman, who had been lagging behind somewhat, complained that his right leg was hurting him. I suggested that he should share some of his load between the rest of us, but this he declined to do. We sat down to argue the point for a moment, when all of a sudden he began shivering, and I realised that he was starting an attack of fever similar to the one to which I had succumbed five days before. I suggested, therefore, that we should remain where we were. But Tilman would not hear of this, saying that if we did not get to a point from which I could make a useful reconnaissance on the following day, yet another twenty-four hours would be wasted. So we divided his load among the rest of us, and carried on, though how he was able to stick at it throughout a long and weary day I cannot imagine, for the work of making one's way over a badly broken moraine-covered glacier is as tiresome and exasperating a job as I know.

As I have mentioned before, it is impossible to work out a line of march over such country beforehand, and the only thing to do is to go straight ahead, and tackle the difficulties as they present themselves. A long ascent of a steep slope of boulders, poised precariously on the hard black ice, and ready at the slightest disturbance to roll down and crush one's foot; a slender ice ridge, leading across two yawning chasms, one on either side, from which came the dull thunder of a sub-glacial stream; an ice cliff, down which steps had to be laboriously chipped; these followed one another in monotonous succession, and led perhaps to an impasse, demanding a long, tiresome detour, perhaps to a further tangle of cliffs, ridges and towers. Here was a lake whose dark blue waters proclaimed it to be of great depth, infinitely placid, save when some little avalanche of ice and rock, crashing down from above, whipped it to frenzy; further on, a raging torrent, rushing madly in no particular direction, barred the way. Our day's work yielded us but some three miles of progress, and we camped in a perfect wilderness of moraine debris. On arrival, Tilman collapsed into a sleeping bag, and lay for the next thirty-six hours on a rough bed of boulders, waiting patiently for the fever to pass.

The following morning was beautifully clear, and I roused myself out of a half-frozen sleeping bag in time to resect the position of the camp on the plane-table before the clouds came up and obscured the view. In this brief spell of clear weather I was able to get a general idea of the topography of the valley we were in, and in the gathering shadows of a snowstorm Pasang and I set off to reconnoitre the upper part of the glacier. Working our way diagonally across the ice stream, we reached a point where the moraine debris from the left bank of the glacier met that from the right bank. The contrast between these two species of rock was very striking. That from the Kalanka side was almost white, while that from the peaks of the eastern 'rim' was a dark blue-grey. At this junction we found a wide trough running up the middle of the glacier, providing an avenue of easy going. It closely resembled those glacial troughs which provide such an easy approach up the East Rongbuk Glacier on Everest.

By now it was snowing steadily, and the trough provided our only means of steering a direct course up the glacier. We made rapid progress however, and soon reached the end of the moraine-covered part. Here the trough petered out in a level stretch of ice, which provided going even more unpleasant than that which we had encountered lower down. Slush, knee-deep, covered its surface, which was scored into a maze of channels cut by twenty or more swiftly flowing glacier streams, and it was not until the middle of the afternoon that we reached an extensive lake which lay at the foot of a sheer precipice of ice-worn rock, and seen through the haze of falling snow, bore an uncanny appearance. On either side of the precipice was a confusion of ice cliffs, which indicated two ice falls. One, I judged, must come from an extensive ice plateau to the north, from which the Great North Glacier derived the bulk of its strength. About the origin of the other ice fall I could form no idea.

After a short rest on the shore of the lake, we worked round to the edge of the 'plateau' ice fall, worked out a route, and ascended some 700 feet above the lake. Then, as the weather showed no sign of improvement, we returned to the lake, and plodded down to camp, where we found Tilman still very weak, but better, and determined on making a move on the following morning. We discussed matters, and decided to push a camp as high as possible by the side of the ice fall which Pasang and I had visited that day.

Snow fell gently throughout a most uncomfortable night, and despite the dreariness of the morning I was glad enough to get going. Our loads were light, as we were carrying only enough food for three men for three days, and we had with us merely the larger of the two tents. The plan was for Tilman, Pasang and myself to occupy the high camp, while Angtharkay and Kusang went down again to the one we had just left. Three is a safer number than two when travelling on extensive snow-covered glaciers as, if one man falls into a crevasse, it is extremely difficult for a single companion to pull him out.

Just before reaching the trough, we passed a curious phenomenon. We were walking along the brink of an ice cliff about 100 feet high, and below, flowing directly towards the face of the cliff, was a large stream which, when it reached the cliff, entered by way of a tunnel in the ice. A few yards to the left it reappeared, flowing exactly in the opposite direction, until it disappeared once more into another ice channel.

The weather cleared somewhat while we were going up the glacier and, when we reached the lake, we were greeted by a gleam of sunshine which transformed the cheerless waters of yesterday into a pool of radiant loveliness in which danced the images of a thousand sparkling ice pinnacles. We saw, too, up the valley containing the second ice fall, whose presence had puzzled me on the previous day. It was a narrow gorge-like affair, which bent round to the west and came, we concluded, from the northern foot of Kalanka. Thus its glacier came to be known as the Kalanka Glacier, and Tilman was forced to abandon his 'Changalanka' jest and agree to the name 'Changabang' for the glacier coming in below Junction Camp.

We sat for a while on the shore of the lake, to bask in the sun and to revel in that brief moment of beauty. Then we turned our attention to some precipitous slopes at the side of the 'plateau' ice fall. Here we became involved in some difficult climbing, which was made no easier by the snow, which soon started falling again, accompanied this time by a blustering wind.

At about three o'clock, at an altitude of some 18,500 feet, we started searching for a place on which to camp. The ground was continuously steep, and in the end we were forced to construct a platform on which to pitch our tent. Leaving us to complete the task, Angtharkay and Kusang went off down, climbing at top speed in order to be able to reach the lower camp before darkness cut off their retreat. They had instructions to return in three days' time.

An entry in my diary that evening reads: 'The wind dropped and the weather cleared, and gave us a slight idea of our surroundings. The ridge we are on seems to be covered with ice, and probably leads up to Peak 113 (on our plane-table sheet). We are closer to the glacier than we thought, and above the worst bit of the ice fall. The glacier seems to be split into two sections and the bit nearest us leads up to an extensive plateau, which does not look very far away. I suppose that is the thing to explore first; but the snow is now falling heavily again and I don't know what will happen. We have two and possibly three days' food with us. I hope we will be able to do some good in that time. We are having a spell of vile weather. I don't know if it is the monsoon or not. It does not look like it somehow. We all got very cold this afternoon, but are quite comfortable now – about 6.10 p.m. A miserable outlook, and we will soon have to be fighting our way back down the Rishi with scanty provisions.'

The presence of three bodies kept the tent warm and in spite of the cramped position we all slept well, and I did not wake until Tilman struck a match at 2 a.m. to look at his watch. I cursed him roundly and went to sleep again, until he woke me again at 3.45. I know of no proceeding more dismal than the preparations for an early morning start from the chaos of an over-crowded tent. One man struggles manfully with a stove in order to provide the party with a drink of melted ice, while the others do their best to knock it over in their efforts to find some missing sock, glove or puttee. Tempers are at boiling point, and the whole business of mountain exploration seems utterly futile and ridiculous. Food in any form is repulsive, and the water, when at last it has been obtained from the ice-blocks, tastes strongly of last night's pemmican, and nearly makes one sick. This, of course, is someone else's fault for not having taken the trouble to wash the pot out the night before! Oh! for a really heavy snowstorm which would give one an indisputable excuse to get back to the only place in the world one really wants to be in – in the warmth of the recently abandoned sleeping bag. It is stupid to start now anyway – why not wait until we see what the weather really is going to do! But at length all is ready; freezing fingers struggle for some minutes to close the complicated fastenings of the tent, and the party proceeds in silent churlishness until the sun swamps all gloom in the wonder of his early dawn.

On this particular morning, we were threading our way through a maze of ice corridors whose walls were white, cold, dead, until all in a moment their deathly pallor was changed to a faint rose flush, faint but radiant with life and warmth.

We emerged from the badly crevassed area, and chipped our way up a steep snow slope, at the top of which we found ourselves on the ice plateau at an altitude of over 20,000 feet. Two great ice-peaks rose in front of us. These numbered 110 and 113 on our plane-table sheet. Between them was a saddle, separated from us by a very gentle slope. We decided to make for the saddle, and from it to attempt the ascent of Peak 110, which appeared very easy from where we were standing. I confess that I was vaguely hoping to find an exit from the basin by way of this saddle, though, looking back, that hope seems to have shown poor mountaineering judgment. Peak 113, seen from the plateau, was a wonderfully symmetrical pyramid of the purest ice, standing fully 1,500 feet above the saddle.

The saddle was deceptively far away and, though the snow was still fairly frozen, it took some hours of hard going to reach it. The crest of the saddle we found to be 20,500 feet. Below us to the north and west was one of the most terrific drops I have ever looked down, and it was some seconds before I could adjust the focus of my eyes to see that one could not merely step down on to the moraine-covered Bagini Glacier, 4,500 feet below. It looked as though, if a stone were dropped, it would touch nothing until it struck that glacier, up which Dr Longstaff's party had made their way twenty-seven years before. Beyond, standing out above a belt of dark cloud, was a wonderful panorama of the Garhwal mountains. Close at hand on the extreme left rose the slender spire of Dunagiri, whose delicate structure of ice ridges has presented such formidable barriers to her votaries. Beyond, in the distance, the graceful head of Nilkanta stood in superb contrast to the massive shoulders of the Badrinath group, some of whose secrets we were to be privileged to reveal. Then came my first Himalayan acquaintance, Kamet, ruling despotically over his colony of peaks of the Tibetan borderland; then the untrodden glaciers of Hathi Parbat; and lastly to the north a wondrous mass of mountains of all shapes and sizes, still unnamed and unmeasured.

The wind was too cold to stand for long admiring the view, and we started up the slopes of Peak 110. The snow was soft and powdery, and it was exhausting work making a trail. Tilman had not yet recovered from his fever, which was not surprising, considering that he had only risen from his bed of sickness on the previous morning. He seated himself in a shallow crevasse, which was sheltered from the wind and exposed to the warm sun, and told us to carry on and see what we could do with the peak. Pasang and I laboured on for an hour, through snow into which we sank up to our hips. In that time we made some 300 feet of height, and I decided that we would stand no chance of getting to the top, and regretfully abandoned the attempt. From where we had got to, however, there seemed to be no technical difficulties between us and the summit. It was evident too that the good weather would not survive many hours.

When we regained the plateau, we found the snow in a vile condition. As we got lower down, we were out of the wind, and the heat and glare were intense, and the labour of flogging a trail was a heart-breaking one. But we were in no particular hurry, and every now and then we sat down to gaze at the glorious view over the Nanda Devi Basin which our position commanded. The valleys were filled with great banks of woolly storm clouds, and the peaks of the eastern rim and the twin peaks themselves showed up in splendid isolation, which helped us to get a general idea of their relative size and position.

Once, while we were preparing to glissade down a very steep slope of about thirty feet into a crevasse, Pasang started off before we were ready, and, misjudging the length of the rope, both Tilman and I were pulled head first after him. The landing was soft and the fall was not long enough to have any serious consequences, but the incident was an annoying one, as it was a bad mountaineering error caused by pure carelessness. The badly crevassed section of the glacier required delicate handling, as the complicated system of snow bridges, which had been hard-frozen and secure in the morning, were now very unsafe, and we were constantly breaking through and hearing that ominous tinkling sound of icicles falling into the frozen depths of the crevasses below us. We reached our camp without further mishap, just as the usual afternoon snowstorm made its appearance, and spent the remainder of the day brewing and consuming vast quantities of tea and strenuously debating the subject of our next move.

10   Chapter 10

We had been keen to climb Peak 110 primarily in order to be able to get a comprehensive view of the complicated topography to the north. Our reverse had merely stimulated that desire. Probably a more useful alternative for the morrow would be to continue the exploration of the ice plateau in that direction. By doing this, if the weather were reasonably fine, we would be bound to see much of interest, whereas if we failed on the peak again, it would be a day of our most valuable time in this unknown country wasted. However, from what I had seen, the peak looked easy and eventually its blandishments won the day.

Pasang had had about enough on the previous day, and at 4 a.m. on the 20th Tilman and I left camp, heading once more for the ice plateau. We suffered all the usual early morning torments, but were more than adequately compensated by the splendour of the dawn over the Nanda Devi Basin. Having our tracks of the previous day to follow, we climbed at a great pace, and reached our highest point of the previous day while our mountain world was still frozen; but beyond this we were faced with quite unexpected difficulties. A slope of dangerous snow, through which steps had to be cut into the ice below, led us, after some hours of hard work, into a long snow-filled corridor, running across the face of the mountain between high walls of ice. The snow had been swept into the corridor from the ice slopes above, and was deep and soft. We sank in up to our waists as we beat our way along. We could not see where the corridor was leading us, but it was soon obvious that if we did not escape from it soon, we would have neither time nor energy to go any further. After half an hour or so, I saw a narrow vertical crack or 'chimney' in the wall nearest the mountain. I started up it and, by putting my feet against one wall of the 'chimney', and my back against the other (a method familiar to all rock climbers) I could make slow progress. But we were now at an altitude of nearly 22,000 feet, and I had not got many feet up the 'chimney' before I was gasping like a fish out of water. Also the ice, of course, did not offer much friction to either boot or back, and the tendency to slip was very great. The air in the cleft was deathly cold, and in spite of my exertions my extremities soon lost all sensation. It was not long before I was bitterly regretting my folly in having tackled so severe a climb at such an altitude. The top of the cleft resisted my efforts so sternly that when, eventually, I emerged on to the steep ice slope above, I sat there faint and sick for several minutes before I could summon up sufficient self-control to take in the rope as Tilman climbed up the 'chimney'. If it had been cold for me it was far worse for poor Tilman, who had had to wait below while I was wrestling with the 'chimney'.

When, after ten minutes' rest, we started up the ice slope, we were both very shaky. The slope was steep and covered with three inches of slush, which made the job of chipping steps a difficult one. Higher up conditions became worse, and we soon realised that our struggle with the ice-chimney had left us too weak for the labour of hacking a safe pathway up ice of such a texture. Also the work called for absolute steadiness, as a slip on the part of either of us would have been impossible to check, and must have resulted in disaster, and we were both too tired to be able to guarantee safe movement. Again we had to admit defeat and turn back. Of course, if we had had time to spend on the job, we would have been able to make a bivouac in one of the crevasses nearby, and so eventually to hack our way up those relentless slopes. But we had come here primarily to explore the Nanda Devi Basin, and we could not afford the two days which would be necessary for a serious attack on Peak 110.

The descent to the plateau called for unremitting care, and I was mightily relieved when we got clear of those vicious ice slopes.

Our second reverse on this peak was another clear demonstration of the tendency to under-estimate mountaineering difficulties in the Himalaya.

After a close observation of the mountain, we had expected to have no serious difficulty in climbing it, and yet we had twice failed to do so. Our camp was only 18,500 feet high, and 4,500 feet is a lot to have to do in a day at that altitude, but this was not the reason for our defeat. In time, when these mountains become more familiar, a great many of their difficulties will be looked upon with less respect; but one wonders if mountaineering technique will ever reach so high a standard as to allow men to climb the more formidable giants of this vast range.

When we reached the camp we found all three Sherpas waiting for us. After slaking a raging glacier thirst, we packed up the tents and sleeping bags, and hurried on down.

When we reached Great North Glacier, we found that the streams were enormously swollen. There had been a terrific increase in the rate of melting of the surface ice. I imagined that this was a sure sign that the monsoon was at hand, and we became seriously worried about the state of the rivers below.

After an undisturbed night in the open, I awoke at sunrise on 21 June to the song of many birds, which, strangely enough, seemed to be just as numerous far up in these barren moraine-filled valleys as amongst the pastures lower down. At 6.30 on this brilliant morning, while the Sherpas packed up the camp preparatory to going down, Tilman and I started up the glacier once more. We had a busy and interesting morning working with our plane-table at various points about the glacier, and in the afternoon, when the storm clouds had once more re-asserted themselves over the country, we ran at a great speed down the Great North Glacier to Junction Camp. When we reached the main valley, we found that a wonderful change had taken place in the short week we had been away. To a great height the mountain sides were a brilliant green with young grass. Our camp, lovely before, was now set in a garden of wild flowers, whose gay colouring framed the pools and new-born streams, contrasting deliciously with the harsh ruggedness of the higher glacier regions from which we had just come.

That evening we took stock of our food, and found that we had sufficient for only three more days. The weather was very unsettled, and it was evident that the monsoon was at hand. This was surprising, as we had not expected it until after the first week in July. Tilman was suffering from a severe pain in his foot, for which he could not account. There was still much minor exploratory work to be done in the northern section of the basin; this we could not hope to complete.

On the 22nd we took a light camp into yet another side valley leading towards the eastern 'rim', and Tilman and I spent that night at an altitude of 18,100 feet, while the Sherpas returned to Junction Camp. We slept as usual in the open, and that evening, after a sharp hail-storm, we experienced again that vision of divine beauty which is, I suppose, the chief object of the strange pilgrimages which men make to the less accessible regions of the earth. It does not come to one at any particular place or time, and may elude the hunter over hundreds of miles of arctic waste or on countless mountain summits, to be found only on rare occasions, when the mind is unexpectedly attuned to the realisation of a delicate perfection of form and colour.

Before us, rising out of a misty shadow-lake of deepest purple, stood the twin summits of Nanda Devi, exquisitely proportioned and twice girdled by strands of white nimbus. This was backed by a liquid indigo, changing to mauve as it approached the south-west, where the icy pyramid of Trisul stood in ghostly attendance. Then, after passing through every degree of shade and texture, the colour died, leaving the moon to shed her silver light over a scene of ravishing loveliness, and to revive within me childish fancies, too easily forgotten in the materialism of maturer years.

We had intended to attempt, on the following day, the ascent of an attractive peak of some 21,500 feet, above our camp. Tilman's foot, however, appeared to be getting worse, and it was deemed wise that he should rest it in preparation for the heavy work which our retreat down the Rishi Nala would involve. Without his early-morning energy to assist me I found it more difficult than ever to summon up the strength of mind necessary to extricate sleepy limbs from the warmth of my sleeping bag; particularly as the morning was dull and cheerless. Vanished were all the lofty enthusiasms of the previous evening, eclipsed by the hateful obligation of having to expose swollen lips and sore hands to the damp cold. Leaving the bivouac at 7.20 a.m. I crossed Glacier No. 5 on dry ice and climbed up the ridge which divides that valley from the Great North Valley, reaching a height of some 20,000 feet. Although the sky was overcast, the clouds stood well above the peaks and from my perch I obtained the most comprehensive view I had yet seen of the northern section of the basin, and spent an interesting and instructive hour filling in minor detail on the plane-table sheet. Towards one o'clock a bitter wind started blowing from the east, and snow fell. I made an unpleasant but quick descent to the Great North Glacier and reached Junction Camp at 4.30 p.m. to find Tilman and the Sherpas already arrived with our high camp kit. Tilman's foot was now badly swollen, and had caused him intense pain on the descent. It was now apparent that the trouble was a carbuncle on the upper surface of the foot.

On 24 June, while the others moved the camp across the Great North Glacier to the side of the lake, I had a long walk up the side of the Main Glacier, principally with the object of sketching the features on the northern face of Nanda Devi. The going was easy and pleasant along the level grassland beside the glacier. It rained steadily most of the day and although my attention was constantly occupied by flowers, lakes, and herds of bharal, I was able to see very little of topographical interest and returned down the valley earlier than I had intended, reaching camp at 4.20 p.m.

I had hoped that by cutting our rations down slightly we might have time to explore the head of the Changabang Glacier, but it was now evident that the monsoon had broken and that we could not hope for more clear weather. Also we were far from sure how long the return journey would take us and one of the party was lame. We decided, therefore, to begin our retreat at once. And lucky it was that we had no great temptation to stay on in the basin, for our food dumps proved inadequate as it was!

A heavy mist hung over its grey waters as we said goodbye to the lake which had greeted us more than a fortnight before with so much sparkling life. We started very early and had reached the snout of the Main Glacier by midday, to find our fears regarding the state of the rivers only too well founded. The one issuing from the Main Glacier was now a raging torrent, despite the fact that the ground over which it was flowing for the first half mile of its course was relatively flat, and to ford it seemed at first to be a hopeless proposition. Moreover, the alternative of crossing the glacier above its snout and getting to the opposite side of the river in that way was out of the question, owing to a formidable line of overhanging cliffs thereabouts. For a moment our position looked serious, and I began to visualise the unpleasant consequences of having our retreat cut off. We waded out in several places, only to find each time that we could not stand up to the force of the current. After repeated attempts we were standing disconsolately at the water's edge when Pasang suggested a line which appeared to me to be at least as bad as the rest. However, he seized me by the hand, and I was led into the water's edge with a sinking heart. We immersed our lower halves in the seething turmoil, and advanced slowly. One of us moved forward a few inches supported by the other, then he would stand firm while the other moved, and so on. The rushing water made me giddy, and I knew that the least mistake would put us in a false position, from which there would be no hope of recovery. When the water touched my waist I knew that I had reached my limit, and any increase of pressure must sweep me off my feet. Pasang was splendid; never did he relax his concentration on himself or me for a fraction of a second. At length, after what seemed an age, the depth of the water began to lessen, and we bounded out on the other side, Pasang, who had done much more than his share of the 'supporting', letting out wild cries of joy.

With the help of a rope stretched across the river, the others got over without mishap, though Angtharkay had an extremely bad time of it and required much support from the other two. Our relief at getting across without mishap was shared by the Sherpas, who danced with delight. But there was no time to waste in celebration, and we started down at full speed towards the junction of the northern and southern streams. To reach it we had to cross a spur coming down from Nanda Devi, and here we became involved in some difficult rock climbing. However, at three o'clock we reached the southern stream just above the junction. After a short search, we were fortunate enough to find a place where the river, running over a stretch of mud flats, was very sluggish and, though the water was deep, we managed to get across without further unpleasant adventures. We found a nest, hereabouts, with three grey-blue eggs belonging, we supposed, to snow pigeons. These birds were very common in the basin.

We climbed diagonally up the steep slope beyond the river, heading in a south-westerly direction until, about a thousand feet above the junction, we came upon a little grassy shelf with a spring of clear water. Here we settled down for the night, deliciously conscious that a heavy day's work had taken us clear of two serious difficulties, and that we were now well on our way to the Rishi Nala. But as we sat round our blazing fire of juniper wood in the gathering dusk, watching the heavy rain clouds float lazily over the rolling moors of the basin, my content was marred by a feeling of sadness at having to leave so soon this country, which had provided us with a deep and lasting happiness, and whose beautiful secrets it had been our privilege to explore.

26 June was a terrific day. During an early breakfast we caught a last fleeting glimpse of Nanda Devi's mighty head through a rift in the heavy monsoon clouds which hung over us. Then we started off towards the west, moving across the steep grassy slopes at a breathless pace which never slackened throughout the morning, and by midday we reached the little cave in which we had camped on 5 June. The Sherpas were as anxious as we were for speed,

and I think that the mind of each of us was on the 'flesh pots' of the Dhaoli Valley. But this was not the only reason, for the supplies of food left in the dumps were meagre and did not allow for any hitch which might easily occur on the return journey, on account of the early breaking of the monsoon.

Most of us were feeling fairly fit, but Tilman was rendered very lame by the carbuncle on his foot. He insisted, however, in carrying his share of the loads, and never breathed a word of complaint, though the furious pace over such difficult country must have caused him very considerable pain. We halted at our old camp for about twenty minutes, in order to eat a cup-full of satu mixed with cold water. The scramble from there down the very steep slope of 2,000 feet to the river took us two hours on account of the awkwardness of the loads. The river was many feet higher than when we had made its acquaintance before, and of course our little bridge had been swept away. On we went through the afternoon, and darkness found us encamped in a little clump of silver birch beyond the dreaded 'Mauvais Pas'.

I passed the night in a tiny recess between two boulders, and throughout the first half of it a thunderstorm raged above the gorge. The boulders provided inadequate shelter from the heavy rain which accompanied the storm, and I got very wet. The scene, however, was one not easily to be forgotten. Lightning flashes played continuously upon the grim precipices about me, while the fleecy rain clouds, entwining themselves about ridge and gully, accentuated their already stupendous size. Echoes of the thunder and hissing of rain provided fitting accompaniment.

The next morning, in thick mist and steadily falling rain, we continued our way along the delicate traverses which constituted the only practicable route across the gaunt precipices forming the southern wall of the canyon. The long tedious task of discovering the way and relaying our loads along it had made us familiar with almost every yard of the route, so that in spite of the bad visibility we were now experiencing, we made no mistakes. We were assisted too by the cairns which we had built at various points, and at one o'clock that afternoon we reached our base camp on the shore of the river we had left nearly a month ago. We had all been looking forward to a good square meal, but on arrival we found that by some mistake we had left only half the quantity of food which we had intended leaving, and that we now had sufficient only for three more days. This allowed for no contingencies, and there was no time to lose.

Below our base camp we had a choice of several routes. Dr Longstaff had made his way to this point along the southern slopes of the valley, but he had encountered considerable difficulties, and with our loads and in such weather we would certainly take two and possibly three days to reach the place where he had bridged the Rishi Ganga. The route by which we had come with the Dotials was out of the question, owing to the impossibility of crossing the river in its present state where we had crossed it before. The only alternative then was to cross by the natural bridge to which I have referred before, ascend the Rhamani Nala until we found a place where we could cross it, and try to get on to the high line of traverse which Dr Longstaff's party had taken after they had crossed the Bagini Pass in 1907. So shortly after four o'clock that afternoon Pasang and I set off to investigate the possibility of this alternative.

We crossed the river by the natural bridge, which Pasang had not seen before. He was delighted, and seemed to think that it solved our last remaining problem. In gently falling rain we climbed up a difficult cliff to Longstaff's old campsite, some 200 feet above the Rishi. From here we edged our way along a narrow shelf which gave us access to the Rhamani stream, but at a point where the river, issuing from a deep-cut ravine, descended in a series of waterfalls, and offered no hope of a crossing. We retraced our steps, and in some anxiety scrambled up along the steep rhododendron-covered slopes above the ravine, whose smooth unbroken walls overhung the river. We were forced to climb some 1,500 feet up before we found another break in these walls, and were able to get down to the river again. This time, however, we found ourselves at a fairly level stretch between two waterfalls, and decided after some discussion that the crossing could be attempted at this point. It was now getting late, and we had to get back quickly if we were to avoid being benighted, but I would have given much to have been able to continue our investigation of that remarkable gorge.

At the base camp we deposited our plane-table, some lengths of rope, candles, 'Tommy's cookers' and a few items of clothing, to be picked up when we returned in August for the exploration of the southern section of the basin. This lightened our loads somewhat, and on the following morning we were back at the crossing place by ten o'clock. We got over without much difficulty, and climbed a further 500 feet up on the other side. This brought us on to a prominent ridge, from which we had a clear view down the Rishi Nala. Fortunately visibility remained good until three o'clock, by which time we had covered about a mile and a half on a fairly horizontal line. Then mist enveloped us, and for the next two hours, in pouring rain, we floundered helplessly about the intricate hillside until we came upon a spacious cave, where we decided to spend the night. There was a quantity of juniper growing nearby, and we were soon drying our sodden gear by a blazing fire.

The weather was still bad when we awoke next morning, and we did not get started until eight o'clock. Groping our way through heavy mist, we got on to exceedingly difficult ground, and by eleven o'clock we had covered only a quarter of a mile. However, soon after this the weather cleared, and we found ourselves close to the terrace from which we had descended to the river nearly five weeks before. On reaching this we were on familiar ground once more and made such excellent progress that by the middle of the afternoon we were running down the pine-clad slopes to Dibrughita – 'the horizontal oasis in a vertical desert'. The alp was more beautiful than ever – a vast meadow of lush grass interwoven with forget-me-nots, deep red potentillas, large blue gentians, and flowers of a dozen other varieties, while the stately army of tall dark pines stood in a wide circle as if guarding this little shrine from the demons of the Rishi Gorge.

Our troubles were now over, and as we lay on the damp ground in the gently falling rain before an immense log fire, we basked in contentment undisturbed by sordid considerations of time, distance, and food.

A long slog up the steep slopes of the 'curtain' ridge the next day (30 June), took us to Durashi, where we found that the shepherds from Lata village had been installed for about ten days. These were the first human beings, besides ourselves, that we had seen since discharging the Dotials on 29 May, and our arrival startled them considerably. However, we managed to persuade them that we were not the mythical devils of the upper gorge, and they supplied us with quantities of goat's milk, which I thought at the time was the finest drink I had ever had. It must have strengthened us considerably too, for on the following morning, we made astonishingly quick time up to the Durashi Pass. I had been hoping that some snow would still remain in the gullies, as this would have enabled us to glissade some of the way down to Tolma, but except for a few patches here and there it had practically all gone. We decided to descend diagonally to the Lata village, instead of going down to Surai Tota. We had not much idea of the way, but before we had gone far we struck a sheep track which led us through an intricate network of cliffs in the forest, and soon blossomed out into a sizable path, down which we ran recklessly. Kusang lagged behind to gather considerable quantities of wild strawberries. He gave me all he had picked, and when I asked the reason for his generosity, he said that he had damaged his knee and that eating strawberries would make it worse! I failed to see the connection, but did not argue the point too strongly. We reached Lata village just before four o'clock, and immediately set about trying to persuade the inhabitants to sell us some food. We were bitterly disappointed, for the net result of our scrounging was a few unripe apricots and a cup-full of flour. There were no chickens, and therefore no eggs. There were cows, but no milk, and the last year had been a bad one for grain and, with the next harvest still so far off, the villagers could not afford to part with their flour. It was evident that the land of plenty was not yet reached, and we tightened our belts with a grim resolve to reach Joshimath the next day.

That evening we paid a social visit to the village, which we found in a great state of excitement on account of the arrival of an itinerant trader. His wares consisted of a miscellaneous assortment of buttons, matches, Jews' harps, soap, etcetera, for which the villagers were eagerly exchanging the grain which had been refused us earlier in the day, though we had offered money some five times the value of the ridiculous trinkets supplied by the pedlar. We could not find out how he disposed of the grain, but it must have been a slow and precarious method of livelihood.

Early next morning, a large section of the village turned out to see us depart and accompanied us for some distance in order to see that we got on to the right path. It was a tedious march and we all felt very lethargic, the cause being, no doubt, our enforced underfeeding for the past few days. In the pouring rain we sped down the Dhaoli Valley practically without a stop. Each of us, I suppose, was thinking of hot tea and lots of food; but to a passer-by (if there had been such a phenomenon) we must surely have resembled the demons of the Rishi to whom we had been likened by the shepherds at Durashi. Early in the evening we entered Joshimath, exactly six weeks after leaving it.

Part 3

The First Crossing of the Watershed (Badrinath – Gaumukh)

11 Chapter 11

We had over-estimated the joys of Joshimath. After three or four days of idleness and over-eating we were quite ready for a move to the north, where we fondly hoped we might be beyond the reach of the monsoon. We were bound for the Kedarnath-Badrinath group of mountains which are of great topographical interest since in them lie the sources of three of the main affluents of the Ganges, the rivers Bhagirathi, Mandakini, and Alaknanda, and close to these sources are the well-known temples of Gangotri, Kedarnath and Badrinath.

Our object in wishing to visit these was to cross the range which forms the watershed between the Alaknanda and the Bhagirathi, and so to link up the two chief sources of the Ganges. The range was but twenty miles north of Joshimath and it seemed very likely that there we should escape the influence of the monsoon and enjoy fine weather. (This theory was sound enough – in theory; but like most it did not work out in practice and we found that we were in the same predicament as if we had gone to see the English Lakes in the hope of avoiding a wet summer in the south.)

We knew that in 1912 Mr C. F. Meade and his two Swiss guides had gone from Badrinath up the Bhagat Kharak Glacier, climbed the ridge at its head, and looked down on the Gangotri Glacier. They did not descend on the other side, but they thought the pass was practicable, and it was our intention to find and cross this pass and thereby not only cross the range, but also explore the unknown head of the Gangotri Glacier.

But there is more than geographical interest in this district. It is believed to be the home of the gods of Hindu mythology, and every feature of the landscape is sanctified by some legend and is traditionally memorable.

It seemed that from earliest Vedic records (Hindu writings), the geography of the mountainous regions sheltering the Ganges sources was well known. In those distant times when men still worshipped the elements, a region which saw the birth of great rivers and greater storms was naturally regarded with awe; and so, when the worship of the elements was supplanted by the worship of gods, it began to be revered as their home.

The learned and the pious were drawn there for meditation and adoration, and hill and valley, peak and waterfall, came to be associated with particular gods and embellished by stories of their lives. Indeed, in the Hindu legend of the creation, Brahma, Siva and Vishnu assumed the form of mountains. When

Brahma desired to create the earth he began by assuming the visible form of Vishnu, the whole universe being covered with water on which floated that god, resting on a bed supported by a serpent. From his navel sprang a lotus from which issued Brahma; from his ears issued two Daityas (or, when transferred to an earthly sphere, Dasyus, the aboriginal black race as opposed to the fair Aryan), who attacked Brahma; and Vishnu and Brahma fought with them for 5,000 years until Vishnu finally killed them and from their marrows made the world.

Vishnu then assumed the form of a tortoise and raised the earth out of the water and asked Brahma to create all that the world was of earth, sky, and heaven; divided the earth into nine parts and created wind and sound and time; past, present, and future; work and desire, and anger; from the last-named Siva was created as making the third of the great trinity, Brahma the creator, Vishnu the preserver, and Siva the destroyer.

The story then goes on that during the terrestrial reign of one Prithu, all plants perished by reason of his tyranny, which so angered him that he determined to destroy the earth. The earth sought pardon, and begged the king to remove the mountains which prevented the spread of vegetation. Prithu uprooted the mountains and heaped them on top of each other, but then from the earth proceeded to milk all plants and vegetables. Other gods and demons followed his example and milked the earth of all its virtues, who then fled to Brahma to complain of this everlasting milking. Brahma took her to Vishnu, who made the following promise: 'Soon the head of Brahma will fall upon thee [at Brahm Kapal a great rock in the river at Badrinath]; Siva will come to sit upon the mountains of Tankara' [at Jageswar in Kumaon]; 'Bhagirath Raja shall bring down Ganga [Ganges] to thee. Then I myself will come in my dwarf incarnation and all the world will know that Vishnu has descended on thee. Then thy pains shall be removed and the mountains cease to afflict thee with their load, for I shall be Himalaya; Siva will be Kailas [a mountain in Tibet north of Kumaon]; Brahma will be Vindhyachal and thus the load of the mountains shall be removed.'

But the earth asked 'Why do you come in the form of mountains and not in your own form?' and Vishnu answered: 'The pleasure that exists in mountains is greater than that of animate beings, for they feel no heat, nor cold, nor pain, nor anger, nor fear, nor pleasure. We three gods as mountains will reside in the earth for the benefit of mankind.' (An answer which mountaineers would do well to learn in order to baffle the all-to-frequent inquiry of why they climb mountains, for it leaves the questioner no wiser than before, yet it has an authority sufficiently impressive to silence him!)

Thus Himachal, the Snow Mountains, were invested with sanctity, but the holy of holies is Mount Kailas, in Tibet, and the sources of the Ganges and the mountains which surround it, and here are the ancient temples of Badrinath,

Kedarnath, and Gangotri. They are all reached by roads having a common origin at Hardwar, another holy city which marks the place where the Ganges debouches from the hills on to the plains. The three temples are within a circle of twenty miles radius, but between each rises a 20,000-foot ridge of snow and ice, and to pass from one to the other pilgrims must retrace their steps for more than one hundred miles, so to outflank this great barrier.

Kedarnath was particularly associated with the worship of Siva, whose adventures there are definitely not of the kind associated with the life of that grim and terrifying god, the very apotheosis of lust and cruelty. The legend is that the god took refuge here when pursued by the Pandavas (a tribe of the Dasyus whom we have already met) by assuming the form of a buffalo and diving into the ground for safety. Unluckily he left his hinder parts exposed on the surface, and there is still a mountain here which is supposed to resemble in shape the hindquarters of a buffalo and is now an object of adoration.

These high-spirited Pandavas were effectually subdued later, and when told that their power had left them and that they should begin to think on heaven, it was to the Himalaya they retired. The account of their departure is most moving, a pathetic touch being that of the dog who, I suppose, had taken a too prominent part in the buffalo hunt. We read that, 'Yudishthira, their ruler, then took off his earrings and necklace, and all the jewels from his fingers and arms, and all his royal raiment; and he and his brethren, and their [sic] wife Draupadi, clothed themselves after the manner of devotees investments made of the bark of trees. And the five brethren threw the fire of their domestic sacrifices and cookery into the Ganges and went forth from the city following each other. First walked Yudishthira, then Bhima, then Ayuna, then Nakula, then Sahdeva, then Draupadi, and then a dog. And they went through the country of Banga towards the rising sun; and after passing through many lands they reached the Himalaya Mountain, and there they died one after the other and were transported to the heaven of Indra.'

Close to Kedarnath on the north, but reached by a different road, is Gangotri. There is a celebrated temple here and close by is Gaumukh, the Cow's Mouth, which should have proved an even greater attraction, but from what we saw and what I have heard since, is visited by only a few. This is the snout of the Gangotri Glacier, fifteen very rough miles above the temple, and the sacred source – or rather the most sacred, for there are others – of Mother Ganges. Apparently when the world was young and man was in a state of innocence the Ganges rose at Benares, so that it was an easy matter for believers to visit it. As the earth increased in years and wickedness, the source retreated successively to Hardwar, Barahat, and now to Gaumukh, whither the long and arduous pilgrimage may atone in some measure for the sins of a more vicious age.

In the temple at Gangotri are two images representing the Ganges and the Bhagirathi, and below in the river bed are three basins where the pilgrims bathe. One of these is dedicated to Brahma, one to Vishnu, and one to Siva, and the water of these basins will not only cleanse away all past sins, but ensure eternal happiness in the world to come. It is almost as efficacious if taken away – and returning pilgrims may then hope to get back some of their expenses! The water is drawn under the inspection of a Brahman and by him sealed for a small consideration, and when carried down to the plains it realises a high price. The mighty Ganges is here only about fifty feet across and at Gaumukh perhaps half of that, but in the summer when the snows are melting the current is very fierce.

Such are the interesting legends attached to the Kedarnath-Badrinath country and, the flesh-pots of Joshimath having so quickly palled, we were glad to begin drawing up food lists and to engage the necessary coolies. Unfortunately our eight deserters from Surai Tota had so blackened our characters that we had great difficulty in finding anyone else, but at last we collected six coolies, and two days' march along what is called the 'Pilgrim Road' brought us to Badrinath on July 11th. At a village on our way up we stopped to sample some exciting-looking sweetmeats and were led to believe that all the inhabitants were positively clamouring for work as coolies. Now our six were only coming – and that reluctantly – as far as Badrinath with us and we wanted eight to come on to the Bhagat Kharak Glacier, so we promised to give eight villagers the work and received in return an ardent promise that we could rely on them presenting themselves next day in Badrinath at dawn.

This was excellent, and on the 12th we were up at five o'clock and had all the loads in readiness, but when eight o'clock came and there was still no sign of any porter, we began sending out into the highways and byways of Badrinath for recruits. By nine o'clock we had five men and we then moved over to the bazaar, where we sat, with what small patience we could muster, beside the three extra loads until men could be found for them. Every man in the bazaar joined in the search – which meant that no spare man could be found, but two hours later our complement was somehow made up and we gave the word to start. By then, of course, the first five had drifted off to see their friends or to buy food, but we were assured they would follow. So in ones, two and threes did we straggle out of Badrinath – a distressing sight to an orderly-minded man.

But our fellow-marchers were as happy-go-lucky as ourselves. They had started from Hardwar, a journey of some thirty days from Badrinath and were for the most part townsmen or peasants from the plains; the former in 'dandies', or walking before a plodding coolie carrying their baggage: the latter walking – without the coolie. For the majority baggage was not a serious hindrance as a brass bowl for food and a pilgrim's staff was generally enough. One additional thing was carried by all, whatever their station in life. This was an umbrella. Indeed, the almost universal use of this very European article was most striking, and I must admit that the umbrella was a highly incongruous adjunct when borne aloft by a hardy shepherd of the hills, clad in a long, blanket-like coat of homespun fastened across his chest by a metal skewer and chain for want of a button; but seemingly he was sensible enough to prefer dryness to a picturesque appearance.

The pilgrims were of both sexes, and we inclined to believe there were more women than men. Many of the former, could they afford it, were carried in a basket or a 'dandy'. The basket was high, narrow and cylindrical, not much bigger than a dirty-linen basket, and was hitched to the coolie's back, he carrying a T-shaped staff to support its weight when at rest. The passenger sat facing the rear with only his head showing, and the many we passed appeared to be asleep, with handkerchiefs over their faces to keep off the flies. The 'dandy' was rather like a sedan chair without any sides and was carried by four coolies, thus making it a very expensive mode of transport. Slung at each end from a pole which rests on the bearers' shoulders, it was so arranged that they might walk in echelon, and not side by side. The passenger is literally and metaphorically 'in the hands' of his carriers, as the following story shows.

Tradition relates that the ruling family of Kumaon, at that time the Katyuris, had their origin here. There is a story about the last Katyuri Rajah which illustrates the steep contours of this country more vividly than can any descriptive writing. Rajah Dham, the last of his line, ruled so tyrannically that he went in fear of his life. In such circumstances the usual safeguard is to wear an extra steel waistcoat or to change the cook, but in this case the Rajah took the precaution of having iron rings fastened to the shoulders of his dandy-bearers. The poles passed through these rings, and so it was impossible for the bearers to drop their royal burden over a cliff without themselves accompanying it. But no one is secure against desperate men, and when oppression grew intolerable, four men were found ready to sacrifice themselves for the sake of their country, who flung themselves off the road, with the Rajah, to their deaths.

The profane like to recount a more recent tradition which also shows how the country lends itself to the arranging of 'accidents', but puts the dandy-bearers in a less pleasing light. The pilgrim season is short: it starts in May and none leave Hardwar after the end of August, and so like other seasonal workers the dandy-men try to make the most of it. It is the custom to contract for transport and pay in advance, but if the dandy-men went the whole way, they could at the best make only two full journeys. They therefore hit on the happy plan of tipping their passenger over any convenient cliff into the river, many marches short of Badrinath, and hastening back for a fresh load. They argued that the arrangement satisfied both parties, the pilgrim bathed in the sacred waters as he had desired, and the coolies could earn twice as much in the season. The practice died out with the coming of the British raj, who probably regarded it as a too free interpretation of the contract.

The pilgrims, so we have been told, found the fruition of all earthly desire in a visit to their sacred places, the shrine of Vishnu at Badrinath, the Panch-Sila, the Five Rocks and their respective pools which encircle the throne of Vishnu, and what is called 'The Holy Circle of Badrinath', which includes a tract of country from the shrine of Kanwa to the peak of Nanda Devi, on the summit of which is supposed to be a lake, the abode of Vishnu himself. Their day's stage was usually about nine miles and at each halt they found accommodation in long, low sheds open in front to the road and surrounded on the remaining three sides by stone walls supporting a grass roof. The floor was of beaten earth which received daily a fresh wash of mud or clay and along the roadside were a dozen or more little circular fireplaces, also of clay, spaced at four-feet intervals. There were also shops, at which the pilgrims might buy their food and fuel, the purchase of which entitled them to a free night's lodging. Some of these rest-houses were provided with big thatched-reed sleeping mats, but there was no other furniture. Certainly everything looked very clean (owing probably to the frequent washing with yellow clay) but, fortunately perhaps, we were never called upon to put this supposed cleanliness to the test.

The government, having made the 'Pilgrim Road', a well-engineered bridle-track seven to ten feet wide and maintained by the P.W.D. of India, were rightly concerned about the health of the pilgrims, for an outbreak of cholera at any of the rest-houses would be most serious. The greatest difficulty was sanitation, and therefore inspectors were employed along the route to see that at least the most rudimentary regulations were carried out. At most of the villages, too, pipelines had been laid down to bring drinking water from high up the hillsides, where the chances of contamination were less. Even despite these precautions dysentery and, in the lower valleys, malaria took toll of the pilgrims, many of whom, weakened by unaccustomed effort and the cold, were in no condition to resist an attack. We were told that at Badrinath alone that year there had been thirty deaths – but as probably there had been some 30,000 pilgrims this did not strike us as being an alarming proportion. Besides, more than a few of them were most likely caused by weakness and starvation, since many of the poorer classes start out with little or no money and are soon reduced to begging their way – no easy task in such a sparsely populated district. Doubtless such a method answered well enough for the professional beggar (for whom India is renowned). He had only to pass through a bazaar and thrust his bowl under the noses of unfortunate shopkeepers to have a handful of rice or ata put into it. In this walk of life a disgusting appearance is a positive asset, and I have never once seen the most repulsive-looking individual turned away empty-handed. At Badrinath itself the temple authorities dispense every day quantities of free food: at mid-day a great bowl of cooked rice is carted into the main street and anyone who asks may be filled.

We were much puzzled by the complete apathy which most of them betrayed. Here was no 'Happy Band of Pilgrims', but a procession of woebegone miseries that reminded us of refugees, driven from their homes by an invader. None seemed to derive any pleasure from the performance of a duty which to them meant the principal thing in life, or from the glorious scenery through which this duty led them. One and all went along with downcast head, bestowing no glance upon the grandeur of the hills and deigning but a sour look at passers-by. Possibly, of course, this latter was reserved for ourselves – the outcasts and unbelievers defiling holy ground. (After all, a European on the road to Mecca during the pilgrim season would be lucky to receive nothing more harmful than angry looks.)

But these Hindus were not so fanatical in such matters as the Mohammedans, and on several occasions we found them pleased to show us their temples, so we came to the conclusion that a possible cause of their indifference lay in their awe and fear of mountains. To nearly all of them rocks, hills, snow and ice, were things outside their previous experience and, as we told ourselves, we had not to go so very far back to find similar emotions in our own forefathers. Whether their faces showed these we cannot tell, but what they felt they have very clearly expressed, as, for example, in the writing of Defoe in his *Tours*: 'Here we entered Westmorland, a country eminent for being the wildest, most barren, and frightful of any that I have passed over in England, or even Wales itself. ... Nor were these Hills high and formidable only, but they had a kind of an unhospitable terror in them. ... But 'tis of no advantage to represent Horror as the character of a Country, in the middle of all the frightful Appearances to the right and left.' And a writer of yet later date describing an ascent of homely Saddleback seems to be even more moved, though he does omit the capitals: 'views so tremendous and appalling that few persons have sufficient resolution to experience the emotions which those awful scenes inspire.'

In addition we had to remember that every rock or pool was supposedly the abode of some god, so that a fearful and downcast air on the part of the suppliant were understandable. In very truth, these pilgrims might exclaim with Kim: 'Surely the gods live here. This is no place for men!'

12 Chapter 12

Interested though we were in the behaviour of the pilgrims, the country ahead was yet more interesting, and soon we left the last pilgrims behind, for only a few go much beyond Badrinath.

Three miles from Badrinath we passed through the village of Mana, the last inhabited village on the road to the Mana Pass into Tibet. Its site was picturesque, overlooking the mouth of a terrific gorge and backed by a bleak hillside studded with prodigious boulders, some of which had rolled down, thus completely spanning the ravine. Here the low huts, roofed with rough flat stones, appeared to grow like some fungus out of the landscape, and here the Alaknanda Valley bent abruptly to the west and three miles up gave birth to a river at the adjoining snouts of the Bhagat Kharak and the Satopanth glaciers. But contrary to expectations our pilgrims did not visit this source: instead, they resorted to a place called Bhasudhara, about a mile short of the glaciers. Here, in truth, was the spot where 'the slender thread of the Lotus flower falls from the foot of Vishnu', a spot far more fitted to witness the birth of the sacred Ganges than the desolate, moraine-covered ice of the Bhagat Kharak. Almost as soon as one rounded the bend at Mana the eye was drawn, without conscious volition, to a narrow white ribbon of water outlined against a wall of reddish rock at whose feet was a grassy alp. Here the water, cascading from some hidden glacier, dissolved at the bottom into a fine mist with which the wind sported, and so sprinkled a rude shrine and the pilgrims who bowed before it.

This part of the Alaknanda above Mana was a favourite resort for those who wished to commune alone and to practise austerities. We came upon several living the lives of hermits in caves and under sheltering boulders – an existence pleasant enough during the summer months, away from the flies and smells of Badrinath, and sustained by the milk of the goats which were herded here in great numbers. (In winter, no doubt, these folk descended to a kindlier climate as did the entire population of Badrinath, since from November to May their temple is shut.)

But a far more interesting ascetic than the hermits of the Bhasudhara was a Professor Ram Serikh Singh, known to all in the district as 'the Master'. We had met him first in Badrinath, whither he came every year, not to stay in the town but to withdraw, with a single attendant, to a tent pitched on a green alp in the shadow of the beautiful Nilkanta. There, in the midst of scenery grand and inspiring, he passed his time in reading and meditation. Deeply learned in Hindu religion and in philosophy, and also in the traditions of these mountain regions, his learning had not been gained from books alone since he was a lover of mountain travel and had journeyed extensively, even to Mount Kailas in Tibet, which lay some hundred miles to the north-east and was of the greatest sanctity to both Hindu and Tibetan. We spent many delightful hours with 'the Master' in his wild and secluded valley, and the memory of them is among the fondest of our travels. His genial countenance and robust figure had at once a resemblance to Mr Pickwick and to Friar Tuck. Sitting talking in his tent, or poring over a map with his spectacles athwart his nose, his likeness to the former predominated; outside on hillside or road, sturdy of frame, his thick gown girdled at the waist, a mighty staff in his hand, he recalled a favourite picture of Robin Hood's trusted companion. That there is no portrait of 'the Master' in these pages is what we call 'our fault'. He, however, out of the depths of his philosophy, refers to it as Providential (in the strictest meaning of that word). Before setting out to visit him at his camp we constantly reminded each other about a camera, hoping that he would permit us to photograph him – and in the end, both of us inevitably forgot it! When we told him of this omission of commission he displayed great satisfaction, laughingly told us that never had he had his photograph taken, and saw, in this last narrow escape, the directing hand of some Higher Power determined to protect his immunity.

But it is high time we left 'the Master' and the 'Pilgrim Road' and concentrated upon our reconnaissance of the Kedarnath–Badrinath group!

Our stay in the village of Mana was lengthened by our inability to collect our still scattered followers. But having at last mustered them all, we crossed the grim gorge of the Saraswati by a natural rock bridge and followed the Alaknanda Valley westwards. The valley was pleasantly open and was the grazing ground for all the Mana herds and flocks, and the abode of many anchorites engaged in meditation and the practice of austerities. Had there been juniper wood as well as grass we would have liked it better, for we had no wish to vie with the anchorites in mortifying the flesh. When we camped that night one mile short of the Bhagat Kharak Glacier all hands had to range far and wide to collect enough pitiful little twigs to boil a kettle. Just across the river, tantalisingly close, was a little birch spinney but it might as well have been fifty miles away.

Before reaching the glacier we had to ford a side stream of which we had been warned at Mana and advised to go up it for a mile before attempting to cross. After the Rishi it looked fairly harmless, as indeed it was if taken in the right place, and we scorned to be driven by it two miles out of our way. While we were looking for an easy place the Sherpas tried a line of their own, and Pasang got into serious difficulties. He lost his footing and went right under, but luckily for him his load came free (we again noticed the merit of head straps), and he was pulled ashore, bruised and badly shaken and minus his ice axe. The load, containing his own and my kit and bedding, went bobbing downstream, on the way to Calcutta and the sea, and in trying to stop it, Tilman's ice axe fell a victim to the hungry river. The load grounded lower down on some shallows but the axes were never recovered, and from now on the Sherpas had to use sticks which later proved a serious handicap.

The moraine on the north side of the glacier made a fair path, and two days later we camped at 16,000 feet near the head of the glacier and sent the local coolies back. The glacier was about seven miles long and as soon as we rounded a bend in it half way up we could see there was no pass at the head; there were, however, four subsidiary glaciers flowing in from a south-westerly direction so our hopes were by no means extinguished. The first of these, close to the head of the Main Glacier was disposed of before camp was pitched, for I went round the corner to look for a better campsite and saw, with disgust, a most forbidding cirque of cliffs at the head.

From the camp we climbed a small peak (19,000 feet), from where we saw enough to rule out a second possible pass, and we also obtained a good view of the northern bounding wall of the Bhagat Kharak, which was to prove useful to us later. We then made a traverse of our peak and came down a new way, in the course of which Tilman made the discovery that glissading on steep ice was too rapid, even in these fast-moving times, and we reverted to slow but safe step-cutting.

Our camp on the ice was not very home-like so we moved it across to a grassy flat on the north side where conditions were pleasant, and where we were well placed for a fresh move, the necessity for which was now looming ahead of us. A walk up the third glacier confirmed our fears, and after much heart-searching we decided the fourth was best left alone. We had caught a glimpse of the col at the head of this on the way up and it seemed to offer some hope, but the approach to the glacier was up a steep and difficult ice fall which, moreover, was raked by avalanches from the tremendous north face of Kunaling, the giant of this range, some 23,400 feet. The roar of an intermittent bombardment of this glacier from the slopes of Kunaling was ever in our ears.

(Since returning to England we have learnt that it was up here that Mr Meade went, but he got on to the glacier by some route which avoided the ice fall and the avalanche-swept area.)

Defeated in the Bhagat Kharak we fell back on a fresh plan. In 1931 the Kamet expedition had gone up the Arwa, a valley system north of the Bhagat Kharak, and in one of its branches had found a pass which obviously led to the Gangotri side of the range, although it was not completely crossed. We therefore decided to cross first to the Arwa and, if our food allowed, to attempt to find a way over the great Gangotri Glacier.

So on 18 July we started relaying loads (including a quantity of juniper wood) to the top of the 20,000 feet ridge between us and the Arwa. The direction we wanted to take was due north but the only place by which the ridge could be crossed lay well to the east of north, and we were reluctantly driven farther from the watershed. In four days we established a camp on the ridge, where we stayed two days while Tilman and I climbed a peak of about 21,500 feet. It was an interesting ridge climb, but the pleasure we expected, and in fact received, from it was secondary to getting the hang of the geography of the Arwa glaciers on to which we were about to descend. In this object we were disappointed, for the weather which earlier was so good that we flattered ourselves we had outrun the monsoon, now broke up, and snow, rain, and mist were our daily portion.

But our two-day halt here enabled us to eat some of the weight out of our loads and when we started the descent we were just able to carry everything in one shift – everything except our juniper which we abandoned regretfully. The descent was not as exhilarating as descents should be; indeed, soft snow and heavy loads made it purgatorial. We towed the loads behind us like sledges, lowered them in front of us, or sent them rolling down under their own steam; any method rather than carrying them which only sank us deeper and deeper in the snow. At last, after passing at great speed under some hanging glaciers, where the Sherpas called loudly and effectively upon their gods, we reached dry glacier; the first of the Arwa branches which we called 'A'.

The sun had come out and now blazed down on us as if bent on making up for past deficiencies, and we spread ourselves and the loads out to dry. The Sherpas stretched themselves like lizards on rocks, bottom upwards, for they were over partial to sitting glissades and suffered accordingly. We had dropped over 3,500 feet from the pass and the barometer now registered only 16,200 feet, though it was surprising it could register anything at all after the treatment the load in which it travelled had received. Pasang and Tilman had a little joke of their own about that barometer. When he saw us consulting it so earnestly he often asked Tilman what its name was, and upon being told 'Shaitán' (Satan) he seemed to appreciate the name and thereafter took an affectionate interest in 'Shaitán's' welfare.

The glacier on which we were camped was three-quarters of a mile wide and the watershed was now two miles west of us, but there was no crossing it here and we had to go still further north. On the opposite side of our glacier two subsidiary glaciers flowed down from the north, and of these we chose the westernmost for our route to the next branch of the Arwa.

The col at the head of this was about 18,000 feet and the approach to it not difficult. We left a small dump of food at our camp on 'A' glacier, went up to the col and crossed it, and in the afternoon camped on the 'névé' of what we called 'B' glacier at 17,000 feet. From here we could see where our pass lay, still two miles north and 2,000 feet higher, and the condition of the snow had up till now been so bad that we began to despair of reaching it. Soon after making camp it began to rain and as we had omitted to pitch the tents door to door and there was only the one 'Primus', the party of five assembled in one tent to advise and assist in the cooking, thereby raising a very satisfactory 'fug'.

The rain turned to snow in the night and the morning was overcast, but by 8.30 we were ploughing slowly to the north with the watershed now close on our left hand. Had there been any drying power in the sickly sun which leered at us out of a big halo, sure presage of foul weather, Tilman would have made a passionate appeal for a later start. It was his privilege to carry the tents and he preferred them dry, the extra weight being a consideration but not nearly so objectionable as the water which seeped through on to his back.

That virtue is its own reward we were beginning to learn, for in the matter of early starts we found there was no other. At whatever hour in the day we were afoot the snow crust would never bear our weight, and we sank to our knees or waists as much at dawn as at midday. Today we encountered an exceptionally bad patch in which we wallowed to the point of exhaustion, but as we neared the col conditions improved and by midday we gained the top (19,500 feet). A desultory snowstorm prevented us seeing much but it was very noticeable how, as we came north, the hills assumed a more Tibetan aspect; the rock being reddish and loose, the slopes more gentle, and the tops flatter.

Below us a steep, loose gully led down for 300 feet to a small glacier. The bottom of the gully was iced, and below the *bergschrund* gaped hospitably. We descended one at a time in order to avoid the danger of loose stones. On the icy bit Pasang parted company with his load which headed straight for the abyss, but fortunately jumped it and was fielded by myself on the far side. Long-suffering 'Shaitán' had had yet another narrow escape!

The glacier we were now on was badly crevassed and to Tilman, who was in front, it seemed to fulfil somebody's definition of a sieve, 'a lot of holes held together by wire'. He duly fell into one but his load got wedged and held him up very comfortably. Pasang, the next man, was unaware of this and before Tilman could explain matters had nearly pulled him in two with the rope, thinking, not unnaturally, that he was dangling over space. For the next fortnight every deep breath fetched a groan from poor Tilman's battered ribs, the burden of their groaning being 'save me from my friends'.

Above a deep ice fall we forsook the glacier for a scree slope and were soon at the bottom on another much bigger glacier, fortunately 'dry', and flowing due west. We camped on some rocks in the middle of this and now the snow which had fallen fitfully all day, stopped for a moment. There, looking down the glacier, we saw in the distance the wall of another valley crossing it at right angles, unmistakably the Gangotri. This was a cheering sight – moreover we now had water at hand instead of snow to melt, and one of us, gifted with a strong imagination, conceived the happy idea of mixing raisins in the dough for our 'chupatties' – and so in great content to bed.

Again it snowed all night and was still at it in the morning, so we stayed in bed singing doleful songs which presently had the desired effect, for the snow stopped. Dumping two days' food here we started down the glacier, doing the first mile on 'dry' ice very quickly. Then we got into a jumble of moraine and spent the next two hours clambering in and out of great hollows. Finally we won clear and got on to a smooth lateral moraine on the right bank, and soon the sight of a few flowers gladdened our ice-weary eyes. We made five miles that day in spite of a long, luxurious halt at midday, when the sun came out and we basked and dried our sodden loads. The colours in this valley were most striking, for besides the vivid patches of green provided by the grass there were bold splashes of red, blue, and white rock. As yet we had found no juniper but we promised ourselves a fire next day.

We camped that night in a pleasant alp only two miles from the Gangotri ice stream, but our friendly moraine had petered out and the going promised to be rough. For once we woke to a fine morning (27 July) and looking out of the open tent flap we saw a sight which fairly made us spring from our bags. West across the Gangotri floated, high up, a silvery spire, graceful as that of Salisbury, and sparkling in the early sun[1]. It seemed poised in mid-air, for the base on which it rested was momentarily hidden and revealed by the mists writhing upwards from the valley.

By ten o'clock we reached the junction of our unknown 'X' glacier [2]and the Gangotri, and we halted on a friendly alp to discuss our next move, watched by an inquisitive herd of bharal from the cliffs behind. We had imagined that the glacier which we had come down would join the Gangotri five miles above the snout, and we were now, at a guess, ten miles from the head. We much wanted to visit both, the head because no one had seen it, and the snout because many had. We felt that to come to the Gangotri Glacier and not see Gaumukh, the Cow's Mouth, the birthplace of Mother Ganges, would be like going to Cairo without seeing the pyramids; at least one of us felt this but the other was not so sure, and an interesting debate began as to whether sightseers and trippers (which we were in danger of becoming) were to be emulated or despised. Before the question was put, the debate being still in progress, the clearing mist revealed a river not three miles away, a sight which altered things considerably for it meant we could go down to Gaumukh and back in the day. We camped where we were and unashamedly set forth as trippers.

We made our pilgrimage to Gaumukh from the wrong direction, and if the merit acquired is proportionate to the energy expended, ours must have been

---

1 Probably Shivling

2 The Chaturangi Glacier (Editor)

great. There was no lateral moraine on our side and we toiled by devious ways through chaotic hills and valleys of ice strewn with gigantic boulders, the short two and a half miles taking us a long two hours. On the way we passed the mouth of a valley lying parallel to the glacier we had descended, but there was no indication of it on our map and this omission gave us a feeling of quite unmerited superiority to map-makers in general and the author of this map in particular. We ought to have blessed him for giving us something to correct, whereas we made lofty and scornful remarks about slipshod work; but in less exalted moments we did appreciate at their true worth the labour and skill which had gone to the making of a map that was never meant for mountaineers.

Drab though the scene was, like the tongue of any glacier, it was impossible to be unmoved at sight of the turbid flood rushing from a black ice cave under the towering wall of ice which marked the end of the Gangotri Glacier, and to reflect that here, where it was a bare thirty feet wide, the Ganges began a journey of 1,500 miles to the Bay of Bengal into which it poured through many mouths, one alone full twenty miles wide. When one further reflected that from sea to source it was regarded with veneration by more than two hundred million human beings who, in life, believe that to bathe in it is to be cleansed from sin, and at death ask no more but that their ashes may be cast upon its waters, one had a combination of stupendous spiritual and physical marvels which could hardly be equalled elsewhere in the world.

Not wishing to acquire a double dose of merit, we returned by an easier way on the south side of the glacier where, beyond a high moraine, were grassy flats brilliant with flowers and watered by meandering streams. Opposite to our camp we recrossed the mile-wide glacier and the Sherpas welcomed us with a cheerful juniper fire and a dish of wild rhubarb, not quite equal in flavour to that of the Rishi Ganga, but rare and refreshing for all that.

We had left dumps of food on the way for the return journey but we still had two days' food in hand, and the question was what we should now do. Our tripper instincts being satisfied, the explorer instinct was asserting itself. We wanted to traverse the whole length of the Gangotri Glacier, but with only two days at our disposal we could not get far. As we were discussing alternatives inspiration came to us, borne perhaps on the wings of the wild rhubarb, and such was the attractiveness of this fresh plan that we decided to return to Badrinath forthwith to put it into execution.

On 28 July we started back up 'X' glacier and two days later camped at the foot of the small glacier leading to the pass; the weather was clearer than when we came down and we could now sketch in the many lateral branches. Mindful of the loose stones in the gully we made an early start on the 29th and went up to the pass as fast as we could in order to tackle the gully while it was yet frozen up. Tilman, as last man, was in the best position for feeling the results of and criticising careless movements on the part of the others, but thanks to our early start, and the Sherpas' Agag-like tread, we reached the top without shifting a stone. On the other side snow conditions were now better and we pushed on past our old camp and straight down 'B' glacier, for instead of crossing the second pass back to 'A' glacier and our food dump, we had decided to go round by the Arwa Valley and camp at the foot of 'A' glacier, retrieving our food next day.

By the time we were clear of 'B' glacier and heading down the valley the weather became very thick and we had some difficulty in locating the snout of 'A'. At last we came to a stream issuing from a glacier, and assuming it was 'A' we camped. Next morning Angtharkay and Pasang started early up the glacier, which we devoutly hoped might be the right one, though any doubts we had we kept to ourselves. They found the dump, but did not get back till afternoon, by which time it was raining, so we declared our half-holiday a whole one.

We now held all streams, of whatever size, in the greatest respect and to avoid having anything to do with the one by which we were camped, we went up to the glacier and crossed on the ice. In these uncongenial surroundings we were surprised to meet a large flock of goats going up the valley, and it is to be assumed the shepherds knew where they were going for as yet we had not seen a blade of grass, and even a Tibetan goat would jib at a stone and water diet.

The nearer we approached to home the worse became the weather, as it had in the Rishi, and a searching wind blew up the valley, bringing with it a cold rain. We huddled in the lee of a boulder to brew the last of our tea and then, pushing on, we got on to the track which came down from the Mana Pass. Here we met a Tibetan and two women living in a tent which was remarkable for its superior ventilation, and with them the Sherpas had a long chat. In appearances there was not much to choose between our party and the Tibetan; of both it was true to say that they were there without visible means of support. But it seemed that they were less destitute and they presented the Sherpas with a handful of twigs. I was struck with the kindness of the gesture, for it was no more than that, the twigs hardly sufficing for tinder, let alone a fire. In this, however, I was under a misapprehension, because when I mentioned it to the Sherpas I was told that the gift was tea!

We carried on till five o'clock, getting wetter and colder, hopefully expecting to find some juniper wood, but at last resigned ourselves to the bleak prospect of one more fireless night which a brew of the Tibetan's firewood did something to ameliorate.

Next day, 2 August, we crossed the upper end of the same remarkable Saraswati gorge whose lower end we had crossed on the way out. It ran for half a mile to the mouth of the Alaknanda Valley like a gigantic slit, and was but a few yards across at the top, while the river roared through, heard but not seen, two or three hundred feet beneath. The track crossed it here, as below, by a natural rock bridge and passing through the village of Mana we were presently in Badrinath and busy with letters and preparations for our next venture.

Part 4

The Second Crossing
of the Watershed
(Badrinath – Kedarnath)

13   Chapter 13

Two days' rest enabled us to explore Badrinath and its surroundings more fully. On our first view of the town itself we had been greatly disappointed as, upon breasting the last steep rise from Joshimath, our minds filled with the severe grandeur of the country through which we had passed, we looked down on a hideous huddle of tin huts and were grieved by the thoughtlessness of man in introducing such ugliness to the mountains. The roll on the drum, which welcomed all incoming pilgrims and had its length and loudness nicely adjusted to the stranger's probable generosity, was an added irritation and the temple itself did nothing to modify our first impressions. It was of no great height and so hemmed in by houses that little could be seen until close up to it, while even the façade, upon which there was some really fine carving, had a ramshackle appearance.

But on our second visit, when we viewed the temple from the far side of the river, we realised better the extraordinary atmosphere of the place and the lure that had drawn men to it throughout the ages. For at Badrinath, Krishna, probably the best beloved of all Hindu gods and one of nine incarnations of Vishnu (a tenth is expected in the future) was supposed to have, 'practiced austerities', as the saying goes. Since 'he stood here for one hundred years on one foot, with arms aloft, subsisting on air, with his outer garments thrown off and his body emaciated and with veins swollen,' and since but one of his exploits was to lift a huge mountain on one finger to shelter some milkmaids from the wrath of Indra, the god of the skies and rain, we felt that 'austerities' was an understatement to say the least.

On the bank opposite the temple was a bathing pool fed by a hot spring, with steps leading down from it to the leaping, icy waters of the Alaknanda, where a ring-bolt was sunk in the rock so that the pilgrim might cling to it while undergoing his ceremonial bath. By this baptism and by worship by Badrinath a man might obtain whatever he desired and all sins of former births were cleansed if the deity was supplicated through the priest. A legend proving the efficacy of this relates how one Janami Jaya slew eighteen Brahmans (whether rivals for or guardians of the lady we are not told), in order to possess a beautiful girl whom he met out hunting. Even for this enormity a visit to Badrinath was sufficient atonement! When one remembers that the Rawal or priest here, and at Kedarnath and other important centres, is usually a

Brahman from southern India of the Vaishnava sect, and that he is assisted by a secretary or clerk who is also from these parts, the above story seems all the more remarkable.

The origin of this custom of a Brahman priest seemed very remote, but apparently, at one time the ancient religion was supplanted by Buddhism until there arose the reformer, one Sankara, a native of Mysore. The century in which he lived is doubtful but is thought to be about the eighth A.D., and he was particularly active in Nepal and Kumaon, where he drove out the Buddhists and unbelievers and restored the ancient faith. He displaced the Buddhist priests of Badrinath and Kedarnath and in their places introduced priests from the Dhakin and Mysore. Everywhere through his followers he preached the efficacy of pilgrimage to the holy shrines, and there is no doubt that the consequent – and lasting – influx of orthodox pilgrims prevented Kumaon from a second relapse into Buddhism.

Brahmans, the priestly caste, are thus seen to be very powerful, but in many proverbial sayings the lower castes have published their defects. The most glaring seems to be an eye for the main chance, as hinted at in the saying: 'Brahmans and vultures spy out corpses' ; while in another instance we see a case of diamond cut diamond or two of a trade when we are told: 'The Brahman blessed the barber and the barber showed his glass.'

But these legends, if believed in and acted upon wholesale, might lead to results which would tax the forgiving powers of even the Badrinath deities, and to offset this there is another little story which inculcates more desirable conduct. A wealthy trader who had ten sons was told to go to Badrinath with his family and his property, there to give all his possessions to the Brahmans and to make his home, thus securing his admission to Paradise. But while living there his wife (who seemingly had her own views as to property) lost a valuable ivory ring, and the sages then told her that as penance for this duplicity in holding back a valuable article, the family must once more do the round of the 'tirthas' or places of pilgrimage. When this had been accomplished and they were back in Badrinath, the elephant whose tusk had provided the ivory for the ring suddenly appeared and conveyed the whole family at once to the paradise of Vishnu.

Of men brought up on such traditional tales, none who believed could resist the promises of desires fulfilled and past misdeeds forgotten, and at some period in their lives the majority of Hindus visit one or more of the holy shrines. Judging by the swarms of pilgrims met with on the road and in the town most of them had chosen Badrinath.

Among the many legends of these parts believed to have been founded on fact is a story that, many hundred years ago, there was no high priest of the Kedarnath Temple, and that the high priest of Badrinath used to hold services in the temples of both places on the same day. The shortest known route between the two temples was well over one hundred miles, and over a high mountain pass at that. Tradition has it that a quick way across the watershed was known to the priests of those days. But although the natives believe that the two places are only two and a half miles apart, in actual fact, the distance is some twenty-four miles as the crow flies.

Our observations from the Bhagat Kharak had suggested to us that if a pass could be found from the head of the Satopanth, it would lead us into the Kedarnath Valley system. If this proved to be the case, we should stand very little chance of getting down on the other side, owing to the immense depth of the valley there. However, a view from the crest of the watershed would solve for us many interesting problems.

We had intended to return to the Rishi Ganga about 10 August, and August had already come round. But by now we were thoroughly absorbed in the manifold problems of this range, and to have come away without investigating the head of the Satopanth Glacier would have left our task only half finished.

We did not have the same difficulty as before in collecting men to accompany us, but on the morning of our departure, the porters, despite an early appearance, had neglected to have any food before they left their homes three miles away. Consequently we had to fume for a full hour while they made good this oversight – an unpropitious start!

A dense mantle of cloud still hung over the peak as we began to plod up the valley towards Mana and, remembering our little contretemps with the Bhasudhara river of a few weeks earlier, we kept this time to the southern bank of the Alaknanda. This provided us with only a narrow walking space under great perspiring, mossy cliffs, down whose black sides streamed a thousand tiny waterfalls, but luckily there was quite a presentable sheep track which allowed our attention to wander from the main business of getting along to the enjoyment of impressive scenery about us, and, a mile or so further on, the valley widened out and provided a stretch of moderately flat grassland.

Suddenly, with a shout of joy, the Sherpas dumped down their loads and set to work collecting some small, light-blue berries which grew in great quantities amongst the grass. They brought us handfuls of these with great enthusiasm, saying that the berries were considered a delicacy in Sola Kombu, where they came from. On tasting them we found that they had a flavour remarkably like that of toothpaste, and were certainly pleasanter to look upon than to eat.

At three o'clock we came to a small isolated wood of birch and rhododendron about half a mile below the snout of the glacier. We had seen this from the opposite side and had looked forward with relish to the luxury of a blazing campfire. But by now it had started to rain again and the locals were still a long way behind. Before we could get the tents pitched we were wet through. There was no dry wood at hand and it was an hour or so before we had sufficient fire to brew some tea, and that only by dint of continuous blowing on the part of Kusang. The rain having cheated us out of a blissful lounge before blazing embers we retired to our leaky tents with an unpleasant foreboding of what was in store for us higher up.

Awakening to the song of birds and the exhilarating freshness of a perfect morning, our spirits rose and eclipsed the gloom of the night before. Our meal of satu and tea completed, we were content to sit and dry ourselves and our tents in the slanting rays of the morning sun.

It was with an effort that we packed up and started up the boulder-strewn valley. We found that the locals had spent the night in a nearby cave in company with some shepherds, who when we passed their shelter appeared to have not the least intention of stirring themselves for some time to come. What a delightfully carefree life they must lead, requiring nothing but the bare necessities of life, living always up in this wonderland of nature, with little to worry about and nothing to hurry about; knowing nothing of the filth and squalor of our modern civilisation!

Shortly after leaving camp we came to the corner of the Satopanth Valley and turning half left we made our way along the grass slopes at the sides of the glacial moraine. The slackness of the morning remained with us and we made frequent halts to gaze up at the huge ice-clad precipices about us.

Soon we came in sight of the head of the glacier, still many miles away, and were able to get an uninterrupted view of the gap we hoped to cross. From now on little else interested us and we talked of nothing but the 'col'. Was it practicable even from this side? Where would it lead us? Back on to the great Gangotri Glacier? Or over the range to Kedarnath? We argued that point over and over again. I felt most convinced that if we succeeded in reaching its crest we would see a great snow field descending gently before us, turning northwards and forming eventually the Gangotri ice stream which we had reached a few weeks before. Tilman on the other hand held the other view, that the main Gangotri-Kedarnath watershed was to the north of us and that if we succeeded in crossing the gap we would find ourselves amongst the Kedarnath valleys. The discussion waxed heated in spite of Tilman's common-sense suggestion that we should wait and see.

As was the case on the Bhagat Kharak Glacier our chief concern now was how far we could go up the glacier before our supply of firewood ended. We could not expect the locals to spend a night above the limit of firewood, though we could transport sufficient for one night. So we had to aim at pitching our camp as near as possible at the upper limits of the dwarf juniper. As the valley ascended at a very gentle angle this line was by no means easy to gauge.

The going was easy and we made rapid progress, walking on the crest of a kindly lateral moraine which ran for miles down the southern end of the Satopanth Glacier.

Late in the day we came upon a lateral glacier flowing into the main ice stream from the south. This glacier was fed almost entirely by ice-avalanches falling from the ice cliffs of Nilkanta, and in the angle formed by the junction we found an alp whose attractions as a campsite were irresistible. So we spread ourselves out in the sun and basked until the chill of evening sent us to our sleeping bags. Mine that night was squeezed in between two rocks, a position which was more suitable for contemplation of the infinite than for sleep.

The Mana shepherds occasionally brought their sheep far up these moraine-covered glaciers, and we came across a great many piles of stones hung with prayer flags as in Tibet. These prayer flags were simply bits of rag on which were written prayers. Each flap was supposed to emit one repetition of the prayer written thereon, and consequently on a windy day the hanger of a flag could get through many thousands of prayers in the course of a few hours.

(A similar, and, I should judge, a more effective praying-machine is the prayer-wheel which is commonly used in Tibet. This consists of a drum wrapped round with paper on which are written countless thousands of prayers. Each revolution of the drum emits one repetition of all the prayers written on it. The large prayer-wheels are worked by water power and must get through sufficient praying in one week to insure for each member of the village a high place in the hereafter.)

The going now became very rough as we had to cross a succession of side glaciers, each bringing down on its surface a perfect wilderness of boulders. This meant the usual wearisome performance. Toiling up a long slope of large stones balanced precariously on the ice, balancing along an edge above a yawning crevasse, jumping from a boulder or slithering down some icy slope beyond.

At about two o'clock on 7 August we reached a point at which the moraine-covered surface of the Main Glacier gave place to bare ice only half a mile or so from the cliffs which enclosed the Satopanth Glacier. Across the valley we recognized our old friend Kunaling, from this side presenting a very much more formidable appearance. [1]

We decided that this was the best point from which to launch our attack on the gap, and dismissing the Mana men, we pitched our tents just before a strong wind descended on us from across the ice.

Shortly after an ominous dawn on the following morning we shouldered our heavy loads and tramped slowly across the ice in the direction of the col.

It appeared to us that there was not much choice of route. A steep ice fall descending direct from the col seemed to be the only way. The line of rock cliffs which bounded it on the left appeared far too steep in its lower section to offer much chance even of getting a footing on them from the glacier. The ice

---

1 The peak referred to is probably Chaukhamba – the highest in the Gangotri area. (Editor)

fall did not look too difficult, though it was certainly very broken in its upper section. So it was towards the ice fall that we turned.

Over the level stretch of ice we made quick time, but when the angle steepened up our heavy loads made themselves felt and the straps bit cruelly into our shoulders. It was a sultry, windless morning and we were oppressed by an intense lassitude. The ice was bare of snow and steps had to be chipped, though the angle was quite moderate. Our pace became painfully slow.

Soon the ice became broken and complicated, and we came to a section where climbing with a load on one's back was impossible. The leader had to cut steps up the rickety piece of ice and haul the loads after him. The section was only some thirty feet high, but it cost us a good hour to negotiate, and from here the climbing needed the utmost care and called for much step cutting. However, it had the advantage of taking our minds off our sore shoulders and aching thighs.

We climbed steadily for some hours, making long detours to avoid crevasses and ice cliffs and we were within a thousand feet of the crest of the gap when we were brought up by a yawning chasm whose bottom was lost to view, hundreds of feet down the icy depths below us. Dumping our loads, we hunted this way and that, but could find no place which offered the slightest chance of crossing this formidable obstacle.

This was a bitter disappointment. After all that weary toil we had but 1,000 feet to go to learn the solution of the riddle which had been occupying our minds for so long.

We descended for a few hundred feet when it occurred to us that we might be able to find a way off the ice on to the upper part of the rock cliffs to the south. Dumping our loads once more, we worked our way over towards the edge of the ice fall. Reaching it we saw that just below us was a point at which we could get on to the rocks immediately above the steep section below. We could not see how far the rocks would take us, but it was worth trying, and with fresh hope we returned to our loads and pitched camp in the midst of the tangled mass of the ice fall.

By now it was snowing heavily, and our small tents soon resembled chips off the great ice-blocks which surrounded them. Night fell to the accompaniment of an almost continuous roar of ice-avalanches from the great cliffs of Kunaling above us, and into the early hours of the morning the thunder of falling ice continued. Though our position was quite safe, being well protected by the crevasses and ice cliffs about us, several times during the night I was brought to a sitting position, trembling, as some particularly large avalanche fell close at hand.

Snow fell gently all the while, and was still falling when we awoke to a grey and unpromising dawn. In consequence of this we made a later start than we had intended. The tents were wet and the loads were heavier in consequence.

Through the mist we could see only a small section of the face of rock above us. Several of the gullies showed signs of recent stone falls and the rock was damp and slippery. When we reached it, however, we found that the angle was easier than it had appeared from below and we mounted at quite satisfactory speed, hurrying here and there when we were obliged to cross one or other of the stone-swept gullies.

Higher up the mist became really thick and we had to grope our way up the rock face – through the still gently-falling snow as if blind-fold.

On the previous day Tilman had fallen and injured another of his ribs, and climbing under such a heavy load as he was obliged to carry caused him considerable pain.

The route finding now became complicated and we had to trust mainly to a sense of direction. Ridge, gully and rock-facet followed one another in monotonous series, until after a step round an awkward corner we found ourselves at the base of a blunt ice ridge which we had seen from below.

Chipping small steps in the ice we mounted to the crest of the ridge. From here we caught a glimpse below us of the ice fall in which we had camped. We followed the crest along until it landed us on what appeared to be a great ice plateau. The mist was still thick about us and we could only guess at the direction to be followed. We plodded on for half an hour and then halted and pitched the tents.

Our height was 18,400 feet and we calculated that we must be just about on the crest of the col.

Snow was still falling lightly and a southerly wind was blowing. All five of us crowded into one of the tents and sat huddled up waiting for the Primus stove to melt some ice and heat the water sufficiently to make tea. But the Primus had sprung a leak somewhere and had to be pumped up continuously. We waited for two hours before the water was sufficiently warm to absorb any colour from the tea leaves, and we began to realise that if we were to have a prolonged sojourn on the glaciers we would not have enough fuel for anything but the simple production of water.

That night we were content with a cup of tepid pemmican soup before we turned into our sleeping bags. At dusk it started to freeze very hard and we became more hopeful about the weather.

Our cheerless camp had done nothing to damp our excitement at having reached the col, and we could hardly curb our impatience for the view which would tell us where the col was leading us.

I still held to the theory that we were at the mysterious head of the Gangotri Glacier. The level stretch of ice over which we had come seemed to indicate the head of a long, gently-flowing glacier. Shortly after dark there was a momentary clearing of the mists above us and we caught the sight of the great buttresses of Kunaling to north of us and those of another, unnamed peak to the south. But in front, a great sea of cloud still withheld from us the secret of our whereabouts.

I spent much of the long, cold night praying fervently for a fine morning, which the frost gave me good reason to expect.

I was disappointed, however, and when I looked out of the tent door at dawn it was into the same 'pea-soup' as on the night before.

After a cup of warm satu, Tilman and I left the camp and started off in a south-westerly direction to reconnoitre.

The surface of snow we were on soon began to fall away in front of us in an ever steepening curve. Shortly after leaving camp we were jumping over and threading our way through a network of small crevasses, and we had not gone far before we were brought up short by a vertical drop of about one hundred and fifty feet. Beyond this a great tangle of ice cliffs showed us that we were on the brink of an ice fall.

It was useless to attempt to find a way through it with a visibility of only fifty yards, and we sat down on the edge of the cliff and waited. The outlook was pretty hopeless as the glacier was narrow at this point and the ice cliffs seemed to stretch the whole width.

We had been waiting for half an hour when all of a sudden the fog rolled away from below us, and we found ourselves looking down into the immense depths of a cloud-filled valley at our feet. The glacier we were on descended in a steep ice fall for about a thousand feet, then flattened out into a fairly level stretch of ice before it heeled over for its final colossal plunge into the gloom of the gorge 6,000 feet below us.

This was obviously not the Gangotri ice stream, which at its snout, some twenty miles from here, is 13,000 feet high. Tilman had been right and we were looking down into the Kedarnath Valley system, from the 'pass' said to have been known to the ancient high priest of Badrinath.

Our little problem was solved, but the grim aspect of the ice falls below us offered little hope for our succeeding in our project of finding a direct route between the two temples.

After some search we were able to trace a route through the first ice fall. We hurried back to the camp, reaching it just as Angtharkay and Kusang were starting out to look for us, fearing that we might have come to grief in a crevasse.

Packing up the tents we shouldered our loads once more and made our way down towards the ice fall. By now the clouds had enveloped us again and we had a difficult job to find the route we had traced through the maze of ice cliffs and crevasses of which the ice fall was made up.

In and out of great ice corridors, past towers and turrets of all shapes and sizes, we worried our way; balancing across slender ice bridges, which spanned gaping crevasses whose icy depths seemed illimitable; toiling up some bulge which obstructed our path and clinging our way down the slippery banks of its further side.

At length we found ourselves on the flat stretch of ice we had seen from above. Going to its further edge we halted for a few moments to gaze down upon the head of the second and very formidable ice fall. It was appallingly steep, and for a long time we could not see any way of attacking it which offered the slightest hope of success.

Immediately in front was a sheer drop of some hundreds of feet to the head of the ice fall itself.

After a careful examination it occurred to us that it might be possible to descend the ice fall for some distance on its right-hand side, and then force a way off on to the cliffs which bounded it in that direction. Beyond this we could not see, but these cliffs appeared to fall away vertically to the valley still some 5,000 feet below.

We worked over to the right and descended for some time before we were brought up by an impassable crevasse. Search as we would we could not find a way of descending a yard further or of reaching the rocks to our right; so very slowly we toiled our weary way back to the level section where we sat for some minutes sucking lumps of ice in vain attempt to assuage a burning thirst.

By this time the weather had cleared somewhat and as we made our way over to the left-hand side of the glacier we saw that by traversing along an ice ledge under some evil-looking séracs we might get down 500 feet below the level section. Beyond this the glacier disappeared from view on account of the steepness of the angle.

We started to traverse below the séracs and the Sherpas as usual burst into their monotonous praying chant, evidently beseeching the demons of the ice world not to throw things at us.

Hurrying across the debris of a recent fall, we found ourselves at the brink of the glacier's final downward plunge. So steep was it indeed that we thought that we must be standing on the upper part of a hanging glacier.

We dumped our loads on the ice and set off down on what seemed to be an utterly futile errand. But it was the last chance, and we thought we might as well finally prove the thing to be impossible so as to be able, later, to find comfort in that fact. Also the Sherpas, for some reason, were almost frantically keen to get down, and would not admit that the thing could not be done. Whether this attitude of theirs was an outcome of their extreme loyalty to us, or whether they were taking a personal interest in the exploration I cannot say. But in any case it was typical of the fine spirit of these men that, from the time we had left the Satopanth Glacier, they seemed willing to go almost to any lengths to get over that pass. Their loyalty to the expedition did not cause them merely to carry out our instructions; they understood our aims and did everything in their power to see that we realised them.

With these allies we hope, one day, to reach the summit of Mount Everest; without them we would have little hope of doing so.

I have often found that towards the end of a long, tiring day's mountaineering one gets a sudden rejuvenation, particularly when faced with a problem of unusual severity. It was certainly the case this evening and we set about that ice fall as if our lives depended upon our getting down.

The work was intricate and needed delicate handling as a slip would have had serious consequences. The further we advanced the steeper became the ice until further downward progress on the glacier itself became an impossibility.

We worked our way over to the left until we came to the left-hand edge of the ice fall. Standing on a small promontory we looked down a sheer drop of some 200 feet into a steep gully which separated the ice fall from the rock cliffs bounding it on that side. We saw that if we could reach the floor of the gully we might be able to work our way down between the ice and the rock. But the 200 foot drop at our feet appeared quite impossible. Tilman and I sat down feeling that we had reached the end of our tether.

But Pasang and Angtharkay refused to admit defeat and asked to be allowed to try the wall below us. We consented; and they roped up on a short rope and gave us an exhibition of calm, surefooted climbing whose equal it has rarely been my fortune to witness.

After some twenty minutes they were back with us admitting that the face below was too much even for them. But Angtharkay's blood was up and no sooner had he recovered his breath than he started traversing to the left and soon disappeared from view behind an ugly ice bulge.

Minutes passed as we waited with bated breath. Then, crash! a great chunk of ice hurtled down and smashed itself into a thousand pieces on the floor of the gully, sending up along the cliffs a rolling echo. I think my heart missed several beats before a shout from Angtharkay assured us that all was well. Presently his head appeared from behind the ice bulge, and we saw that his face wore a broad grin.

He informed us that he had found a ledge from which it might be possible to lower our loads and ourselves.

With this hope we raced up our steps back to the loads. It was beginning to get dark and we had yet to find a suitable campsite and get ourselves fixed for the night. To have attempted to get down into the gully that night would have been too much to expect of them. Also, lower down, the gully was overhung by some ice cliffs and it would be dangerous to pass under these at any other time than the morning.

I spent most of the night tossing about our uncomfortable perch, though it was not so much the discomfort of my bed as excitement which kept me awake.

14   Chapter 14

We had decided not to bother about food or drink in the morning, and as soon as it was light we were packing up the tents and getting ready to start. It was a fine morning and for the first time we were able to get a view down into the valley we were making for, the upper part of which was now only 2,000 feet below us.

A level stretch of glacier some three miles long ended in what looked like a pleasantly wooded valley. About a mile below the glacier there seemed to be a bit of a 'cut-off', and below that dark vegetation stretched away as far as the eye could see. This we took to be pine forest, while far beneath we could see patches of light green interspersed amongst the forest.

Two days marching at the most, we thought, would take us through this pleasant looking country to some habitation. Also it seemed reasonable to suppose that we would strike a forest path or game track and be able to cover, if necessary, some twelves miles a day. We knew that it could be no very great distance from the snout of the glacier to the great Kedarnath pilgrim route.

Working along Angtharkay's ledge, clinging close to the cold clammy walls of glacier ice, we reached the little platform from which we were to lower ourselves and our kit. It was an unpleasant place, enclosed on all sides by walls of sickly green ice, and it required but the slightest slip to send one crashing into the depths below, while the most careful handling was needed to save the loads from a similar fate.

Pasang was lowered down into the gully and he stood there ready to receive the baggage. It was painful work. The rope, wet from contact with the snow on the previous day, was now frozen stiff and cut cruelly into our numb fingers.

It took us two hours of hard work before we were safely assembled on the floor of the gully, and it was with feelings of some relief that we turned our backs upon the scene of our labours.

Now the climbing became more straightforward and for the first time since leaving the Satopanth Glacier we were able to dispense with the rope. Hurrying over the section threatened from above by the ice cliffs we were soon able to break out of the gully to the left where the angle of the cliffs eased off about a thousand feet above the level stretch of glacier in the valley. This we managed to reach by means of an intricate zigzag course down the intervening slopes.

After a few moments 'breather' we raced down the glacier at top speed, leap-ing the crevasses in our stride. We were full of pleasant anticipation of a camp in some grassy meadow below the glacier. We were doomed to disappoint-ment. For on leaving the glacier we found ourselves immersed in a tangle of sappy, green vegetation about eight feet high through which we had to hack our way. So thick was it, that we could not see where we were going and all we could do was to stumble on blindly.

We cleared a small space and sat down for a meal, after which we flogged our way on in the hope of finding a better camping place before nightfall. By now it had started raining and the contact with the sodden undergrowth soaked us to the skin. In addition to this the floor of the valley was made up of large boul-ders which were completely screened by the undergrowth, and at every few steps one stumbled into some pothole between the rocks. Brambles soon made their appearance and added to our difficulties.

Late in the evening, after some two hours of this work, we reached the edge of the great cut-off which we had seen from above. This proved to be a sheer drop of some 1,200 feet in the floor of the valley. There was no time to look for a way down the gaunt crags and we had to make shift for the night. After an hour's work we had cleared a muddy space underneath a boulder and col-lected some sodden stumps of juniper with which to make a fire.

Squatting huddled up under the boulder which afforded scant protection from the rain, vainly trying to dry our sodden garments before the smoulder-ing logs, we discussed our position. Our supply of food was beginning to run low and we had no idea how far we would have to go before we reached the first habitation where we could obtain more supplies with which to carry on. If the going had been good, there would have been little doubt that we could force our way through, however pressed we were for food. But our experience since leaving the glacier had given us an unpleasant taste of what we must expect lower down. The precipice below us might prove to be impassable or cost us much of our valuable time; and with time went food.

Again: what of the side-streams which we must meet further down the val-ley? By now we had considerable respect for this form of obstacle, which we knew could not only hold us up but completely block our way.

The only alternative was to struggle back up the ice fall and over the pass back to Badrinath. The matter had to be decided here and now, for as it was, we would have to go all out to get back over the pass before our food and fuel ran out altogether.

The prospect of retracing our steps and committing ourselves once more to the icy slopes we had just left did not appeal to us in the least. Moreover, the weather showed no signs of improvement and we might quite well be held up by a fall of new snow on the pass.

Starvation high up on the glacier, besides being more unpleasant, would be very much harder to fight against than it would be in a forest, where at least we would be able to make a fire. On the other hand, in going down we were taking a step into the unknown. The difficulties of the forest might easily take us some weeks to overcome, though, of course, we might strike some sort of a path tomorrow, or the next day. It was a difficult problem on which to make a decision, and we sat discussing it long into the night before retiring to our damp sleeping bags.

On visualising the position over again I think undoubtedly the wisest plan would have been to go back up the ice, and several times during the week which followed, we sincerely wished we had done so. I am afraid that the fact that we wanted to make the complete crossing of this most intriguing range weighed too heavily on us all, and the downward course was decided upon.

The rain had stopped by the morning and we optimistically delayed our departure in order to get some of the water out of the tents and sleeping bags. That this was a mere waste of time we were soon to realise. However, it gave us time to look around and decide on the best course of action for attacking our immediate problem, the descent of the thousand foot cut-off.

It was an impressive affair. The river, here of quite sizable dimensions, disappeared underground for a short distance above the bank of the precipice and issued forth in a great waterspout to crash down into the depths below. Owing to this we were able to get from one side of the valley to the other without difficulty and could choose either side down which to make our descent.

A short examination of the left-hand side of the valley convinced us that there was no practicable route to be found there, and so, striking camp, we committed ourselves to a search on the right-hand side. Here we fought our way for a quarter of a mile up and along the side of the valley and then began to descend. Clinging on to handfuls of matted undergrowth we clambered down, cursing our loads the while for their insistence on slipping sideways and often nearly dragging us down with them.

Soon we came to a vertical cliff whose rocky sides were too steep to hold any scrub, but whose cracks and crevices were filled with damp earth and moss. Balancing ourselves precariously above this we lowered Angtharkay, the lightest member of the party, on a rope, until he was able to get a footing on a grassy ledge below. Our loads followed in a similar manner. Then, tying two lengths of rope together and doubling them over a convenient juniper root, we slid down to join Angtharkay on his perch below.

Fortunately the side of the valley on which we were was made up of a series of terraces, which were not too widely separated from each other, and by repeating the process described above we eventually reached the densely forested floor of the valley.

Under the spread of the giant forest trees the undergrowth was not so thick and, walking for once in a normal attitude, we made fairly good progress until we reached the upper limit of bamboo. There, at least, was help against the exhaustion of our meagre food supply, and at one o'clock we called a halt and set about gathering a goodly quantity of the small soft cylinders which form the edible portion of the bamboo shoots. This, and the fact that lately we had not been battling through bramble scrub, put us in better spirits, and we almost forgot to call down curses on the rain which had by now started to fall again.

The bamboo was certainly our ally and was later to prove our salvation, but it was not an unmitigated blessing. Really dense bamboo provides an obstacle second only to thickly matted bramble, and when the valley narrowed and we were forced up on to its steep sides, the bamboo jungle reduced us once more to our weary hack, hacking of a way.

The almost impenetrable density of the jungle down by the river forced us to climb up the steep sides of the valley until we were about 1,500 feet above the stream. There we found ourselves in a zone of tall straight plants about nine feet high. The plants were crowned with a spray of most beautiful blue flowers, in shape rather like snapdragons. The growth was as dense as that of a good stand of corn, and, viewed from above, the general effect closely resembled a forest of English bluebells.

Through these lovely blue flowers we waded for three hours, each taking it in turns to go ahead and flog a path with our ice axes.

Constantly throughout the day we came across fresh spoor which provided ample evidence that large numbers of bears inhabited the forest we were in. These animals, though not wantonly vindictive, possess very poor senses of sight and hearing and should one stumble upon them by accident they are liable to attack through sheer fright. The Sherpas were very alarmed at seeing the tracks of these beasts, and kept up a continuous shouting to give warning of our approach. They were very anxious too that the party should keep well together.

At about five o'clock the ground in front of us began to fall away steeply and, from the change in the tone of the river's roaring, we realised that we were approaching a sizeable side stream, coming down from the peaks of the Satopanth range. Pressing on through the forest we soon arrived at the edge of a ravine from whose unseen depths the thunder of a mighty torrent reached our ears. Looking up to the right we could see the turbulent white river booming its way down towards the gorge.

Here was a problem the seriousness of which we were not slow to recognise, for, if we could find no way of crossing the stream in front of us, we would be in a sorry plight, as now it was too late to think of a return across the pass by which we had come.

Going to the edge we examined the cliffs below us and saw at once that a direct descent into the ravine was out of the question. Moreover, even if we could get across thereabouts, it would be impossible to scale the sheer walls which formed the opposite side of the gorge.

Two alternatives were open to us. Either we could go down to the junction of this torrent with the main river, or we could follow the stream towards its source in the hope of being able to cross it higher up.

We could see that, above the junction, the stream issued from the confines of the ravine and ran for some twenty yards between moderately sloping banks before emptying itself into the main waterway. But here the stream was very broad and there appeared to be but small chance of bridging it at this point. On close scrutiny of the cliffs above the ravine, however, it seemed to us that there was one point where the opposing walls of rock met high above the level of the water.

At first I was sceptical about this and declared it to be an optical illusion produced by a bend in the river; for, although we had seen many such natural bridges during our travels in this amazing country, such formations are rare.

But after studying it for some minutes, I agreed with others that it was indeed a natural bridge. To reach it, however, would involve a climb of some 2,000 feet, over difficult ground, and we decided to pitch camp as soon as we found any water. This was not an easy matter and we had climbed a long way up towards the 'bridge' before we came to a small trickling spring shortly before dark. We were lucky in finding a nice level space on which to camp, and, after pitching the tents and collecting a vast quantity of firewood, we settled down to an evening which for sheer enjoyment would take a lot of beating, despite the fact that five yards from the camp was a bear's lair. Luckily its recent occupant kept well clear of the vicinity during our occupation of the camp.

Growing close at hand we found small clumps of forest fungus, which the Sherpas declared to be edible. We collected a large quantity, but each piece was subjected to a searching scrutiny by Angtharkay, and, for some obscure reason, more than seventy-five per cent were rejected. However, in solidity they made up for what they lacked in taste, and, together with the bamboo shoots, the remainder provided us with a square meal. And this was more than welcome, for on unpacking our sacks we found that what remained of our satu was soaking wet and was rapidly going bad; this in spite of the fact that it had been carefully packed in canvas bags. Indeed, by now almost all our kit was water-logged and we resigned ourselves to living in a state of perpetual wetness.

By now the rain had slackened, and after Kusang had blown the sodden logs for an hour or so we sat before a blazing fire. But though it blazed and needed no further encouragement, Kusang continued to blow late into the night. Tilman conjured up a pleasant picture when he remarked that should Kusang happen upon a house on fire, while others were fighting the flames, he would be unable to resist the temptation of blowing on them!

Lying on a soft, sodden bed of leaves we basked in the glow of the fire. Warm now and, for once, not hungry, we allowed our tobacco smoke to drug us into forgetfulness of the worry which had seemed so acute throughout the long day.

It is astonishing how quickly warmth and a well-satisfied belly will change one's outlook. We were too happy to question whether the bamboo and mushrooms would remain with us all the way along, or whether kindly nature had provided natural bridges over all the side streams which would cross our path. Considering that we had had the 'cut-off' to negotiate that morning our estimated distance of a mile and a half did not seem bad. Later we came to look upon a mile and a half as good progress for a day's labour! Meantime we lay peacefully in a half-doze, watching the firelight flickering on the great gnarled branches above us and making weird play with their shadows.

It was raining more heavily than usual when we shouldered our loads next morning and toiled on and up through the forest. Soon we came to dense bramble and began once more the tedious job of fighting our way through it. Our water-logged kit made our loads doubly heavy, weighing us down and causing us to overbalance as we bent and twisted to rid ourselves of the clinging thorns. Soon a dense mist descended upon us and we had to grope along the ever-steepening side of the nala with only a hazy notion of where we were going. Every now and then a steep-sided gully would bar the way and we would have to scramble up some hundreds of feet before we could find a place at which we could cross it.

After some hours of this, the mist cleared and we saw that we were near to the place where we thought we had seen the natural bridge spanning the gorge. Immediately we realised that we had been mistaken, and that the supposed 'bridge' had indeed been an optical illusion!

Leaving our loads where we halted, we clambered on through the still-heavily-falling rain towards the stream. The rocks were steep and very slippery and we had to exercise extreme caution, for a slip would have deposited any one of us in the turbulent waters of the torrent some hundreds of feet below.

At length we reached a point from which we could command an uninterrupted view of the stream for some considerable distance above and below us. Below us the cliffs dropped sheer to the water's edge, while above, the river, descending in a series of waterfalls, did not permit the faintest hope either of fording or of bridging the stream.

We held a hurried consultation. Either we could go down to the junction in the small hope of bridging the torrent down there or we could work on upstream on the chance of finding better things above the point to which we could see. The Sherpas were very much against going down to the junction.

On the other hand, to have gone up even to the spot to which we could see would have involved the best part of a day's climbing, and then what chance would we have had of finding a place to cross up there? Fording was out of the question and higher up we would find no trees with which to build a bridge. Much as I respected the judgment of the Sherpas, which in country of this sort had usually proved sounder than my own, at that moment I just could not face, on such a slender chance, the toil which the upward course would involve.

It was decided, therefore, that we should return to last night's campsite, leave our loads there, go down to the junction to examine the possibilities of bridging the stream, and return to the old camp for the night. This latter prospect was the one bright patch in a gloomy outlook.

We returned to our loads and made our way slowly back down the bramble-covered slopes, reaching our old camp at about 3.30. While Kusang blew upon the seemingly dead embers of the morning's fire we stood shivering in our soaking garments and reviewed our position. This certainly appeared unpleasant enough, for, if we failed to get across at the junction, two more days at least would be wasted before we could hope to find a way across on the higher route, and probably more, if indeed we could manage it at all. The work involved in getting along was heavy, and without food it would be well-nigh impossible.

At four o'clock, after swallowing some tepid tea, we raced off down towards the junction, leaving Kusang to build the fire and prepare a meal of the few bits of fungus which still grew near the camp. We were some 800 feet above the junction of the two rivers, but sliding down on the sodden carpet of leaves which formed the floor of the forest we reached it in a few minutes. That is to say we reached a point about a hundred feet above it, for the only way we could get down to the stream itself was by way of a steep gully. From a rock above we surveyed the stream as it issued from the mouth of the ravine. The water was obviously much above its normal level, and carried with it great quantities of mud. In the short stretch between the mouth of the ravine and the actual junction there was only one point which offered the slightest possibility of our constructing a bridge. There two rocks stood up well above the surging water, one close to either bank. If we could balance a tree trunk on these two rocks so that it lay across the stream, we could lay other trees diagonally across it and so make a sufficiently sound structure to enable us to cross. But from above, the rocks appeared much too far apart for us to be able to do this.

We climbed down the gully to the water's edge and, measuring the distance across roughly by means of a rope, we came to the conclusion that the thing must be attempted, then re-ascending the gully we selected some suitable pines which most luckily happened to be growing in small numbers hereabouts.

As it was growing dark we climbed the steep slope back to camp at a pace set by Pasang which left us with aching lungs and thudding hearts. And so we camped in exactly the same position as on the previous night, but with so much less food, considerably less confidence in our ability to cross the stream and with our sleeping bags wetter than ever. As we ate our vegetarian meal, therefore, we lacked much of the content that had been with us twenty-four hours earlier.

The dawn of August 14th saw us sliding once more down the leafy slopes, albeit with more caution than previously by reason of our heavy packs. Dumping our loads at the water's edge, and noting thankfully that the stream was no more swollen than on the previous evening, we clambered back up the gully and set to work on the trees which we had marked the night before.

Pasang gave us a fine display with his kukri and after a few minutes the first tree crashed to the ground. Stripping it of its branches we dragged it to the edge and, heaving it to an upright position, tipped it into the gully, down which it crashed its way to the water's edge. Angtharkay and I then descended the gully to make the necessary preparations while the others worked above.

In a surprisingly short time three more trees had arrived at the edge of the stream and Tilman and the other Sherpas began to climb down the gully. Angtharkay and I were engaged in building a rock platform at the water's edge, when all at once there was a crash and looking up I saw a huge boulder hurtling down. The others seemed to be well to the side of the gully and I resumed my work thinking how lucky it was that they had not been lower down where the route lay in the actual floor of the gully.

A few moments later, chancing to look up, I saw Pasang leaning against one of the walls of the gully some way above me. His face was very pale and he was trembling. I scrambled up to him and found that the boulder had hit him a glancing blow on the left arm and left foot. It had even torn the lacing from his boot.

Helping him down to the foot of the gully I examined the damaged members. The arm, though temporarily useless to him seemed only to be badly bruised. His foot was very badly swollen and he could not move his toes. It looked as if one of the small bones on the top of the foot had been broken.

It was a nasty blow to us all, though I could not help being devoutly thankful for his lucky escape, for had he been a foot or two further on the boulder would have hit his head and would have crushed it like an egg; for the rock weighed a good 200-weight.

After treating Pasang's wounds as best we might we set to work once more on our task of bridging the stream. We tied the end of a climbing rope round the top of the longest tree trunk, and placing its butt on the rock platform we had built, we heaved it up to a vertical position. Then, taking careful aim, we let it fall out across the stream. The top of the log hit the rock on the other side and bounded off into the stream to be swept off by the current. Hanging on to the rope for all we were worth we played it into the side.

Having strengthened the structure of the rock platform, we repeated the process with a similar result, but at the third essay the tip of the log remained balance precariously on the slimy edge of the rock opposite us. We then placed another shorter pole diagonally across the first. This scarcely reached the rocks on the other side.

On this flimsy structure Tilman, with a rope fastened to his waist, started to balance across the raging torrent. We stood watching him with bated breath as, inch by inch, he crept along the swaying poles. It was obvious that he must not either slip or upset the balance of the poles, while the further he went the more difficult was his task owing to the thinning of the tree trunks towards the top and the consequently greater sag of the poles. But at length, with what looked like a cross between a leap and a fall, he landed on the other side. We sent up a cheer which was drowned by the roar of the river.

After Tilman had performed this feat the rest was easy, and with all four poles laid across and lashed together with strips of bark, and a rope stretched across as a hand rail we had a bridge over which we could transport the loads without further difficulty. It was now about 10.30 a.m. and we halted for about half an hour on the further side of the river, partly to give Pasang more time to recover from his shock and partly to distribute his load between us. Of course Kusang and Angtharkay insisted upon adding the lion's share of Pasang's load to their own, which made their packs of water-sodden gear quite enormous.

We followed the bank of the main stream down for a few hundred yards and were then forced by cliffs to climb high up into the forest. Here the going was very bad indeed. The side of the valley was exceedingly steep and we had to hang on to the undergrowth above to prevent ourselves sliding down into the undergrowth below while we hacked our way through. At times it took us as much as an hour to cover twenty-five yards.

At first I went ahead with the kukri in order to cut a passage through. It was gruelling work and my shoulders, already burdened by my load, began to ache fiercely. We soon found that except in a few places we could get along faster without the cutting.

The rain was coming down in torrents, but (while on the march) except for making our loads heavier, it could no longer increase our discomfort.

At about three o'clock a small side stream, which had cut deeply into the side of the valley, caused us some trouble and by 4.30 p.m., being by a small spring of water, we decided that we had had enough and began to prepare for the night.

This was no easy job. There was no place level enough to pitch a tent on, and we had to dig with an ice axe into the slope for a long time before we could construct a suitable platform. In the pouring rain it was out of the question to make a fire in the open. Here again the woodcraft of the Sherpas was equal to the occasion. Cutting great quantities of bamboo they set to work to construct a shelter under which to make a fire.

These various jobs kept us busy and warm until dusk. Meanwhile poor Pasang sat huddled under the lee of a tree-stump, shivering with cold – the picture of misery. And small wonder, for his struggle with the undergrowth on that steep slope must have been cruel, and now he was incapable of lending a useful hand.

At length, the shelter finished, we huddled under its scant protection. With numbed fingers (we were still at an altitude of 9,500 feet) we struck match after match. (It was fortunate that we had got a good supply of these stored away in sheepskin gloves!) In this manner we had got rid of two boxes and had started on the third before we succeeded in lighting a piece of rag steeped in paraffin. Once this was accomplished we soon had a fire going. We found that dead bamboo, however wet it may be, catches fire very easily and makes most excellent kindling. Indeed, without it, in such rain as we were experiencing it would have been impossible to light a fire at all. Thus the bamboo plant was providing us with house, fire and food; and without it our lot would have been a sorry one indeed.

Stripping ourselves of our sodden garments we lay naked before the fire while boiling a large pot full of shoot. With a modicum of 'ghee' added after the water had been drained off, these were served and eaten as one would eat asparagus. Indeed Tilman's imaginative palate detected some slight resemblance to that delicacy. Unfortunately we had found no more fungus, and our meal failed sadly to satisfy our all too robust appetites.

It had been the busiest day of a hectic week, and I fell asleep without much difficulty only to be roused by Tilman in what seemed a few moments to find it daylight once more.

15 Chapter 15

So tired were we that the morning was already well advanced before we woke. Hurriedly packing our loads, we left our lonely little shelter to engage once more in fierce strife with the tangled vegetation. While amongst big trees the undergrowth was fairly sparse, but where the trees were small of spread or few and far between, there did the brambles grow in profusion, their large thorns clinging and tearing at our clothes, hands and faces as we kicked, flogged and pushed our way through them.

Here and there the valley was broken and rocky. Such a place could provide a formidable obstacle, for, fighting one's way along, one would be brought up suddenly at the edge of a cliff and a long weary ascent would have to be made before a way was found round it. Further on maybe, one would fall into one of many booby traps in the form of a deep pit filled with bramble and thus disguised better than any man-made game trap. Down one would crash for ten or fifteen feet with load on top.

But it was the gullies which we came to dread most, for here, on account of some old land slip, or the rocky bed of an ancient stream, there were no trees to keep the lesser vegetation in check, and the brambles ran riot.

There was very little variety. At first, struggling to the crest of a ridge full of hope of better things 'round the corner', we felt disappointed when we saw before us yet 'another ---- gully!' Later we got resigned to it and accepted what came without comment.

Five hundred feet up we went and then five hundred feet down; now to avoid some impassable cut-off, now in the hope of better going above or below as the case might be. Generally speaking we kept between fifteen hundred and two thousand feet above the river.

At one o'clock we made a brief halt and at three o'clock we came to the edge of a steep lateral valley. Through the falling rain we could see two moderate-sized streams coming down the valley in a series of waterfalls, and uniting just before they flowed into the main river far below. Separating the two streams was a high ridge.

Scrambling down a steep slope we reached the first stream and, crossing it without much difficulty, we climbed the ridge beyond. For some while we could see no way of crossing the second stream. The water was coming down with tremendous force and the bank beyond rose in an unbroken line of slimy cliff.

Following the ridge along, however, we soon came to a place where a large tree trunk spanned the torrent. In order to reach this we had to prop a small pine up against it, and clamber up this improvised ladder until we could swing ourselves on to the broad back of the giant – no easy task with our loads.

The further side of the valley provided a steep climb at the top of which, for the first time in some days, we found ourselves on a stretch of level ground. Moreover, owing to the gigantic spread of the branches overhead there was little or no undergrowth. It was now 5.30 p.m. and the temptation to spend the night in this delectable spot was too great. The only snag was the lack of a stream. This difficulty was overcome by spreading the tents on the ground and it was not long before we had sufficient water for our modest culinary needs. During the whole of our sojourn in the forest the torrential rain hardly ever slackened.

The net result of our day's labours in actual distance we reckoned to be one mile. Our altitude was now about 10,000 feet. We had two reasons for keeping so high: one, the fact that the valley was steeper and more broken nearer the river, or so it had seemed from our distant views; two, our fear of getting out of the bamboo zone. (On most tropical mountain ranges there is a narrow belt of altitude where bamboo grows in the forest.) If the bamboo were to fail us our plight would be serious indeed.

An entry in my brief diary for this day is fairly representative of the tone of the rest and runs: 'Pasang is no better. The job is becoming very tedious; always wet, not enough food, and can't see where the we are going.'

Pasang was bearing his lot with great courage. He was hard put to keep up with us, even though he was carrying no load, and the frequent stumbles into potholes must have caused him agony.

The procedure on this evening was the same as before and we had a difficult task to get our various jobs done before nightfall. There was water to collect, firewood to gather and cut and the shelter to build before we could light a fire, strip off our clinging garments and huddle round its insufficient heat.

The level stretch on which we camped enabled us to make good progress next morning for a bare 200 yards, before we plunged once more into a gully where the going was worse than any we had struck so far. For two hours we made hardly any progress at all, and when we had succeeded in forcing our way across that gully we found ourselves in another almost as bad as the first. At one o'clock we halted for a quarter of an hour on the crest of a ridge. Looking back we caught a glimpse through the rain-mist of the ridge where we had camped the night before – about one-third of a mile away. Late in the afternoon we came to a cliff of open rock up which we had to climb in order to continue our traverse along the side of the valley. In two places the climbing was too difficult to be done with loads and these had to be left behind to be hauled up after us.

The weather cleared slightly and from the top of the crag we got our first real view down the valley. A mile away we saw two large patches of grassland, a strangely welcome sight. We saw too that we were about to descend into a side valley from the bottom of which the boom of a river reached our ears.

We had dropped a good thousand feet before we reached the water, and at about 5.30 p.m. we started looking for a campsite. Presently we espied a large overhanging rock which would provide us with shelter and an ideal place to camp. We were some ten yards from it when a large black bear emerged from the darkness of the cave. Angtharkay, who was in front, dropped his load and made as if to run for it. But the bear was in an even greater hurry and ambled off into the forest without a sound. However, we had to alter our ideas of a campsite for the Sherpas refused to remain in the vicinity of the cave.

That evening we found that the bears were our rivals, not only in the selection of suitable campsites, but for that all important commodity, the bamboo shoot. Wherever we went we found that the bears had been there before us and ravished the supplies. We had to search far and wide before we could collect enough even for a frugal meal.

Nevertheless, it was in a more cheerful frame of mind that we sat before the blazing furnace which Pasang had made. This, I think, was wholly due to the fact that for once we were not being rained upon and could hang our things before the fire to dry. For it had been a long hard day and we had no reason to be pleased with our progress. We decided that if we did not strike something soon we would have to leave our loads behind and push on without them.

The next morning the stream provided us with no small problem until we found another friendly tree trunk spanning it. The going now became decidedly better and we made such excellent headway that by midday we had reached the first of the two patches of open grassland. The grass was thick and tall, but, oh! what a relief to emerge for a while from the oppression of the forest. Rain had fallen early as usual, but now it stopped for a space and we actually saw an anaemic sun appear. Perched upon a rock we basked awhile in the feeble rays.

Our respite was short-lived and being forced down again into the forest we found ourselves once more immersed in bramble, the rain falling more heavily than ever.

At 3.30 p.m. we came to a cave which bore the signs of previous human habitation, and hunting about, the Sherpas declared that they had found a track. This latter proved to be a mere figment of the imagination however, though the evidence in the cave certainly made things seem more hopeful.

We continued on our way until 5.45 p.m. and arriving at a small stream decided to halt for the night. By now the bamboo was very scarce and, search as we could, we could find no more than a few pieces for our supper. Darkness fell before we were prepared for it and we passed an uncomfortable night in a small cave high up in the face of a small crag.

The next morning was a most unpleasant one. The going was just as bad as it had ever been and I began to experience that nasty feeling of faintness caused by hunger and heavy work together. So it went on, hour after hour, in and out of those pitiless gullies, flogging every inch of the way.

At one o'clock, suddenly, dramatically and without warning, came relief from our worries.

We had found our tedious way across a gully, resembling in appearance many of its fellows, and clambering up a steep slope had breasted the ridge beyond. The point marked a slight bend in the main valley. In front of us stretched an open grassy hillside. A mile down the valley on the opposite side we saw two fields of standing crops. Leading from these down to the water's edge was a path, ample evidence that the village from which the fields were worked was on our side of the valley.

At first we could not believe our eyes, then with one accord we gave expression to our feelings of joy and relief with a prolonged and lusty cheer.

Two hundred yards beyond the fields a large river joined the one which we had followed for the last week. This we knew to be the Madmaheswa in whose valley was the remote Hindu temple of that name.

Even Pasang's foot seemed to have recovered somewhat as we sped joyously along the steep grass slopes. For two hours we kept up a breathless pace when, mounting a spur beyond, we saw far below us a tiny hamlet consisting of some four oblong buildings. When we first spied it we felt like castaways who had at last sighted land. The Sherpas were if anything more relieved than we were, for it was only in the last day or two that the unpleasant possibilities of our position had begun to dawn on them. It was a suitable moment for an oration on our part, but all Tilman could say, mindful evidently of late descents into some Lakeland dale, was 'we shall be down in time for tea'; while I merely stuttered 'thank heaven for that!' We hurried on rejoicing, the Sherpas yelling with delight when we met a herd of cows, and so frightening the man in charge of them that he took to his heels.

There were but three houses in the village and, when we arrived, only two old women out of whom we could get nothing but a cucumber. It was still raining hard so we billeted ourselves in a barn which some goats kindly vacated for us, and waited on events. Presently a greybeard appeared with some apricots which went the way of the cucumber, and when we had got it into his head that we wanted some real food, he brought along some flour. He was not slow to realise how sore was our need, for only after prolonged haggling did we get four pounds of it in exchange for an empty bottle and one rupee; the bottle representing the actual price, and the rupee a souvenir of the occasion, for it would be of no use to him.

We slept well that night, unmindful of bugs and fleas, but we paid dearly for it as many days elapsed before the last flea evacuated our sleeping bags.

It was pleasant to be once more on a track, but as we got down the valley villages became more numerous and tracks led in all directions. We kept getting off our road and none of the villagers seemed anxious to put us right. At five o'clock we were still three long miles from the place we were making for and, as usual, were drenched to the skin, so at the next village we parked ourselves in the one dry spot under a balcony, and started a fire.

Our reception here was frigid, and the woman of the house flatly refused us the use of an empty room which opened off where we were sitting, and added insult to injury by ostentatiously locking the door. The Sherpas got annoyed at this lack of hospitality, and Pasang had to be restrained from coming to blows with some of the villagers who had gathered to hear the old lady's apparently vivid description of our manners and appearance. But after peace had been restored the owner of a nearby house took pity on us, and offered us the use of his balcony where we had a comfortable night.

As no one was robbed during the night the atmosphere next morning was more friendly, and we opened negotiations for two men to accompany us as porters for we were tired of losing our way, and still more tired of carrying heavy loads. Their indecision would have been amusing had it not been so annoying, for we were impatient to start. After a long wrangle over rates of pay and finally seeming agreement, the men would calmly announce they were not coming, and the whole business started over again. Patience was at last rewarded, and two of the more enterprising recklessly consented to cast in their lot with us for at least one day.

By the time we reached Kalimath, the place we had hoped to reach the day before, it was raining harder than ever and even the inhabitants were heard to complain of the weather. We had now got to something more than a village; there was a temple and, at that moment of more interest to us, a shop. Sheepskins were spread for us and tea made, and hoping for a few luxuries we held an informal stock-taking. First we got hold of some almonds which were good, and then we found some jaggary (lumps of raw sugar), excellent if one was not averse to eating one's obligatory peck of dirt at one sitting. We had been without sugar for a week so we bought two pounds of it, and Tilman, who suffered from a sweet tooth, seized the biggest lump. After only a couple of bites he rose hastily, and showing all the symptoms of violent nausea rushed outside – he had eaten a piece of soap! After this we were more careful but it was difficult to distinguish the soap from the sugar without biting it.

Late that afternoon we got on to the 'Pilgrim Road' leading to Kedarnath and were greatly tempted to turn in that direction, but we had already spent too long on this journey and, turning our backs on it regretfully, we headed south. A long day ended at Okhimath where there was a hospital, a bazaar, and an important temple. As usual now, food was uppermost in our minds and we made straight for the bazaar to get the taste of soap out of our mouths. While sitting there the doctor and the clerk of the temple (a Madrassi) came along and took us over to it. Here we were given tea, a room and beds were prepared for us, and the clerk lent us some of his clothes, as of course all our kit was still wringing wet. Meanwhile he and the doctor plied us with questions about our journey, the news of which had apparently gone before us, and were eager to hear about this legendary pass to Badrinath, the crossing of which had invested our party with some merit, the temple authorities treating us as honoured guests, and the doctor doing what he could for Pasang's foot which was still giving him considerable pain.

The temple buildings were arranged round a courtyard in which stood the shrine, and our room opened off this yard. It served the purpose of the village green and was full of gossiping men and playing children, who with one accord adjourned to our room to have a look, filling it to overflowing. It was several hours before they left us to ourselves.

Our quarters were all that could be wished, but the temple precincts were a bit noisy at night what with praying and ringing of bells, and the dawn of another day was heralded (we thought prematurely) by rolling of drums. When it came to making a start our local men refused to go any further and we had to send out for volunteers. The first to answer the call blanched visibly at the sight of the heavy load which Angtharkay had thoughtfully got ready for him, and incontinently fled. At last we persuaded a sturdy, cheerful little man with an alarmingly large goitre to come with us, and our kind host saw us several miles on our way.

As we were toiling up the long ascent to the village which was our next stage, we had a very pleasant meeting with an old native officer who was going up to Kedarnath with his family. He and Tilman exchanged reminiscences about the War and Neuve Chapelle (the mud and wet had left more impression on him than the bullets), and his fine, open manner and obvious pleasure at our success were very charming. The village was grandly situated only a few hundred feet below a 10,000 foot pass, but the bad weather we were still experiencing deprived us of a view back to the Kedarnath peaks which we much wanted to see.

Five miles of descent through forests of oak and sycamore brought us to a small village where we joined a group of returning dandy-bearers who were sitting round the hut of the village milkman and baker. We got this worthy to boil us up a great bowl of flour, milk, and sugar, and the result was a fine, filling batter pudding. Fortunately the road was still downhill and with this weighty cargo on board we were hard put to check our momentum.

That evening a very violent storm made the thought of our tent so unalluring that we prepared to risk a pilgrim doss-house. Just as we were settling down, one having authority came along and opened for us the Dharmsala, a sort of village meeting-hall. He was an ex-havildar of the Garhwal Rifles with eight years' war service, who besides making us comfortable insisted on bringing us presents of milk, ghee, rice, and pickled mangoes.

Our cash resources now began to worry us considerably. A whip round amongst the five of us produced exactly seven rupees and we still had to buy food for the four remaining days to Joshimath, so it was clear we should have to eschew luxuries. We might have raised the wind by becoming strolling players, for Kusang could juggle with three stones and Tilman and I had a varied repertoire of hymns, but on the whole we thought it would be more dignified to try what our credit would do at Chamoli, the first important place we came to on the 'Pilgrim Road'. Arrived there we went to the postmaster, who having communicated on the 'buzzer' with his colleague at Joshimath, readily advanced us some money.

Chamoli is under 4,000 feet above the sea and the heat is almost tropical; after dinner that night we sat outside the bungalow in long chairs talking with the Tahsildar, a local magistrate. He was very interested in Yog and pronounced the theory that Christ, many years of whose life are unaccounted for, had spent part of this time in India studying Yog.

At our next stopping place, Pipalkoti, there was a little stone-paved square in the centre of the village, and round this the bazaar was ranged. While waiting for our men we sat here with one of the shopkeepers discussing tea and politics. The all-important question for him was not Dominion Status but whether Pipalkoti should have its post office back or not, and he showed a touching faith in our power and influence as Englishmen to right all wrongs. Apparently through some delinquency on the part of the postmaster, the village had been deprived of its post office, which was now placed in a much smaller village three miles away. Our public-spirited friend had been battling manfully to restore the lost prestige of his village, as a file of letters a foot thick well showed; and though we could afford him only sympathy he was determined to spill his last drop of ink in the cause.

On the last march to Josimath we had an interesting encounter with the young Prince of Nepal who was returning from a pilgrimage to Badrinath. He was a boy of about ten, spoke very good English, and was travelling on foot. Unfortunately our Sherpas were a long way behind so that we missed seeing what took place at the meeting of a Prince and his subjects.

And so, on 26 August, once more to Joshimath to get ready for our final campaign.

Part 5

The Second
Nanda Devi Venture

16 Chapter 16

On 27 August we began hurried preparations for our second Nanda Devi venture. We had, by good fortune and the experience of those who had gone before us, met with far more success than we had deserved in the first penetration of the basin which I have already described. But, greatly interested as we were in the Badrinath Kedarnath topography, the major task of exploring the Nanda Devi Basin was yet unfinished.

Now that the monsoon had abated somewhat there was no time to waste and Angtharkay was despatched with instructions to recruit fifteen men from the Mana Valley and to return with them as soon as possible. Meanwhile we were busy working out our ration lists, collecting food, packing up and planning our last little campaign.

Pasang's foot was by no means healed, and I expressed some doubt as to whether we would be able to take him with us. But the mere suggestion that he should be left behind hurt him so desperately that I had not the heart to insist and weakly agreed that, as it was two weeks since the accident and he was no longer feeling pain, he could come along.

The rest of the party, although there was much work to be done, were glad enough of the respite from marching, and a newly arrived batch of letters and papers provided Tilman and myself with a certain amount of recreation, although through these we learnt for the first time and with profound sadness of the terrible disaster which had overtaken the German expedition to Nanga Parbat early in July, when four Europeans had perished together with six of our gallant Sherpa comrades from the 1933 Everest expedition. We thought it wiser to keep this news from our three men, and it was an unpleasant ordeal when, some six weeks later, we broke it to them, for nowhere can be found a more warm-hearted friendship than amongst these great little men of the Himalaya.

Late on the night of 29 August Angtharkay arrived with as tough a squad of men as we could have wished for, amongst whom I recognised several whose acquaintance I had made on the Kamet expedition in 1931. He brought too kind messages of congratulation from His Holiness the Rawal and other of our friends in Badrinath. We were particularly gratified to receive a message from 'Master' Ram Serikh Singh who, on hearing of Angtharkay's arrival had rushed down from his camp in the lovely valley below Nikanta to hear our news. Later I had the pleasure of receiving a long and charming letter from him in the course of which he says: 'When you and Tilman Sahib started from Badrinath to explore the Badri-Kedar snowy ranges the rains began to fall, and they were not only heavy but record rains. I have never experienced such heavy and continuous rain for the several years of my residence in this part of the Himalaya. I was expecting you to return without success. When nothing was heard of you I expected that both you and your porters must have perished in the snow. They were anxious days for me. But when I received your letter in my camp from Joshimath with the news of your unique success I hurried down to Badrinath to send a message of my heartfelt congratulations to you and Tilman Sahib.'

We managed to get away just before noon the following day. The weather was bad and we experienced heavy rain as we marched once more up the Dhaoli Valley. After our recent experiences we were anxious about our food supply getting wet. As usual it consisted mainly of flour in the form either of ata or satu. At Tapoban, where we spent that night, we came across a thermal spring. Near its source the water was so hot that one could hardly bear to immerse one's hand. The Sherpas have very great faith in the benefits to be derived from these springs and even Pasang was persuaded, contrary to his Tibetan custom, to have a bath.

Our next day's march took us to Lata, where we billeted in an ancient barn, innocent of roof. We hoped that we would now be able to obtain some food from the inhabitants so as not to have to broach our new stores until we were well on our way; however, as usual, nothing very substantial was forthcoming. Two cucumbers and some potatoes were brought to us by an old woman. When we asked her how much she wanted for them she burst into tears and replied that as her child had recently died she would rather that we did not pay her. We failed to see the connection, but could not induce her to take any money. However, a gift of matches so delighted her that she seemed to forget her late bereavement. An old man actually brought three eggs for which he demanded eight annas (9d.) each. We told him that we could not possibly pay such a ridiculous price, but when he started to go away with the eggs I panicked and gave him the money without further discussion. At that moment an egg seemed an almost priceless luxury.

We were told that at Tolma rice was obtainable, and Kusang volunteered to start very early next morning and go with one of the Mana men to purchase the rice and catch up the rest of us in the evening by taking a short cut from Tolma. We agreed to buy the rice on condition that there were no complaints later about the weight of the loads.

The weather was fine during the morning and we had a most pleasant march along a well-defined path amongst the tall sombre pines of the forest through which we had raced exactly two months before. Now we were not spurred on by the pangs of hunger and we were going uphill instead of down; so we had time to linger in the shady glades of the lovely, open forest. It was a long pull up however as Lata was under 7,500 feet and the little alp of Lata Kharak which we were making for was nearly 13,000 feet.

We pitched camp at the upper limits of the forest just in time to bundle the loads of food inside the tents as a heavy rain storm burst upon us. But it did not last long, and after it had cleared away we collected great masses of rhododendron firewood, and were soon sitting round blazing fires, I for my part lost in wonder at the sight of the ranges across the valley, flooded in that unbelievable blue light which occasionally follows a heavy evening shower in the hills. From far down in the forest there came a faint shout which was at once answered by the full strength of the party, after which the job of guiding the wanderers was taken in turn and shrill whistles broke the silence of the forest at intervals of a minute or so. Kusang and his companion eventually turned up long after dark and after what must have been a very hard day. They had secured a *maund* (eighty pounds) of rice, the arrival of which was greeted with great jubilation.

The rain came on again and continued to fall throughout the night, with the result that we had some difficulty in getting the men started next morning and did not leave before nine o'clock. By then the rain had stopped but a damp mist enveloped the mountain side and a cold wind beat in our faces. This seemed to have a good effect on the coolies, who displayed a remarkable turn of speed. We managed to hit off the sheep-track which led us once again over the scene of the exhausting labours of our first visit in May. It was interesting to pick out old landmarks – here a ridge to reach which had cost us half a day of weary flogging; there a gully into which we had floundered up to our armpits. Now we were swinging along a well-defined path at the rate of miles an hour. We passed a short way above our old bivouac place, and pointed out to the Bhotias the little platform on which we had passed the night; how different it looked from that little island of rock which we remembered so well!

When still in thick mist we reached the Durashi Pass, the Sherpas, led by Kusang, insisted on building an enormous cairn for old times' sake. On this they deposited various tattered garments which had hitherto clung miraculously to their bodies. Pasang sacrificed his hat in order to create a huge joke by placing it on top of the edifice and leaving it there. I think he would have abandoned his boots if he had thought that it would make a better jest!

The Bhotias were mightily impressed by the sheep-track which ran from here across the face of the cliffs to Durashi, as indeed anyone must be who sees it for the first time. We found some juniper growing in some of the steep gullies, and remembering the scarcity of firewood at Durashi we gathered great quantities so that the party resembled a small army of itinerant bushes. When we reached the alp, we found that a new lot of shepherds had taken the place of those we had met before. With their tall, strong frames, flowing hair and handsome, weather-beaten features, their appearance harmonised wonderfully with the prodigious splendour of their surroundings. They told us that the weather was becoming too cold for their flocks and that they were starting their retreat to the Dhaoli Valley on the following day. This retreat must have meant a long anxious job for them, as most of the new-born lambs were still too small to walk far, and there were hundreds of these little creatures to be carried over the difficult ground which led to the Durashi Pass. Indeed, it was difficult to imagine how they hoped to achieve the passage without a considerable loss. Their dogs were beautiful animals and had wonderful control over the sheep.

The morning of 3 September was gloriously fine and the view from the 'Curtain' ridge appeared to make a deep impression on the Bhotias, who demanded a detailed explanation of the topography. They were very thrilled to see a distant view of their own mountains, the Badrinath and Kamet ranges, and started a heated debate amongst themselves as to the identity of certain features. But it was the sight of the graceful curves of their Blessed Goddess, Nanda Devi, as she stood framed between the dark walls of the upper gorge which most excited their admiration. Several of them asked to be allowed to remain with us until we had finished our travels. What an extraordinarily nice lot they were! Always cheerful, they kept up a constant stream of good-humoured back-chat amongst themselves. They had not, of course, to undergo the hardships which the Dotials had suffered on our first journey, but before very long I came to have considerable respect for them as cragsmen, while their every-ready wit and carefree laughter will remain as one of my pleasantest memories. They and the Sherpas came to be the very best of friends and I think there was a measure of genuine regret when the time came for the Bhotias to leave us. In camp in the forest beyond Dibrughita that evening they treated us to a concert of part songs which reminded me very much of those of the Welsh singers. After this one of their number produced a book which was apparently written in Nepali from which he read laboriously to the Sherpas.

During the next few days, as we traversed once more high up on the flanks of the Rishi Nala, we were able to appreciate the tremendous advantage of possessing local knowledge when travelling over difficult country. Across places which had previously cost us hours of anxious toil we were now able to lead our party safely in half the time. We found, however, a great many landslips had occurred in our absence, and that portions of the country were quite considerably altered. The rains must have been terrific. Small, steep-sided nalas, normally dry, and with very little collecting capacity, showed signs of having had as much as seven feet of water coming down them. We soon realised that the delay which had been caused by our experiences on the Satopanth Pass had been a blessing in disguise, for the Rishi Nala would have been no place to be in during such weather as we experienced in the forests of the Kedarnath valleys.

In order to preserve our rapidly disintegrating climbing boots, we wore rubber-soled shoes on this journey. They slipped about horribly on the damp grass and earth-covered rocks and made the traversing along narrow ledges a most unpleasant business. On one occasion Tilman did slip and for a moment I thought he was lost as he swayed on the brink of a dreadful drop.

From Dibrughita we followed the high level route by which we had returned in June. On 5 September we crossed the Rhamani, 1,500 feet above its junction with the Rishi. The stream was still in spate and we experienced some difficulty in getting across. Most of the Bhotias were very frightened of being swept away and left the task of getting the loads across mainly to two young 'tigers' each of whom made some half a dozen crossings. One old man flatly refused to wade into the stream and was eventually carried across. Later it transpired that he was the 'egg wallah' who had achieved a certain amount of fame on the Kamet expedition in 1931, by being washed away in a river in the Alaknanda Valley, only I had not recognised him. That evening we reached our old base camp at the entrance of the upper gorge. At one period during the monsoon everything had been flooded, though as we had walled in the belongings which we had left we found that they were still intact. There were several things which we did not require, but we soon came to wish that we had pitched them into the river as the Bhotias spent most of the night noisily dividing the spoil.

As we knew every inch of the route through the upper part of the gorge we decided to take ten of the Bhotias on with us, while the rest returned. Huge segments of the cliffs had broken away and it was very lucky for us that none of the vital sections of the route had been touched. One landslip might well have rendered the gorge impassable, though it is possible that it might have the reverse effect. The men climbed splendidly and on the evening of 8 September we pitched camp some miles up the main valley of the southern section of the basin. The Bhotias were astonished at the country. Such enormous areas of splendid pasturage and no one was able to get their flocks through to graze it! Pasang said he would like to bring a few yaks through into the basin and live there in peace for the rest of his life!

Our camp was situated near the junction of the two main glaciers of the southern section, and promised to serve as a useful base for our work. Besides the exploration of the country to the south of Nanda Devi we meant to reconnoitre the southern ridges of the mountain to see if we could find a practicable route to the summit. But our chief ambition was to force our way out of the basin either to the south or to the east, for besides not wishing to return by the way we had come, Dr Longstaff's words, 'I can think of no more interesting or arduous task for a party composed of mountaineers than to follow up the great glaciers under the southern face of Nanda Devi and to cross the ridge on which I camped in 1905 into the Milam Valley,' had fired our imaginations.

Our activities in the southern section were governed largely by this ambition. We had two possible alternatives. One was the col reached by Dr Longstaff from the Lwanl Glacier on the Milam side, the other was the depression on the southern 'rim' by which Mr Ruttledge and his guide Emile Rey had tried to gain access to the basin in 1932. Both these ways were likely to prove extremely difficult, but we were inclined to favour the former proposition as Longstaff had proved the practicability of the further side of the Lwanl Col by climbing it from that direction, whereas from what we had heard of Ruttledge's col it seemed very doubtful whether a reasonably safe route could be found down the southern face even if we succeeded in reaching its crest from the north.

It was mainly then with the object of obtaining a clear view of the unknown side of the Lwanl Col that on 9 September Tilman, Angtharkay and I, after bidding farewell to the Bhotias, left camp heading in an easterly direction. We crossed the stream to the northern side of the valley by means of a snow bridge formed by a huge avalanche cone which had fallen from the cliffs of Nanda Devi. Presently, as we made our way along a moraine ledge under these cliffs, we were alarmed by the ominous whirr of falling stones accompanied by some shrill whistles, and, looking up, we saw a number of bharal high up among the crags above us. Never have I seen a more extraordinary display of rock climbing. The cliffs on which these animals were scrambling about looked from where we were to be utterly unclimbable; and yet here were four-legged creatures, young and old, running about on them as if they were horizontal instead of being almost vertical. Later we found out that owing to the inward dip of the rock strata the cliffs of this side of the mountain are not so difficult as they appear. Nevertheless, although I had often watched chamois in the Alps, I never before believed that these animals could move about on rock faces of such appalling steepness. I do not imagine that such agile climbers would be so careless as to knock stones down by accident and I strongly suspected that they were bombarding us purposely and probably enjoying a good laugh at our obvious alarm as the stones shattered themselves unpleasantly close to us.

Soon we got on to the big glacier flowing from the west under the southern face of Nanda Devi, and crossed it diagonally to its left bank, where we found a well-defined lateral moraine along which we could make good progress. We had gone for some miles before we rounded a corner and came in sight of the head of the glacier. There was a lot of cloud obscuring the peaks, but after we had waited for half an hour or so we got a brief and distant view of the col. What we saw made us somewhat uneasy. From the col itself a steep ice or snow gully descended for about 2,000 feet to the head of the glacier. If the gully consisted of good snow throughout its length it would not be difficult to climb it even if it were steep. But from where we stood it appeared to us to be composed of ice, particularly in its upper part. If this proved to be the case the task of cutting steps all the way up it, at the same time carrying loads of fifty pounds, and being responsible for the safety of the Sherpas, who would be carrying at least seventy pounds was one which neither of us was very keen to face; for on steep hard ice it is almost impossible to check a bad slip, while there is nothing easier than to make one. Moreover, several deep ruts in the gully and piles of debris below indicated that the route was swept by stone falls, while the rocks on either side of the gully did not appear to offer a satisfactory alternative. Our view, however, was too fleeting and too distant to be at all satisfactory or conclusive, but we saw enough to make us decide to examine the possibilities of the Sunderdhunga Col, as Ruttledge has named the depression on the southern 'rim', before making a serious attempt to force a route up the grim precipices of the south-eastern wall.

Across the glacier from where we stood the great southern ridge of the main peak swept up into the drifting clouds at an appalling angle. I could not repress a shudder as I looked at its great glistening flanks and reflected that it had been our intention to look for a route up it. The lower section was hidden from view; but higher up the icy cliffs mounted without a break to support the majestic head of the virgin goddess, near 10,000 feet above us. I do not remember even remarking upon the apparent inaccessibility of the ridge, and I began to hope that we had proved the mountain to be unclimbable.

We returned to camp in the evening by way of the left bank of the glacier. The Bhotias had taken their departure and Pasang and Kusang, having performed their numerous duties about the camp, were busily engaged as usual with their intricate coiffure. As they wore their hair long it was in constant need of attention, and long continued practice had taught them much which would make many a Paris hairdresser sit up and take notice. Sometimes a long and richly ornamental pigtail was allowed to hang down the back; sometimes it was wound round and round the head; on other occasions the hair was bunched coquettishly behind the ears. A parting, when such was worn, was ruled with the most scrupulous accuracy. This evening I watched, fascinated, while Kusang (he did not know I was looking) ran a short stump of pencil up his nose and over his forehead to make sure that his parting ran exactly down the middle of his head. He repeated the process over and over again before he was satisfied, squinting the while so grotesquely that I began to wonder if his smiling eyes would ever be the same again.

17   Chapter 17

On the morning of 10 September we were greeted by a warm sun. As it was the first we had experienced for nearly two months we were tempted to bask in its kindly rays for some time before embarking upon the more serious work of the day. We decided to go up the great glacier which we had seen coming in from the south, at the head of which we suspected the Sunderdhunga Col must lie. We intended to camp near the head of the glacier, push a camp on to the crest of the col if that were possible and spend some days examining the ice cliffs on the southern side in the hope of being able to find a way down. If we were successful we could return to continue our work in the basin for as long as our food lasted, in the comfortable knowledge that an escape over the rampart was possible. If we failed we would have to make an attempt on the great ice gully leading up to Longstaff's col. We started, carrying heavy loads, and were content to take things gently. By the time we got into a position which would command a view of the glacier the clouds had come up from the south and we could get no idea of the type of country for which we were making. The going was good on the dry ice of the glacier and we made steady progress, passing one or two remarkably fine specimens of 'glacier tables'. These somewhat surprising phenomena are caused by a large slab of rock falling on to the surface of the glacier and protecting the section of ice on which it has fallen from the rays of the sun, so that as the rest of the glacier melts the slab is left perched upon a pedestal of ice which it has protected. In the case of smaller rocks the process is reversed, the stone becoming heated by the sun and sinking into the ice instead of being left perched above it.

Soon after midday a bitter wind blew up from the south and sweeping across the glacier drove hail and sleet into our faces. This caused us to put on a spurt and before we camped we were a great deal further up the glacier than we had expected to go that day. With difficulty we erected the tents and got the Primus going. The wind dropped towards sunset, and chancing to look out of the tent I saw that the clouds had retreated down the valley leaving the peaks to the south clear. We saw that we were near the head of a very wide glacier-filled valley from which gentle ice slopes rose to a broad saddle which we knew must be the Sunderdhunga Col. To its right was a massive ice peak. This we concluded must be the triangulated peak, 22,360 feet, which is such a conspicuous landmark when seen from the south, and which is known by the Survey of India as

East Trisul. The delicious purity of the summit snows, tinged as they were by delicate rays of the setting sun, filled me with desire for a closer acquaintance with the peak. Moreover, unlike most of the peaks in the vicinity, there was an obviously practicable route to the summit, and the prospect of a view from such an elevated point in this wonderland was irresistible. Arguments against the present plan were not difficult to find. The col was easily accessible from this side and in order to find out whether a descent on the south was practicable or not, one would have to go down several thousand feet of very difficult ice, and once one had done that, one would probably be disinclined to climb back again. So it was decided to cut out the reconnaissance, and make a full-dress attempt when our work in the basin had been completed.

We passed a very cold night and in consequence did not emerge from our tents until the sun was well up. Carrying one tent, bedding for three and food and fuel enough for three days, we started in the direction of the ice peak. The weather remained fine all day, and as hour after hour we threaded our way laboriously through a badly-crevassed area which stretched for a long way up the mountain side, the heat and the glare from the newly-fallen snow was almost unbearable. We aimed at getting our camp up to 20,000 feet. Tilman had been feeling very unfit all day, and in the afternoon when we were at an altitude of about 19,000 he decided not to go any further, and suggested, most unselfishly, that Kusang should stay up at the camp in his place and attempt the peak with Angtharkay and myself, while he went down with Pasang. I, too, was not feeling in very good form, and was suffering from a bad attack of that mysterious complaint loosely known as 'glacier lassitude', so that I was glad when 500 feet higher up we came upon an excellent camping site in a crevasse.

With three of us crammed into a two-man tent, we settled down to a most uncomfortable night. Lack of space did not permit independent movement and when one man wished to turn over the others had to turn too, in order that each should fit spoon-wise into the curves of the other. The Sherpas thought this a tremendous joke and as far as I could make out simply laughed themselves to sleep. I suppose I must lack much of that priceless gift – a sense of humour, for I could see in the situation very little to laugh at, with the consequence that I lay long into the night hiding my head and trying to decide which of my companions snored the loudest.

I roused them at 4 a.m. and after a great deal of struggling we contrived to melt ourselves a drink and wrap our shivering bodies in all the clothing which we could extract from the tangled mess inside the tent. Boots then had to be thawed out and forced after a frightful struggle on to feet which had apparently swollen overnight. Soon after five o'clock we issued reluctantly out into the bitter morning air.

It is curious how the Sherpas, when they have no loads to carry, seem to lose all power of controlled, rhythmic movement which is such a vital necessity in mountaineering and particularly at considerable altitudes. Their steps become jerky and impulsive, they rush along for a few minutes and then sit down, with the result that they soon become exhausted. All that their life of mountain wandering has taught them about the best methods of walking uphill seems to be lost and they are like raw novices who are amongst the mountains for the first time in their lives.

Today this was very evident and before we had been climbing an hour the party was feeling very sorry for itself. Higher up, too, the snow conditions became bad and the work of kicking steps extremely laborious. We began to feel as we had felt at a considerably higher altitude on Everest the year before. We started off by going for an hour without a halt, then the hour was short-ened to half an hour, half an hour to twenty minutes, twenty minutes to a quarter of an hour, and at length we would subside gasping into the soft bed of snow after only ten minutes' struggle. But the morning was fine and as we lay there, we gazed out over a scene of ever-increasing grandeur until even the gigantic southern face of Nanda Devi became dwarfed by the mere extent of the panorama.

I can never hope to see a finer mountain view: the Badrinath peaks, Kamet, the Kosa group, Dunagiri and the great peaks of the northern part of the Nanda Devi Basin – all mountains amongst which we had been travelling for the past four months, served merely as a foil to set off the stupendous ranges lying beyond Milam and across the borders of western Nepal. What a field of exploration lay there – the heritage of some future generation.

Only one frame of mind is possible when working one's way up bad snow at high altitudes. One must shut out from one's mind all but the immediate task of making the next step. To start fretting about the slowness of one's progress or about the time it is going to take to reach the goal would render the whole business unbearable. On a larger scale, this frame of mind, the firm concentra-tion on immediate necessities, made possible those terrible months of sledging through the blizzards of the Antarctic.

As we approached the summit the wind, which had been unpleasant in the early morning, now became very strong indeed and it was the fear of frost-bite which spurred what little energy we had left. My hope of seeing something of the southern side of the watershed was disappointed, for when we reached the summit ridge we looked down into a boiling cauldron of cloud a few feet below us. This was rising rapidly and soon enveloped us. However, we did get one brief glimpse down to the little Simm Saga range which lay at our feet; and also into the head of the Sunderdhunga Valley which we were so hoping to reach. What we saw went a long way to quenching that hope for there seemed to be very little break in the 10,000 feet of precipice which lay between us and the grassy floor of the valley below. I had refrained from taking any photo-graphs on the way up in order to preserve the exposures for the summit. But before my numbed fingers would open and set the camera we were wrapped in a dense cloak of cloud, and we passed the remainder of our stay on the top clapping our hands and banging our feet about in an attempt to restore rapidly diminishing circulation. Then we bustled off the summit and embarked upon a descent which proved to be almost as trying as the ascent. On reaching the camp we packed up the tent and sleeping bags, and in spite of the loads we had now to carry, we shot down over the lower ice slopes at a tremendous speed, paying little respect to the crevasses which had caused us so much trouble on the previous day. Tilman greeted us with apparently unlimited tea. He had put in a useful day's work with the plane-table and had succeeded in fixing several important points about the glacier.

On the following day we went down to our base and, leaving a dump of flour there just sufficient to enable us to beat a retreat down the Rishi Ganga in the event of our failing to escape from the basin to the east or south, we carried the remainder of our stuff to a pleasant little alp a couple of miles up the left bank of the Main Glacier. By now we had been able to make a fairly lengthy examination of the southern aspect of Nanda Devi. We had seen a curious diagonal spur running down in a south-easterly direction from about halfway up the main south ridge. This appeared to be accessible in its lower section and it seemed to us that we might be able to work our way for some distance along it. We decided to attempt to do this in order to get a comprehensive view of the southern section of the basin, though it did not even occur to me that we might also find a practicable route to the summit.

The morning of 14 September was brilliantly fine, and we started early carrying with us the usual light camp and enough food for Tilman (who was now recovered) and myself for two or three days. We crossed the Main Glacier and made our way again along the valley which lay at the foot of the great black buttresses of the southern ridge, fixing our position on the plane-table as we went and taking shots to distant landmarks. We camped that night by a pool of crystal clear water, on a lawn of close-cropped grass over which snowy edelweiss grew in profusion.

It was an hour after dawn the following morning before we got away. It seemed as if the last remnants of the monsoon had departed. The glacier was silent, bound under the iron grip of frost; and we joyously sped over its desolate stony surface. Forty minutes of hard going took us to the foot of the black precipices which girdle the base of the great southern ridge. Here we found that the rock was well broken but firm and that the strata sloped in our favour which made the climbing a great deal easier than we had anticipated. Within an hour of leaving the glacier we had reached the crest of the diagonal spur which we had seen from a distance. This was as far as we expected to get and we sat down contentedly in the warm sunlight and gazed lazily at our unique surroundings.

We saw that the spur we were on, coming down from the main southern ridge of Nanda Devi, formed a gigantic glacier cirque. In front of us across a deep valley rose a stupendous ice wall which formed the southern face of the twin peaks. We were too close and, for all our 18,500 feet, far too low to get anything but a very foreshortened view of the face and it was a long while before the colossal scale began to impress itself upon my imagination. The ice wall was fringed on top by a band of rock forming the actual summits of the twin peaks and the two mile ridge connecting them. By now the sun had been shining on this band for some hours and had already started to dislodge masses of rock, which set up an almost continuous moan as they hurtled through the air towards us, yet so great was the distance of the peaks above us that throughout the day we did not detect a single of these avalanches which must have involved several hundreds of tons of rock. The whole effect was very uncanny.

As it was such a brilliantly fine day and as yet quite early we decided that we would investigate the possibilities of climbing further up the spur. A virtual tower rising straight out of the ridge blocked a way along the crest, but we soon found that we could traverse along under the tower on its eastern side and climb diagonally towards a gap in the ridge beyond. This we reached in a couple of hours without much difficulty, and were surprised to find that here again the inward sloping strata made progress comparatively easy. By now we were about 19,000 feet high and beginning to get really excited. We had already overcome the apparently inaccessible lower part of the ridge and were still going strong. Was it possible that we had discovered the one key to the innermost defences of this amazing mountain? Of course, we would not be in a position to make an attempt on the summit but to have discovered the way was sufficient to work us into quite a frenzy of excitement. Up and up we went without finding any place which gave us more than a moment's hesitation. Our pace was slow by reason of the fact that the rocks were still under a deep covering of monsoon snow, but our progress was steady enough. The higher we got the more fully could we appreciate the immensity of the glacier cirque on the rim of which we were climbing.

We climbed on until about 2.30 p.m. when we halted and decided that we had come far enough. We estimated our height at close on 21,000 feet. The ridge was certainly showing signs of becoming more difficult but for the next few hundred feet there did not appear to be any insuperable obstacle and we came to the definite conclusion that if a well-equipped party were to spend a couple of weeks over the job that there was a good chance that the ridge could be followed to the summit. It would be no easy task and the party would have to be supremely fit and competent. Prolonged siege tactics (which are so much the fashion in the Himalayas nowadays) would be too dangerous to be justifiable, since this method would involve too many men in the upper camps, and if it were overtaken by bad weather high up such a party would be in a very serious plight. In high mountains, mobility is the keynote of efficiency and safety, and it is for this reason that I find it hard to believe that a large, heavily organised expedition will ever achieve success on Everest.

We were now sufficiently high to get a true idea of the immensity of our surroundings, and even though I had been living for months amid perpendicularity on a huge scale I suffered from a feeling of panic which resembled the delirium of a fevered mind.

Our slow rate of descent was evidence that we had climbed too fast earlier in the day and night was falling as we made our way back across the glacier after yet another unforgettable day.

The morning of 16 September was spent mainly in plane-tabling, on the slopes above the camp, and in making further examination of 'Longstaff's Col'. This more detailed study confirmed our first impressions that an ascent of the couloir with heavy loads would be too difficult and dangerous a job. We could not, however, tell for certain as so much depended upon whether the gully was composed of snow or ice. By now we had become really worked up about our chances of being able to force an exit over one of these gaps. In doing so, we would make a complete crossing of the range, thus linking up with the explorations of those who had attacked the rampart from the south and east; we would see for ourselves those valleys, which though not unexplored, we knew to be of surpassing loveliness; and the last phase of our quest would be through country new to us. If we were to fail we would be forced to retreat once more down the Rishi Nala, and from Joshimath to journey back by the way we had come, thus missing a rare and glorious climax to our little season of perfect happiness.

When we returned to camp early in the afternoon we found that the Sherpas had come up and were busily engaged in their hobby of building cairns. Packing up, we ran off down the glacier, reaching our little green alp before sundown, here to spend one more night lying in the open, dozing in the light of the half moon and waking to watch the rosy light of dawn steal gently down the east-turned face of the 'Blessed Goddess'.

The week which followed has left with me a richer and more varied stock of impressions than any other I can recall. We started up the glacier to the south that morning, staggering under the weight of very heavy loads. I was feeling lazy and lagged behind the others, sitting down often to gaze at each new aspect of the peaks around me. Once I found myself by a deep pool in the ice of the glacier, and stayed as if hypnotised by the reflections on the placid blue surface of the water. It was irresistible. I threw off my clothes, plunged in and swam for some seconds under water along the glistening walls of ice. The day ended in camp far up the glacier, under the icy cirque standing at its head.

A frigid night was followed by an even colder dawn and we were hurried along in spite of our cruel loads by the bitter morning breeze. The snow was iron hard, and as the slope steepened the already burdened shoulders of the leader would ache painfully as he chipped steps, while those behind were frozen with inaction. The arrival of the sun changed all this and we were soon stamping a way, and sinking up to our knees at every step, while a fierce glare scorched our faces unbearably. Several large crevasses caused us some trouble, but we worked at full pressure and at 11.15 a.m. we reached the crest of the 'col'. We found that this consisted of an extensive snow plateau which sloped gently towards the south, so that we were obliged to descend some 500 feet before we could get any view of the southern precipices on which all our thoughts were concentrated. From the edge of the plateau we could look down into the cloud-filled Sunderdhunga Valley up which, as I mentioned earlier, Hugh Ruttledge and his guide, Emile Rey, had come in 1932 to attempt to gain access into the Nanda Devi Basin. In order to save the reader the trouble of referring back to that incident it may not be out of place to requote here, Mr Ruttledge's description published in *The Times* of 22 August 1932, of the obstacle which now faced us:

> 'In a mood of hopeful anticipation our party, on 25 May, trudged up the narrow glacier which leads from Sunderdhunga itself to the base of the wall, of which the greater part has been invisible from a distance. The Sherpas cheered derisively as a little avalanche had an ineffective shot at us from the cliffs above; and raced round the last corner. One step round it, and we were brought up all standing by a sight which almost took our remaining breath away. Six thousand feet of the steepest rock and ice. 'Nom de nom,' said Emile, while Nima exclaimed that this looked as bad as the north-west face of Kangchenjunga in 1930. However, we had come a long way to see this, so we advanced across the stony slopes to a point from which we hoped, by detailed examination, to reduce terrific appearance to milder reality. But the first impressions were accurate. Near the top of the wall, for about a mile and a half, runs a terrace of ice some 200 feet thick; in fact, the lower edge of a hanging glacier. Under the pull of gravity large masses constantly break off from this terrace and thunder down to the valley below, polishing in their fall the successive bands of limestone precipice of which the face is composed. Even supposing the precipice to be climbable, an intelligent mountaineer may be acquitted on a charge of lack of enterprise if he declines to spend at least three days and two nights under fire from this artillery. An alternative is the choice of three knife-edge arêtes, excessively steep, sometimes overhanging in their middle and lower sections, on which even the eye of faith, assisted by binoculars, fails to see a single platform large enough to accommodate the most modest of climbing tents.'

We dumped our loads in the snow and set about our task immediately. Remembering Ruttledge's description we decided that our best chance of success was to get on to one of the three rock arêtes or ridges, for though they were referred to as being 'excessively steep', at least their crests would be safe from the bombardment of ice-avalanches. The clouds had now come up from below and our view was very restricted. After working over to the left for some distance, however, we came to the edge of a tremendously steep gully from which came an incessant rattle of stone falls. Beyond we could make out a dark mass which we concluded was the first of the rock arêtes. After hunting about for some time we found that in order to reach the arête we would be forced to run the gauntlet of the rock falls in the gully. As these were coming down at very short intervals the chances of our getting across without some member of the party being killed was very small, and the risk was quite unjustifiable. So that was that.

The ice fall below us plunged out of sight. We returned to our loads and worked over to the right. In about twenty minutes we were brought up short and found that we were standing on the edge of the ice-terrace overhanging 6,000 feet of polished limestone. It was a wonderful sight. Every now and then enormous masses of ice would break away from the cliffs we were standing on and crash with a fearful roar into the cloudy depths below. After satisfying ourselves that there was not the slightest hope in this direction we waited for some while to watch this unusual scene. It is not often that one gets a chance of watching a display of ice-avalanches from so close, and rarer still to see them breaking away from the very cliffs on which one is standing.

We returned disconsolately to our loads for a meal at 2.30 p.m. A cup of tea and satu put new heart into the party and we set off to tackle the last line of possibility. This was the ice fall which lay immediately below us and which separated the ice-terrace from the rock arêtes. A few feet of twisted and riven ice was all that we could see: beyond this the ice fall plunged out of sight into the whirling mists which filled the depths below. It was useless to attempt to work out a line of attack from above and all we could do was to go straight at it and worry our way down by the tedious processes of trial and error. We had plenty of food with us, however, and we could afford to take our time. As long as we kept fairly well out of the line of bombardment from the ice cliffs of the terrace and avoided a slip we could carry on for several days if necessary.

Soon we found ourselves on ice more torn and complicated and more frighteningly steep even than that which we had tackled six weeks before on the southern side of our Satopanth Pass. It was exceedingly strenuous work trying line after line without success, but as the evening wore on our energy seemed to increase, probably from a growing feeling of desperation. A series of slender ice ledges suspended over space by some conjuring trick of nature would lead us downwards to the brink of an impassable chasm. Then a wearisome retreat back by the way we had come to try a new and perhaps equally futile chance.

The further we went the more involved became the precipitous maze we were in, until my head began to whirl and I began to think we should neither find our way on or back. By dark, however, we had managed to get some hundreds of feet down and we crept into our sleeping bags in a slightly more hopeful frame of mind.

The night was an extremely cold one and we decided not to start before the sun was up on the following morning as our clothes had become sodden in the soft snow of the previous day and an early start would almost certainly have resulted in frost-bite. This decision gave us a moment of leisure in which to watch a sunrise whose beauty far surpassed any I had seen before. In the right and left foreground were the icy walls, steep-sided and grim, enclosing the head of the Maiktoli Valley; in front beyond the brink of the ice ledge on which we were camped, and immensely far below was a lake of vivid colour at the bottom of which we could see the Sunderdhunga River coiling like a silver water snake, flowing away into the placid cloud-sea which stretched without a break over the plains of India.

The day was one of heavy toil, over-packed with thrills. Hour after hour we puzzled and hacked our way down; sometimes lowering our loads and ourselves on the rope down an ice cliff, at others chipping laboriously across the steep face of a tower or along a knife-edged crest, always in constant dread of finding ourselves completely cut off. The bitter cold of the early morning changed towards midday to a fierce heat and glare which robbed us of much of our strength and energy. Our heavy loads hindered every movement and threatened to throw us off our balance. But we were all absorbed in our task, and worked on through the day without pause.

Evening found us working on dry ice 3,000 feet down. Beside us to our right was a prominent rock ridge, which, though lying immediately below the higher line of hanging glaciers, offered us a heaven-sent alternative if only we could reach it. We cut steps to the edge of the glacier and from there we looked down a sixty-foot ice cliff into a steep slabby gully. The gully was evidently a path for ice avalanches, but it was narrow and once in it we could run across in a couple of minutes. By chipping away the ice in a large circle we soon fashioned a bollard. Round this we fastened a rope, down which we slid, recovering the rope from the ice bollard without difficulty. A short race across the gully with hearts in our mouths took us to a little ledge under the overhanging walls of the ridge, which offered a convenient and well-protected site for a camp. No sooner had we got the tents pitched than there came a fearful roar from above and for fully a minute a cascade of huge ice blocks crashed down the gully, sending up a spray of ice dust, while a number of ice splinters landed harmlessly on the tents.

The day, begun with the sight of a dawn fair beyond description and crowded with so much vivid life, closed with us stretched luxuriously on our ledge, perched high up amongst the precipitous glaciers of one of the grandest of mountain cirques. Lightning flickered somewhere to the east; the distant thunder was almost indistinguishable from the growl of the avalanches. Mists floating stealthily in and out of the corries about us, forming and dissolving as if at will. Far to the south the placid sea of monsoon cloud still stretched over the plains, and the silvery light of a full moon lent to the scene an appearance of infinite depth.

Three thousand feet of precipice still remained to be descended and this took us nearly the whole of the following day. Frequently we had to rope down the more difficult sections. On one of these occasions one of the sacks came open; most of the contents fell out, bounced once and hummed out of sight. In the afternoon we were enveloped in mist and had considerable difficulty in groping our way downwards; but Antharkay distinguished himself by a really brilliant piece of route finding and in the evening we reached a collection of rude stone shelters, used by shepherds, and known as Maiktoli. The shepherds had departed some weeks before.

The high mountains were now showing signs of approaching winter, a sharp reminder that our season of freedom and perfect happiness was at an end. But the marches which followed have left their quota of memories. A struggle to find an exit from the grim gorge in the upper Sunderdhunga Valley into which we had blundered in a heavy mist; our last encounter with a swollen mountain river; an enormous feast on wild raspberries and Himalayan blackberries lower down the valley; the generous hospitality of the first villagers we met, and the sweetness of their honey; the sparkling sunlit mornings, as one lay, sleepily watching the smoke of a distant wood fire mounting straight up into the clear air; a dawn on the distant ice-clad giants, whose presence we had just left.

Return to civilisation was hard, but, in the sanctuary of the Blessed Goddess we had found the lasting peace which is the reward of those who seek to know high mountain places.

Shipton at Snow Lake in 1939.

A view down the Upper Rishi Gorge. The path takes a tortuous line along the left-hand slopes. Photo: John Porter

Eric Shipton and H.W. Tilman leaving England for Nanda Devi in 1934.

A difficult section on the path through the Upper Rishi Gorge.

Nanda Devi from the north. The cliffs on the southern rim of the Sanctuary can be seen on the right. Photo: Hamish Brown

The 8,000-foot cliffs on the northern flanks of the East Peak of Nanda Devi.

Peaks ringing the northern end of the Sanctuary seen from the north of Trisul – Changabang, Kalanka, Hardeol and Pt 6992. The latter peak was attempted twice by Shipton and Tilman.

The boulder camp in the bamboo forest. Kusang, Pasang and Angtharkay are preparing a meal of mushrooms and bamboo shoots.

Printed in the USA
CPSIA information can be obtained
at www.ICGtesting.com
JSHW012016140824
68134JS00025B/2454